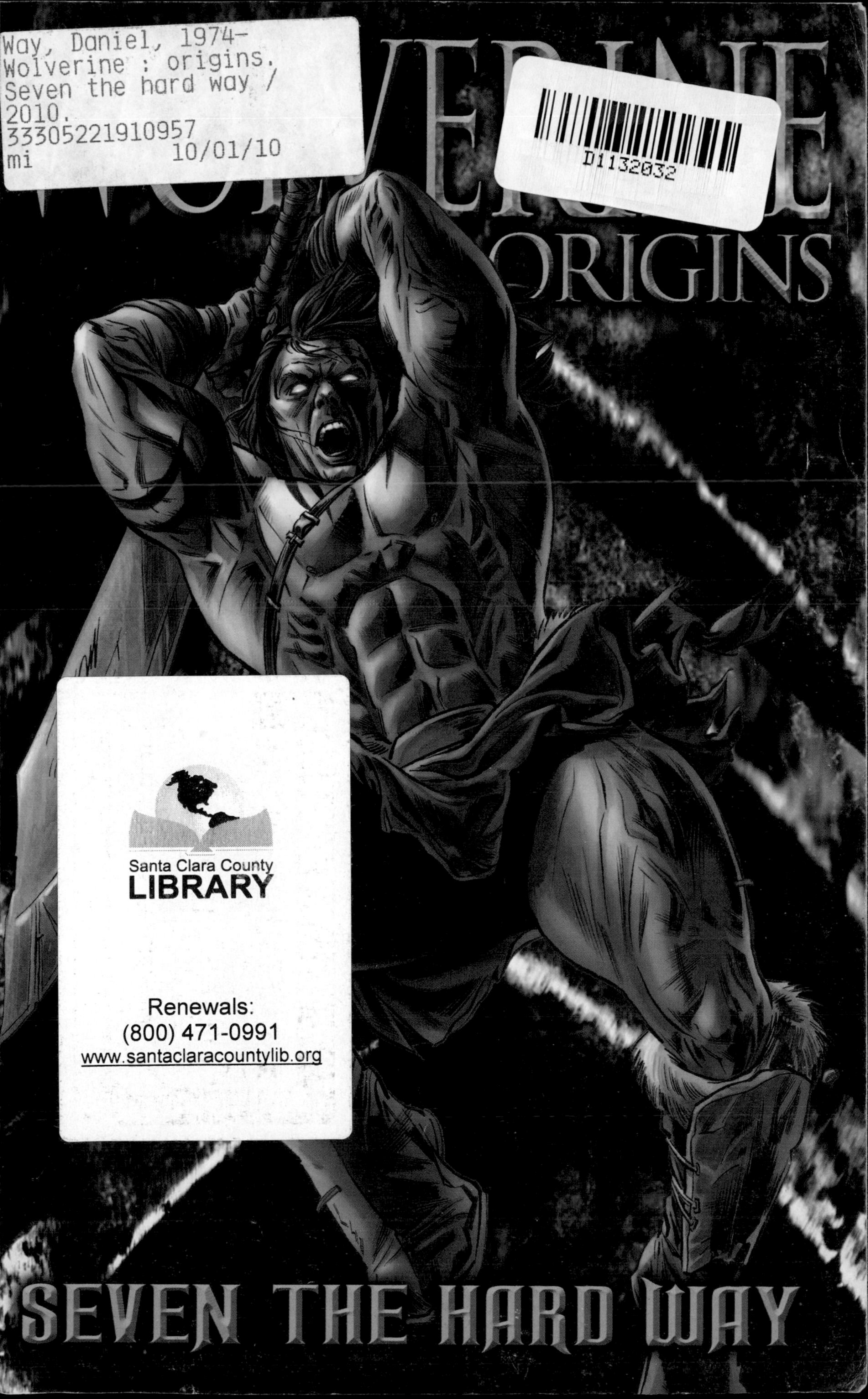
ORIGINS
SEVEN THE HARD WAY

Collection Editor: Jennifer Grünwald
Assistant Editor: Alex Starbuck
Associate Editor: John Denning
Editor, Special Projects: Mark D. Beazley
Senior Editor, Special Projects:
Jeff Youngquist

Senior VP of Sales: David Gabriel
Editor in Chief: Joe Quesada
Publisher: Dan Buckley
Executive Producer: Alan Fine

WOLVERINE ORIGINS: SEVEN THE HARD WAY. Contains material originally published in magazine form as WOLVERINE ORIGINS #41-45. First printing 2010. ISBN# 978-0-7851-4648-3. Published by MARVEL WORLDWIDE, INC., a subsidiary of MARVEL ENTERTAINMENT, LLC. OFFICE OF PUBLICATION: 417 5th Avenue, New York, NY 10016. Copyright © 2009 and 2010 Marvel Characters, Inc. All rights reserved. $19.99 per co in the U.S. (GST #R127032852); Canadian Agreement #40668537. All characters featured in this issue and the distinctive names and likenesses thereof, and all related indicia are trademarks of Marvel Characters, Inc. similarity between any of the names, characters, persons, and/or institutions in this magazine with those of any living or dead person or institution is intended, and any such similarity which may exist is purely coinciden **Printed in the U.S.A.** ALAN FINE, EVP - Office of the President, Marvel Worldwide, Inc. and EVP & CMO Marvel Characters B.V.; DAN BUCKLEY, Chief Executive Officer and Publisher - Print, Animation & Digital Media; . SOKOLOWSKI, Chief Operating Officer; DAVID GABRIEL, SVP of Publishing Sales & Circulation; DAVID BOGART, SVP of Business Affairs & Talent Management; MICHAEL PASCIULLO, VP Merchandising & Communicatio JIM O'KEEFE, VP of Operations & Logistics; DAN CARR, Executive Director of Publishing Technology; JUSTIN F. GABRIE, Director of Publishing & Editorial Operations; SUSAN CRESPI, Editorial Operations Manager; Al MORALES, Publishing Operations Manager; STAN LEE, Chairman Emeritus. For information regarding advertising in Marvel Comics or on Marvel.com, please contact Ron Stern, VP of Business Development, at rster marvel.com. For Marvel subscription inquiries, please call 800-217-9158. **Manufactured between 2/8/2010 and 3/10/2010 by R.R. DONNELLEY, INC., SALEM, VA, USA.**

10 9 8 7 6 5 4 3 2 1

WOLVERINE ORIGINS

ORIGINS

SEVEN THE HARD WAY

Writer: Daniel Way
Pencils: Doug Braithwaite
Inks & Washes: Bill Reinhold
with Doug Braithwaite (Issue #43),
Gary Erskine (Issue #44) & Mike Manley (Issue #45)
Colors: Andy Troy
Letters: Virtual Calligraphy's Cory Petit
Cover Art: Doug Braithwaite

Assistant Editor: Jody LeHeup
Editors: John Barber & Jeanine Schaefer
Group Editor: Axel Alonso

WOLVERINE
ORIGINS

The mutant Wolverine has spent a century fighting those who would manipulate him for his unique powers—razor-sharp claws, heightened senses, and a healing factor capable of miracles. After repeated brainwashing, torture, and reprogramming, Wolverine's past was as much a mystery to him as to anyone. With those long-lost memories returned to him, Wolverine has set out on a mission to punish the conspirators who have wronged him.

Now, Logan has finally caught up with the mysterious figure known only as Romulus, the man that has been secretly manipulating him his entire life. Over the course of the epic battle that ensued, Logan learned that Romulus's grand scheme was for Logan and Daken—Logan's dangerously misguided son—to fight to the death, determining who would take Romulus's place at the top of the food chain. But Logan knows that even if he kills Romulus now, he will be playing into Romulus's ultimate plan…and Daken will inevitably come for him, forcing Logan to kill his own son. The only answer to the problem as Logan sees it is to let Romulus live until he can figure out a solution. But the minute Logan's back is turned, Romulus knocks him unconscious and disappears.

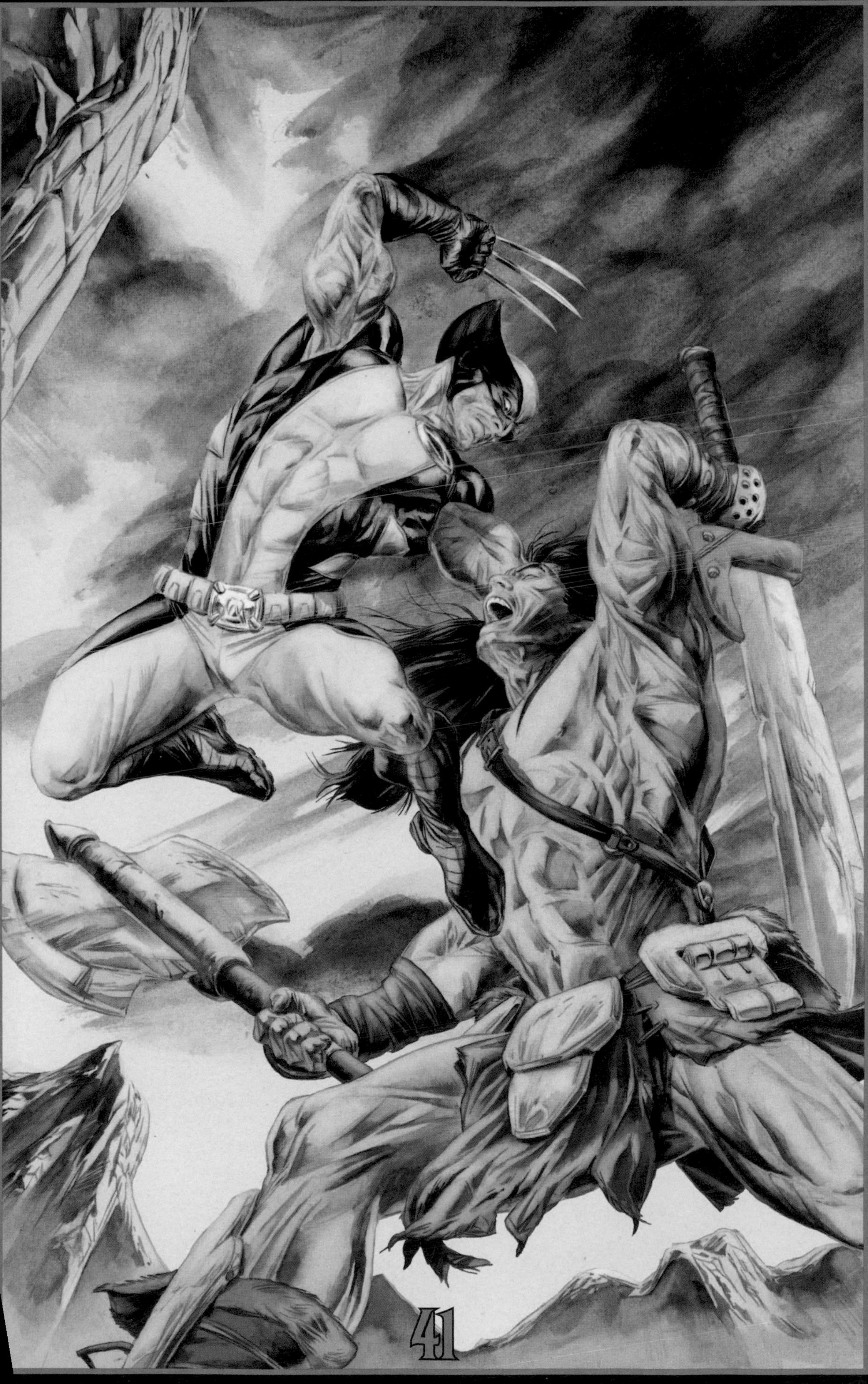
41

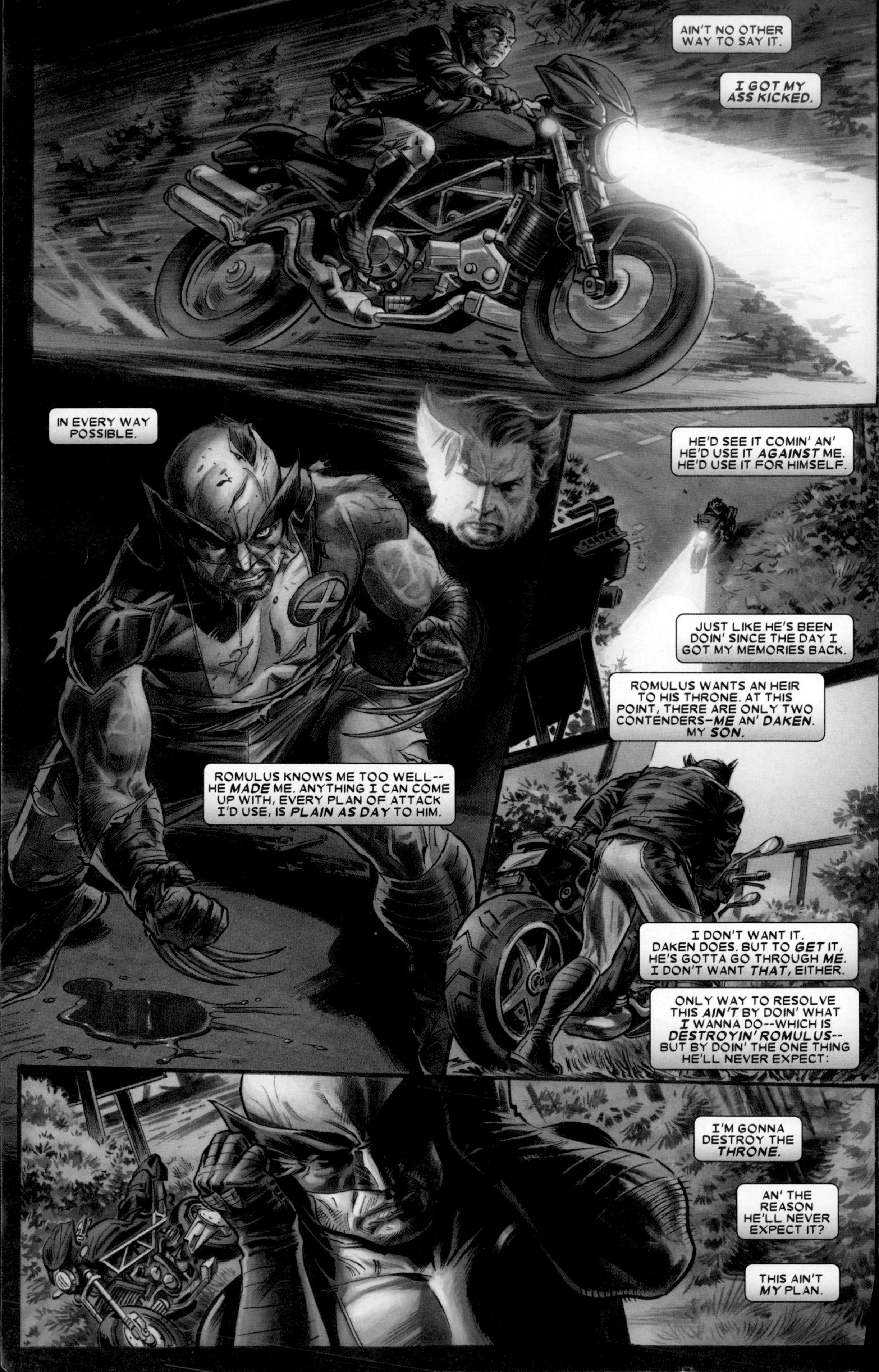
AIN'T NO OTHER WAY TO SAY IT.
I GOT MY ASS KICKED.
IN EVERY WAY POSSIBLE.
ROMULUS KNOWS ME TOO WELL--HE MADE ME. ANYTHING I CAN COME UP WITH, EVERY PLAN OF ATTACK I'D USE, IS PLAIN AS DAY TO HIM.
HE'D SEE IT COMIN' AN' HE'D USE IT AGAINST ME. HE'D USE IT FOR HIMSELF.
JUST LIKE HE'S BEEN DOIN' SINCE THE DAY I GOT MY MEMORIES BACK.
ROMULUS WANTS AN HEIR TO HIS THRONE. AT THIS POINT, THERE ARE ONLY TWO CONTENDERS--ME AN' DAKEN. MY SON.
I DON'T WANT IT. DAKEN DOES. BUT TO GET IT, HE'S GOTTA GO THROUGH ME. I DON'T WANT THAT, EITHER.
ONLY WAY TO RESOLVE THIS AIN'T BY DOIN' WHAT I WANNA DO--WHICH IS DESTROYIN' ROMULUS--BUT BY DOIN' THE ONE THING HE'LL NEVER EXPECT:
I'M GONNA DESTROY THE THRONE.
AN' THE REASON HE'LL NEVER EXPECT IT?
THIS AIN'T MY PLAN.

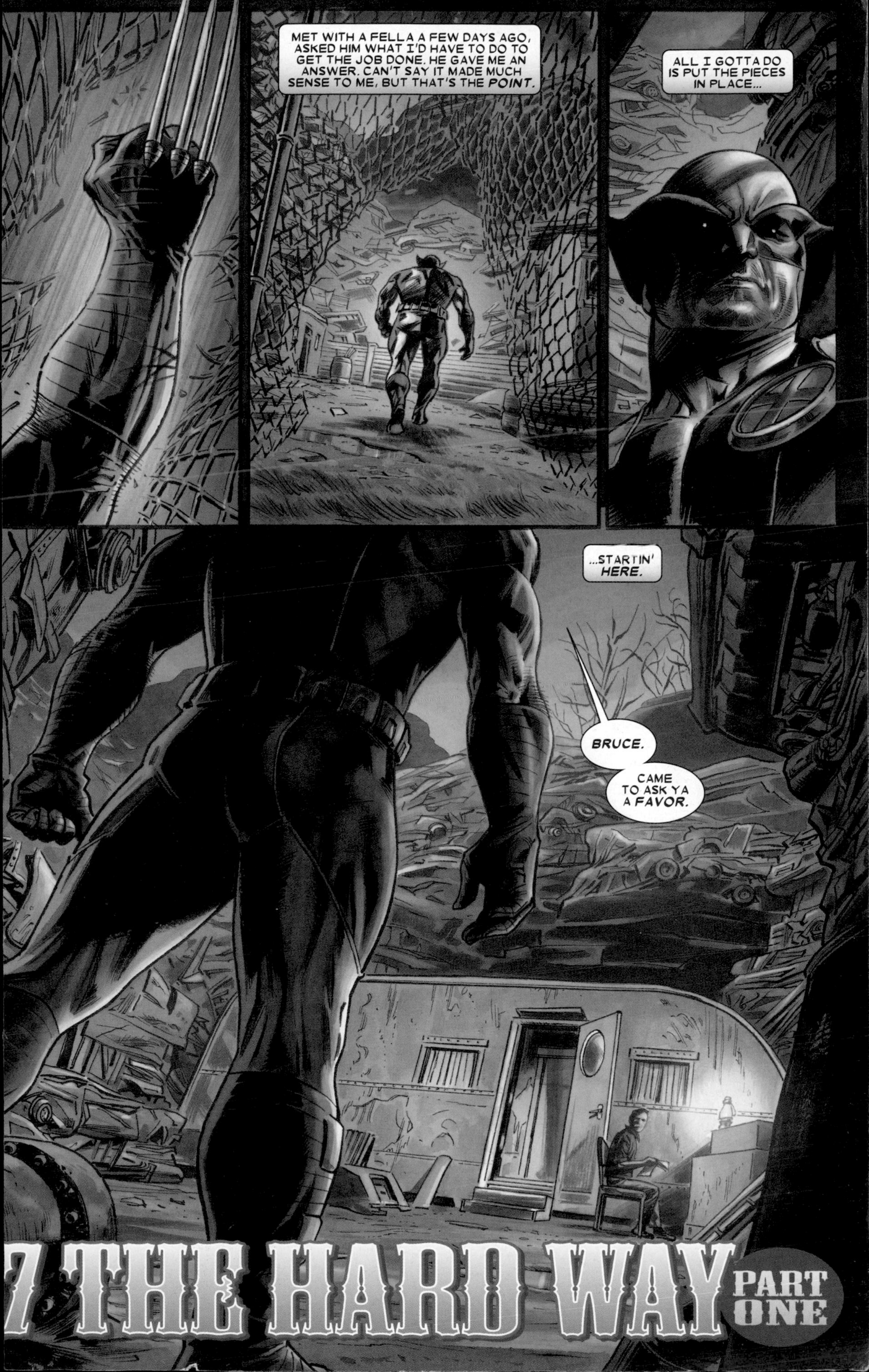
MET WITH A FELLA A FEW DAYS AGO, ASKED HIM WHAT I'D HAVE TO DO TO GET THE JOB DONE. HE GAVE ME AN ANSWER. CAN'T SAY IT MADE MUCH SENSE TO ME, BUT THAT'S THE *POINT*.
ALL I GOTTA DO IS PUT THE PIECES IN PLACE...
...STARTIN' *HERE*.
BRUCE.
CAME TO ASK YA A *FAVOR*.
7 THE HARD WAY
PART ONE

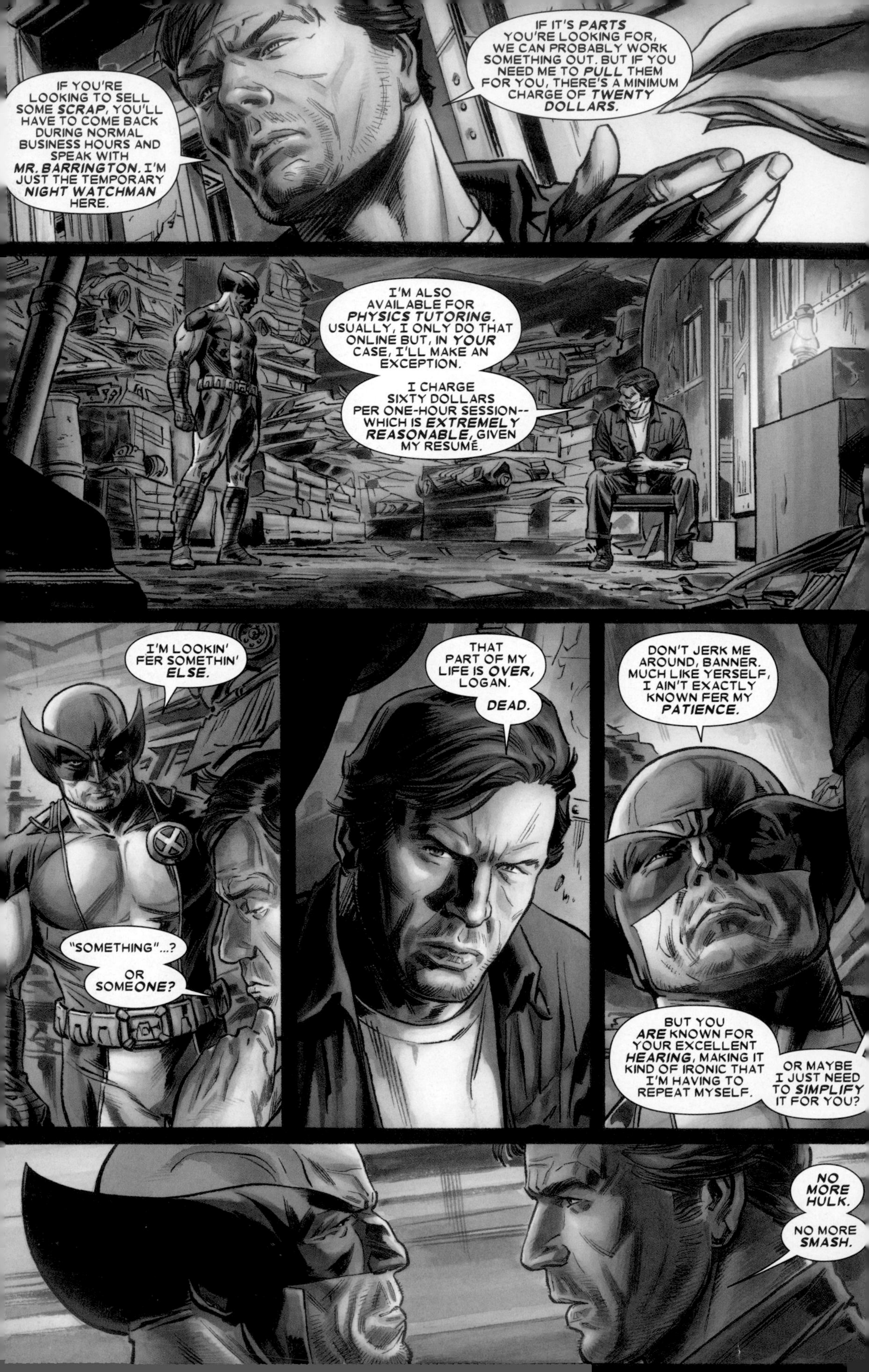

IF YOU'RE LOOKING TO SELL SOME SCRAP, YOU'LL HAVE TO COME BACK DURING NORMAL BUSINESS HOURS AND SPEAK WITH MR. BARRINGTON. I'M JUST THE TEMPORARY NIGHT WATCHMAN HERE.
IF IT'S PARTS YOU'RE LOOKING FOR, WE CAN PROBABLY WORK SOMETHING OUT. BUT IF YOU NEED ME TO PULL THEM FOR YOU, THERE'S A MINIMUM CHARGE OF TWENTY DOLLARS.
I'M ALSO AVAILABLE FOR PHYSICS TUTORING. USUALLY, I ONLY DO THAT ONLINE BUT, IN YOUR CASE, I'LL MAKE AN EXCEPTION.
I CHARGE SIXTY DOLLARS PER ONE-HOUR SESSION-- WHICH IS EXTREMELY REASONABLE, GIVEN MY RESUMÉ.
I'M LOOKIN' FER SOMETHIN' ELSE.
"SOMETHING"...?
OR SOMEONE?
THAT PART OF MY LIFE IS OVER, LOGAN.
DEAD.
DON'T JERK ME AROUND, BANNER. MUCH LIKE YERSELF, I AIN'T EXACTLY KNOWN FER MY PATIENCE.
BUT YOU ARE KNOWN FOR YOUR EXCELLENT HEARING, MAKING IT KIND OF IRONIC THAT I'M HAVING TO REPEAT MYSELF.
OR MAYBE I JUST NEED TO SIMPLIFY IT FOR YOU?
NO MORE HULK.
NO MORE SMASH.

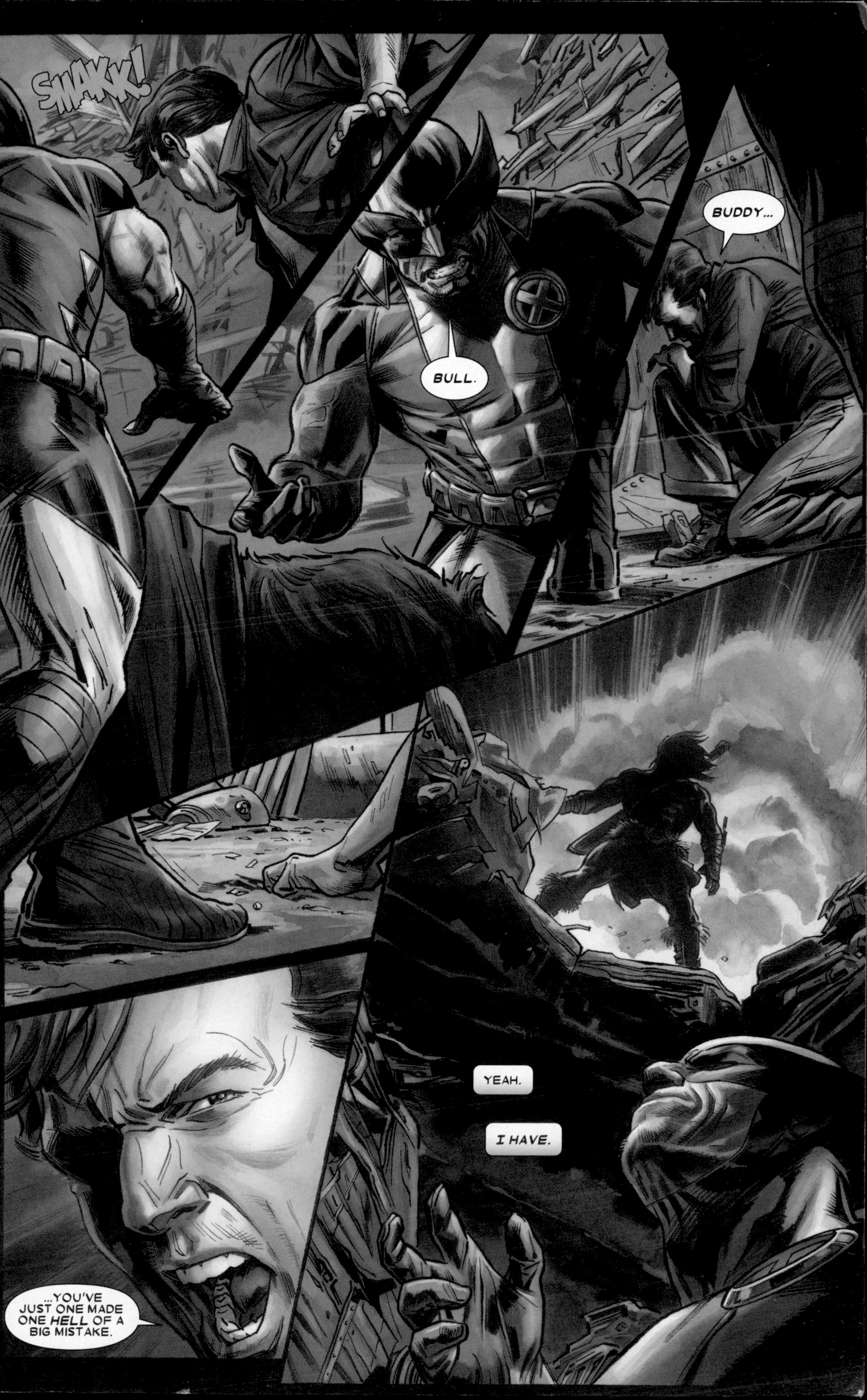
SHAKK!
BULL.
BUDDY...
YEAH.
I HAVE.
...YOU'VE JUST ONE MADE ONE HELL OF A BIG MISTAKE.

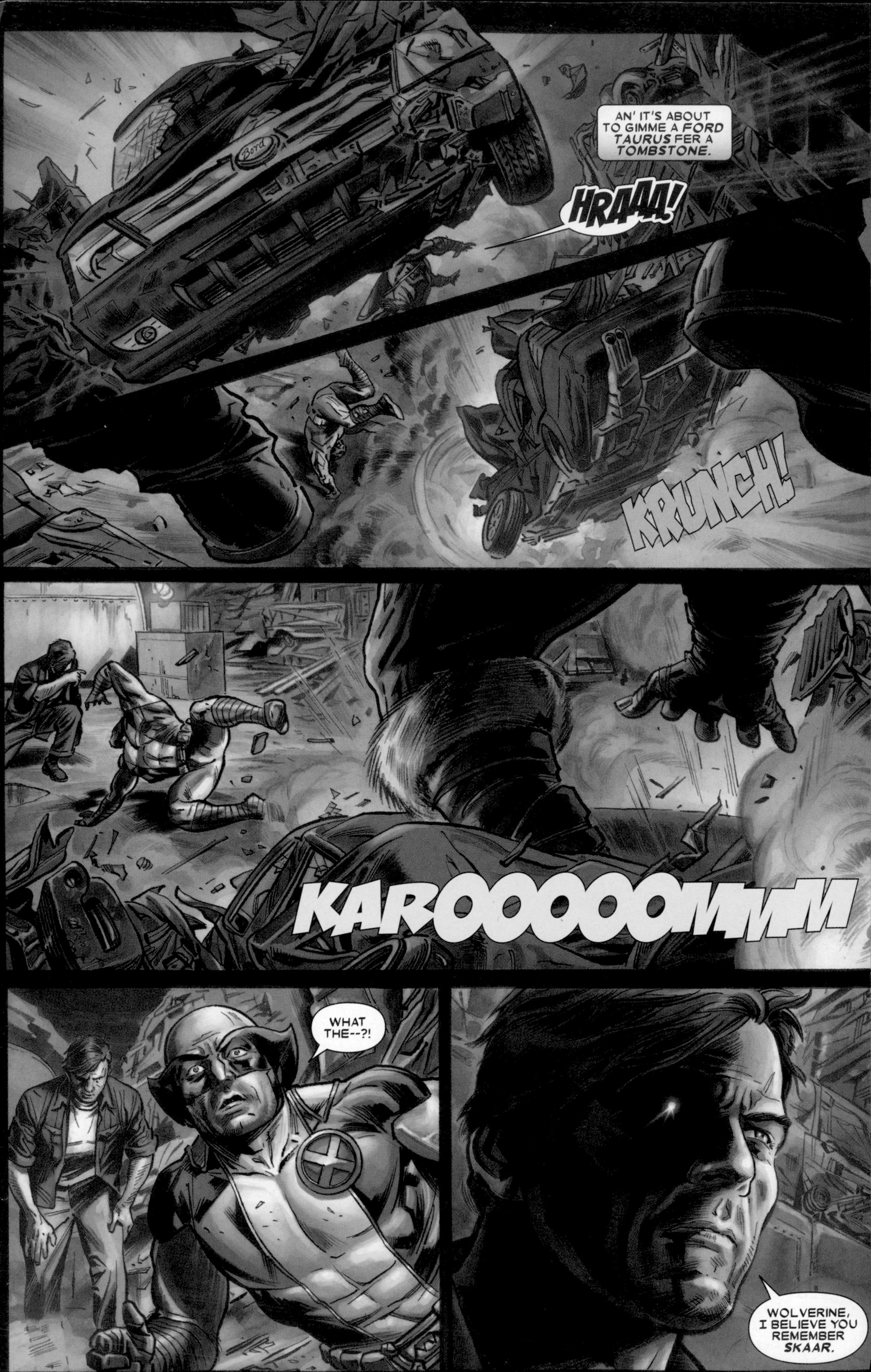
AN' IT'S ABOUT TO GIMME A FORD TAURUS FER A TOMBSTONE.
HRAAA!
KRUNCH!
KAROOOOOOMMM
WHAT THE--?!
WOLVERINE, I BELIEVE YOU REMEMBER SKAAR.

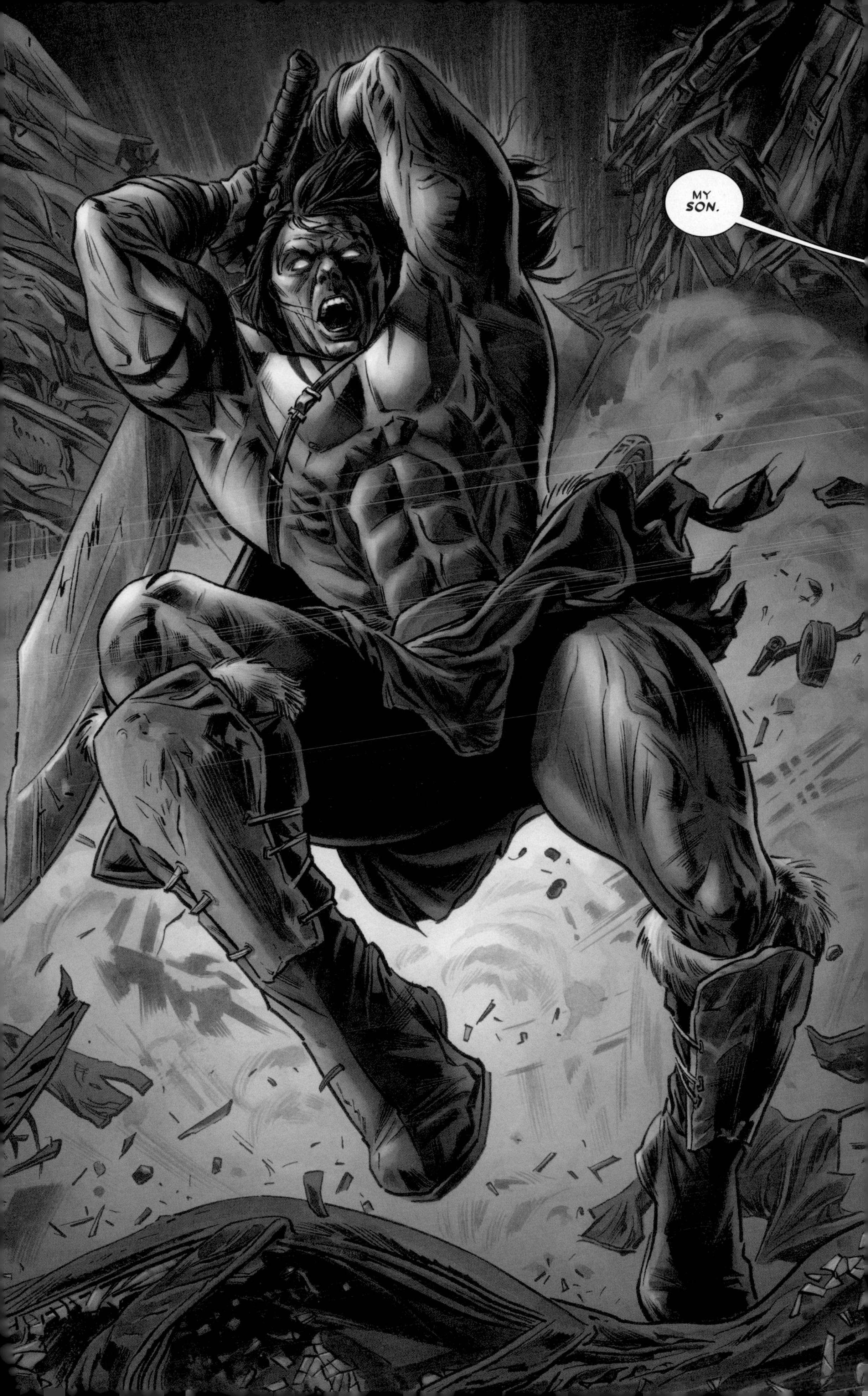
MY SON.

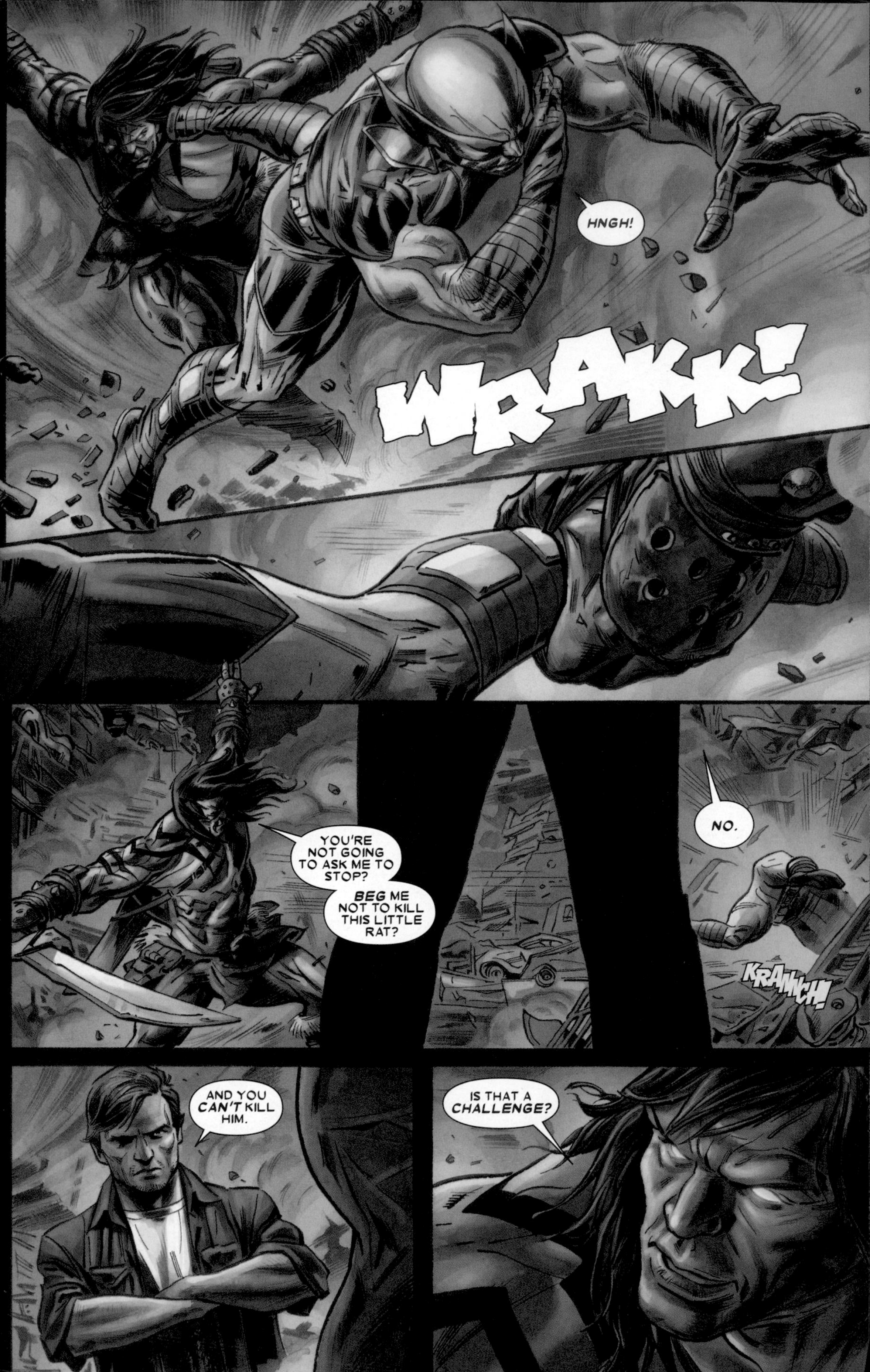
HNGH!
WRAKK!
YOU'RE NOT GOING TO ASK ME TO STOP?
BEG ME NOT TO KILL THIS LITTLE RAT?
NO.
KRANNCH!
AND YOU CAN'T KILL HIM.
IS THAT A CHALLENGE?

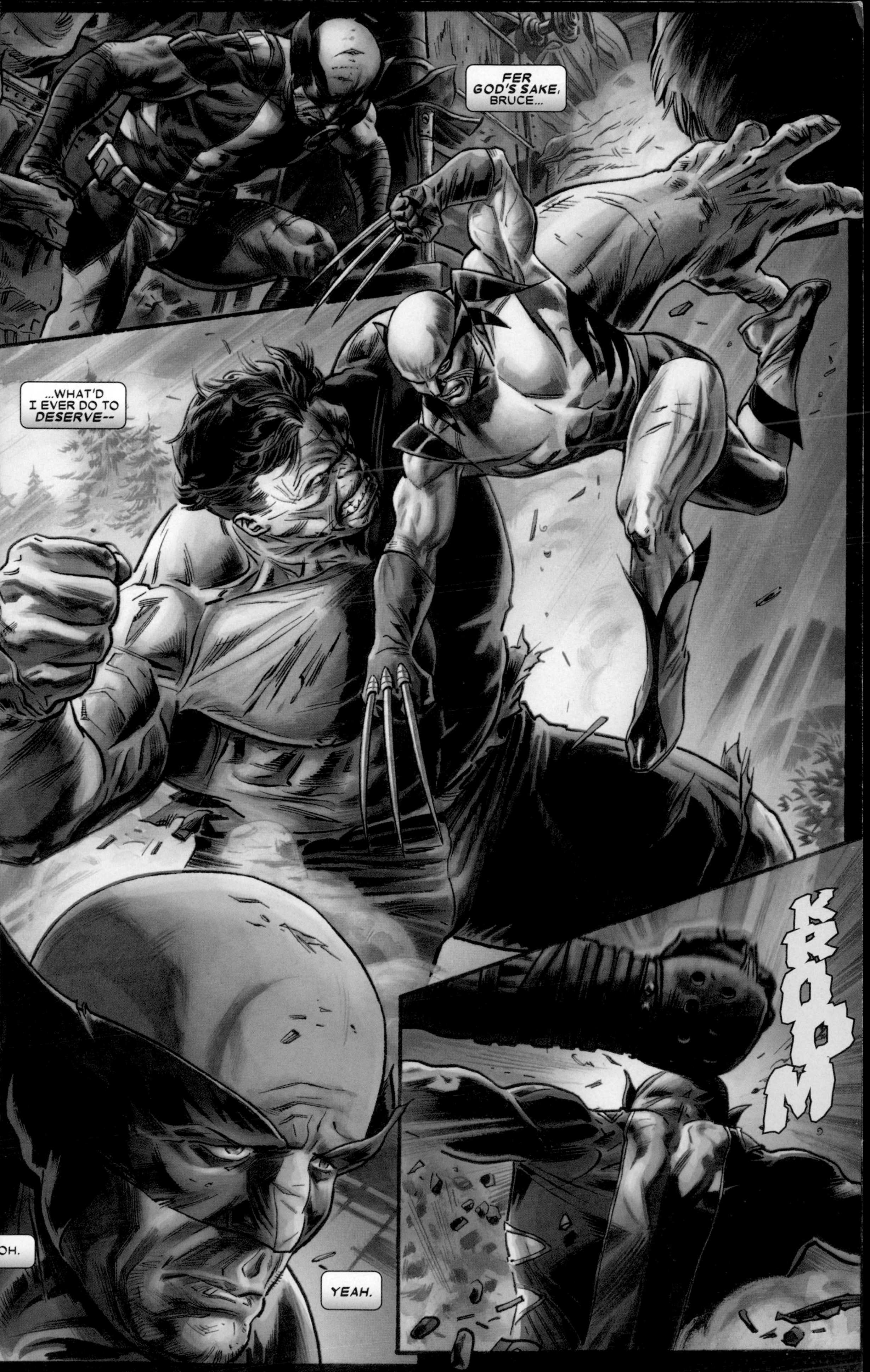

FER GOD'S SAKE, BRUCE...
...WHAT'D I EVER DO TO DESERVE--
KROOM
OH.
YEAH.

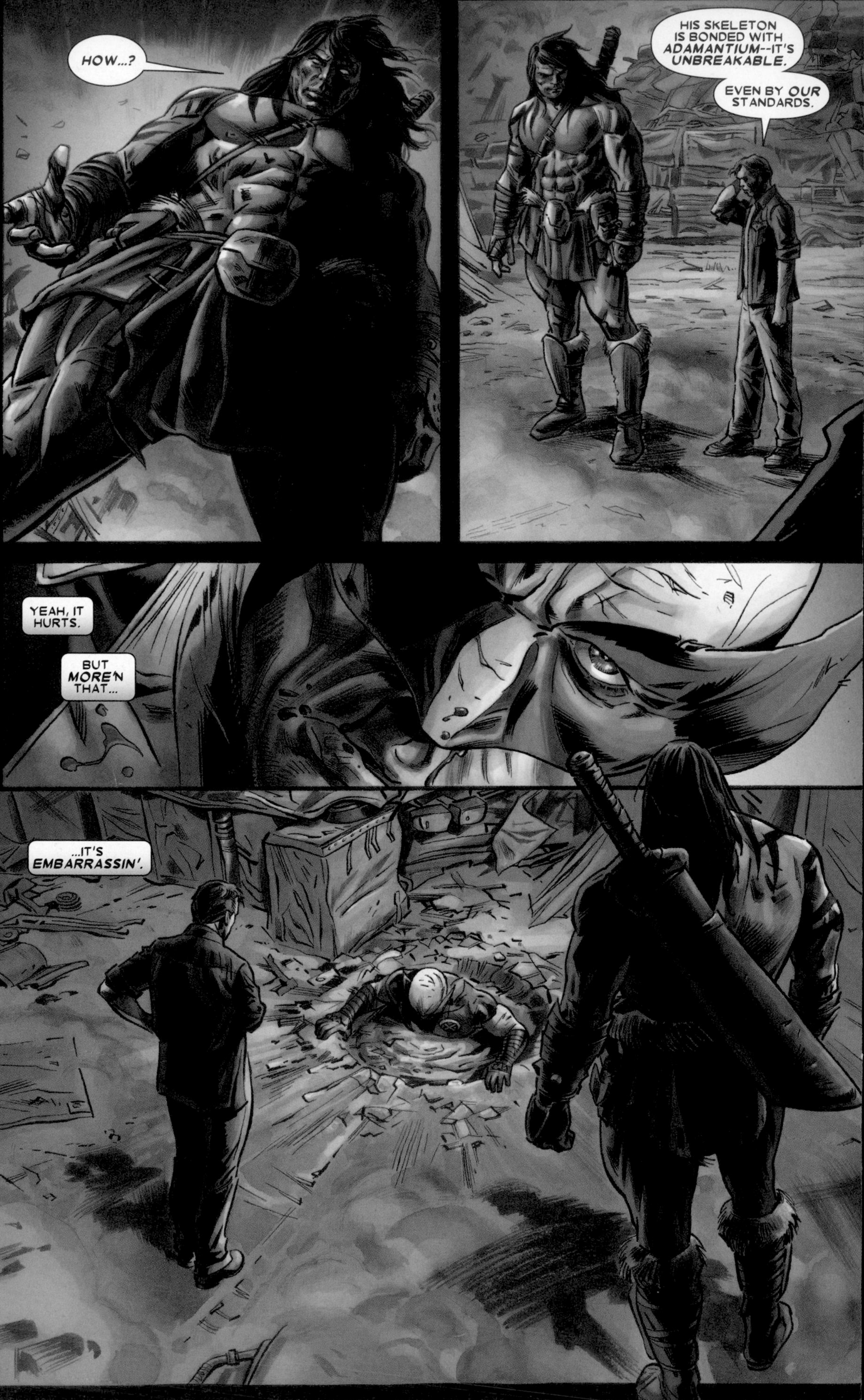
HOW...?
HIS SKELETON IS BONDED WITH ADAMANTIUM--IT'S UNBREAKABLE.
EVEN BY OUR STANDARDS.
YEAH, IT HURTS.
BUT MORE'N THAT...
...IT'S EMBARRASSIN'.

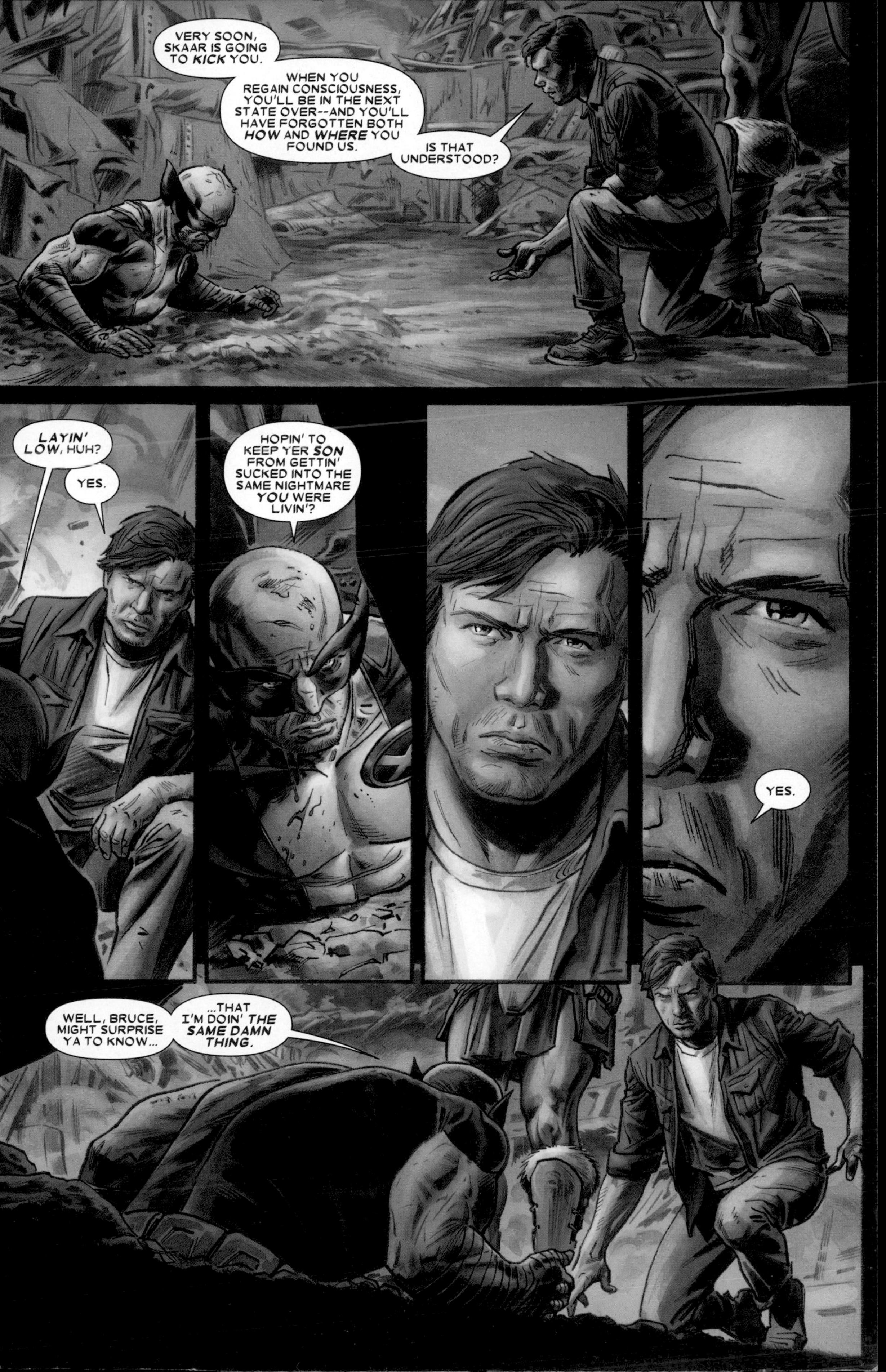
VERY SOON, SKAAR IS GOING TO *KICK* YOU.
WHEN YOU REGAIN CONSCIOUSNESS, YOU'LL BE IN THE NEXT STATE OVER--AND YOU'LL HAVE FORGOTTEN BOTH *HOW* AND *WHERE* YOU FOUND US.
IS THAT UNDERSTOOD?
LAYIN' LOW, HUH?
YES.
HOPIN' TO KEEP YER *SON* FROM GETTIN' SUCKED INTO THE SAME NIGHTMARE *YOU* WERE LIVIN'?
YES.
WELL, BRUCE, MIGHT SURPRISE YA TO KNOW...
...THAT I'M DOIN' *THE SAME DAMN THING.*

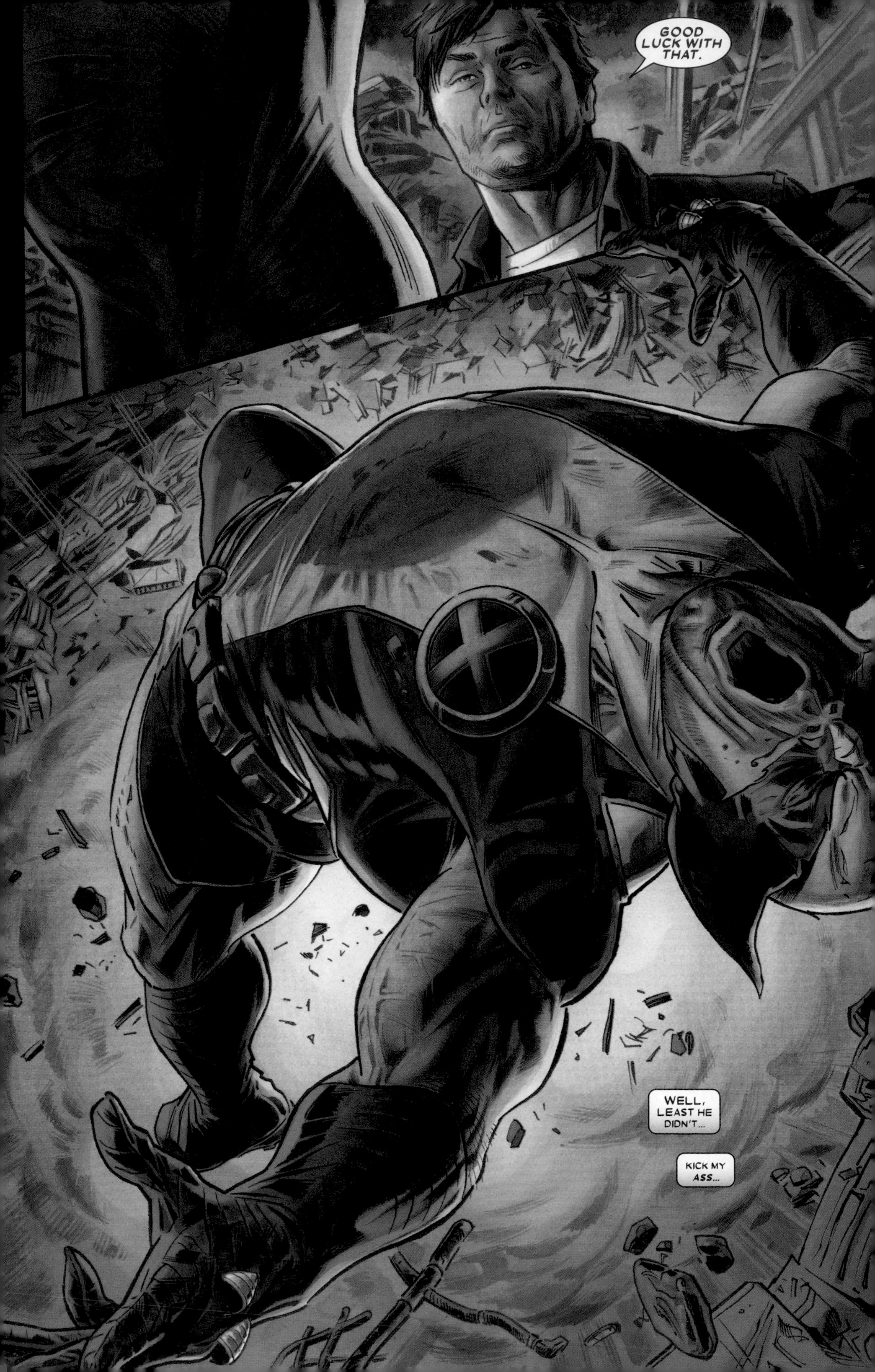
GOOD LUCK WITH THAT.
WELL, LEAST HE DIDN'T...
KICK MY ASS...

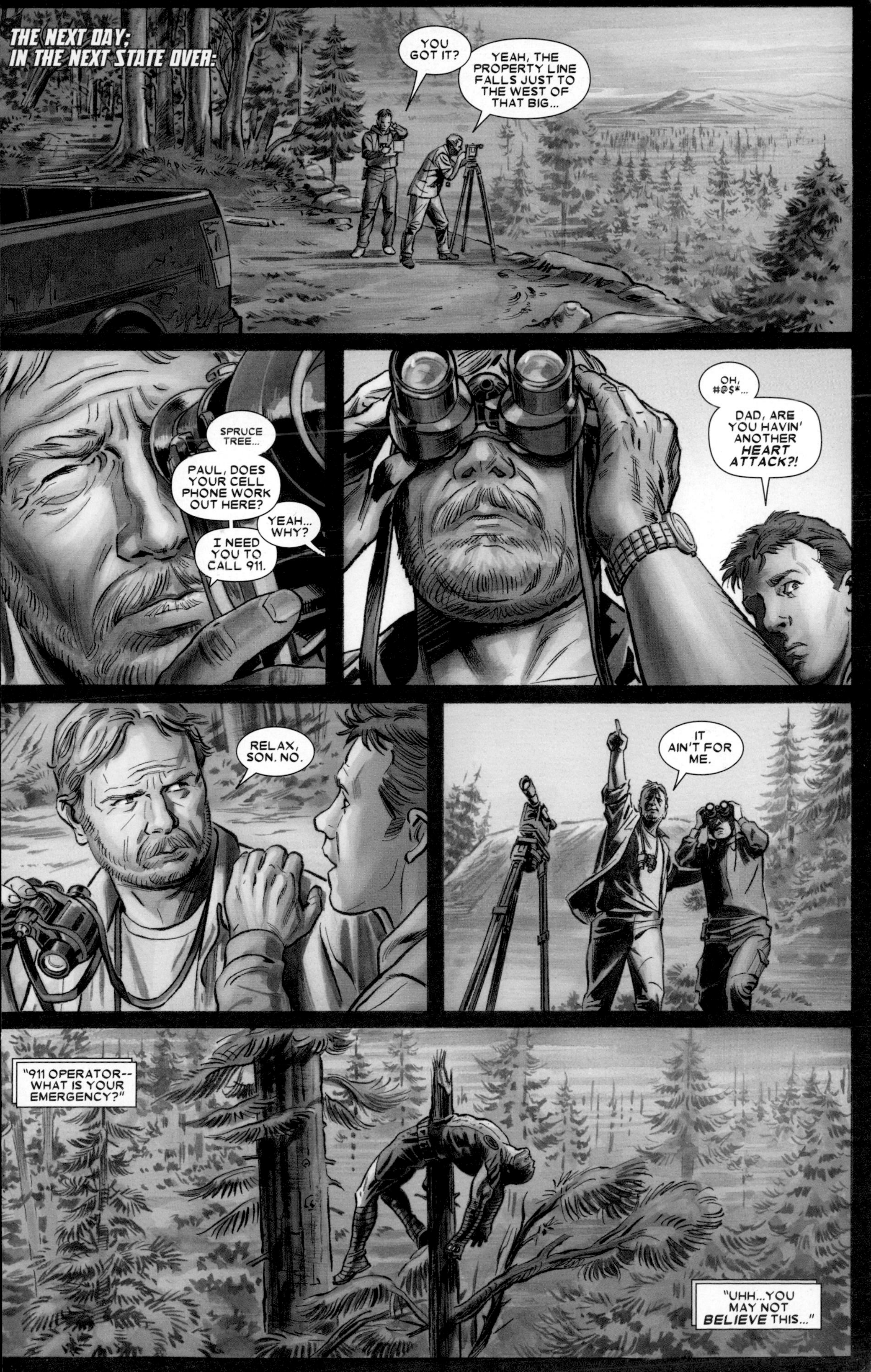
THE NEXT DAY; IN THE NEXT STATE OVER:
YOU GOT IT?
YEAH, THE PROPERTY LINE FALLS JUST TO THE WEST OF THAT BIG...
SPRUCE TREE...
PAUL, DOES YOUR CELL PHONE WORK OUT HERE?
YEAH... WHY?
I NEED YOU TO CALL 911.
OH, #@$*...
DAD, ARE YOU HAVIN' ANOTHER HEART ATTACK?!
RELAX, SON. NO.
IT AIN'T FOR ME.
"911 OPERATOR-- WHAT IS YOUR EMERGENCY?"
"UHH...YOU MAY NOT BELIEVE THIS..."

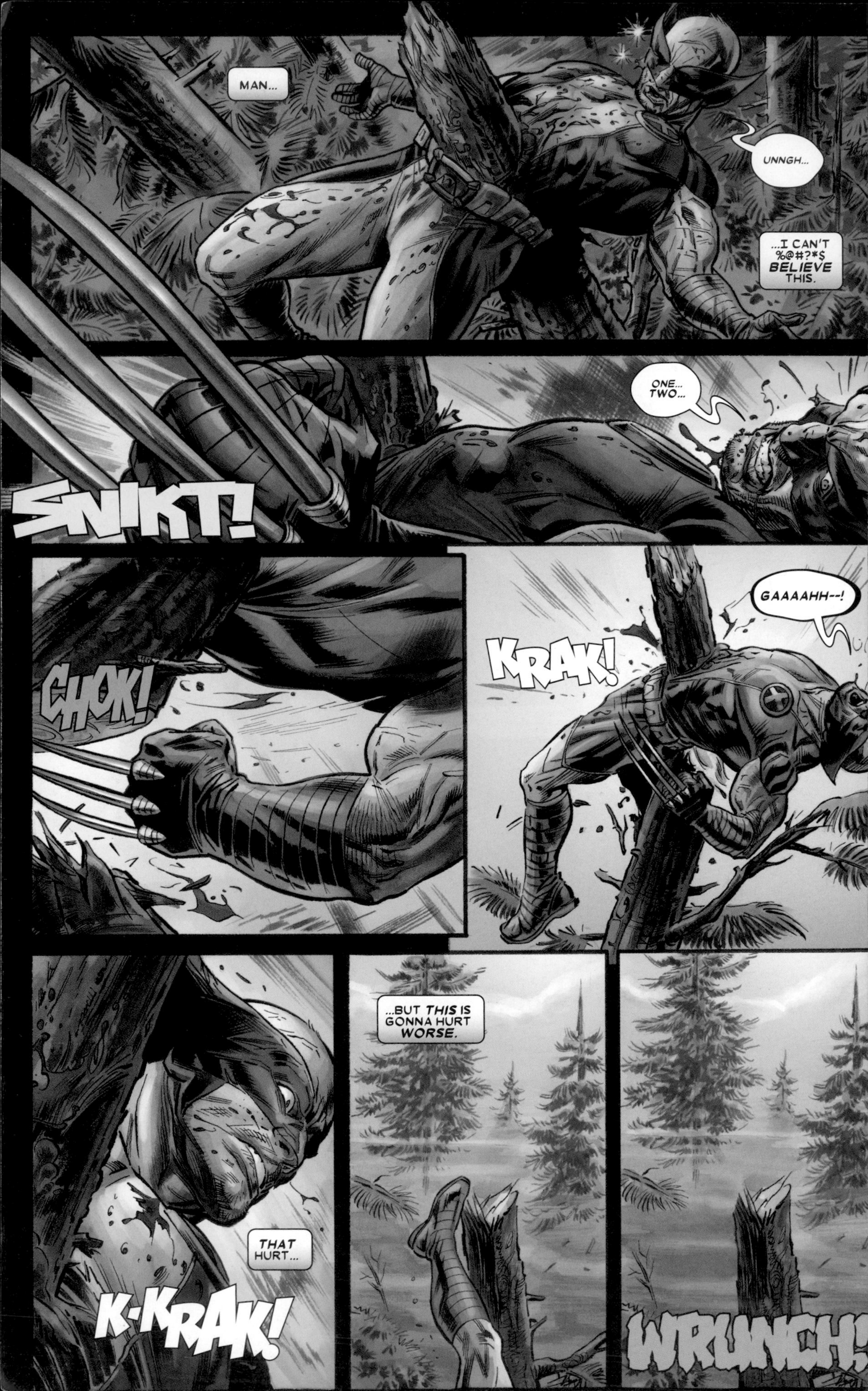
MAN...
UNNGH...
...I CAN'T %@#?*$ BELIEVE THIS.
SNIKT!
ONE... TWO...
CHOK!
KRAK!
GAAAAHH--!
THAT HURT...
K-KRAK!
...BUT THIS IS GONNA HURT WORSE.
WRUNCH!

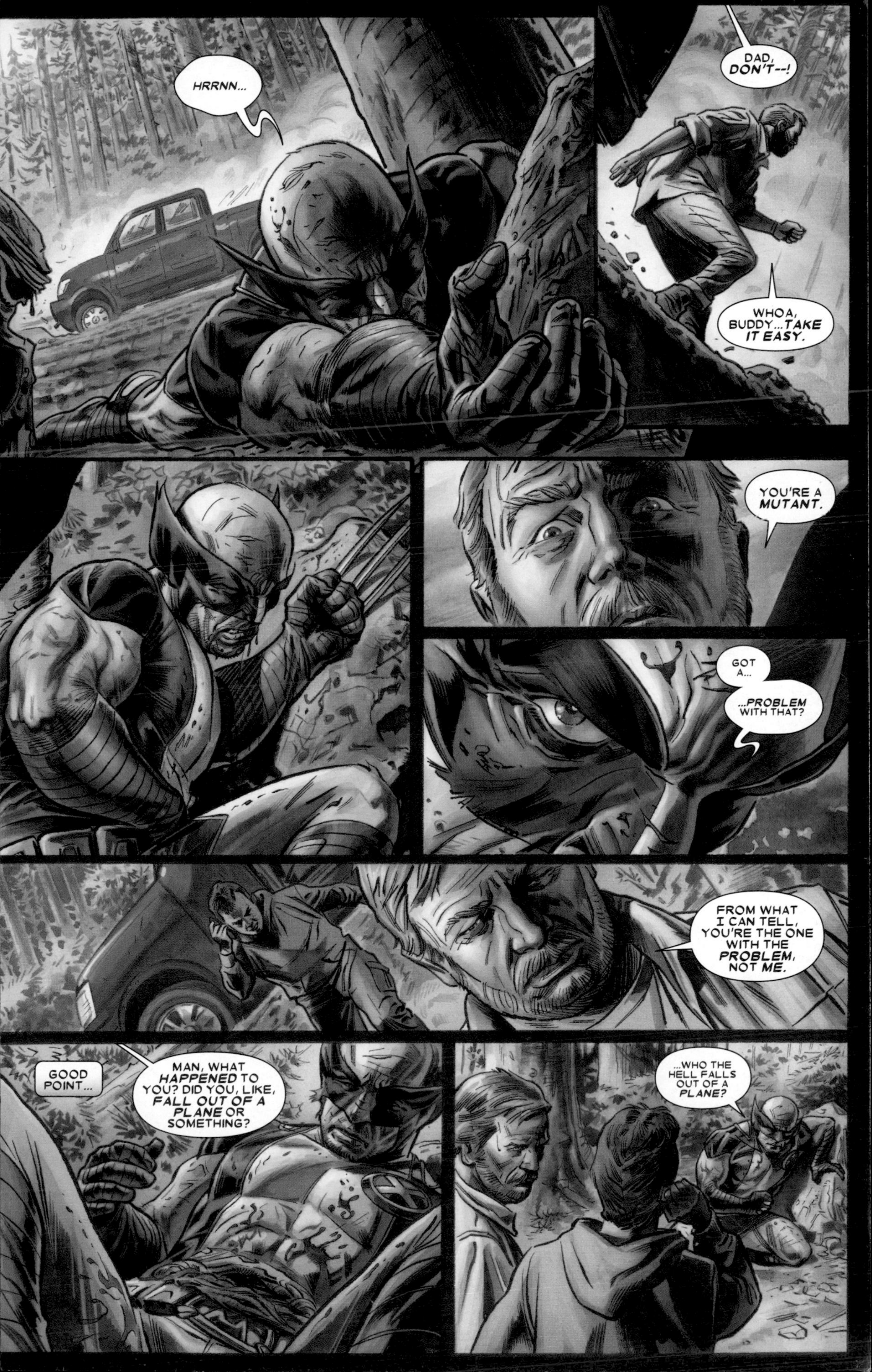
HRRNN...
DAD, DON'T--!
WHOA, BUDDY...TAKE IT EASY.
YOU'RE A MUTANT.
GOT A...
...PROBLEM WITH THAT?
FROM WHAT I CAN TELL, YOU'RE THE ONE WITH THE PROBLEM, NOT ME.
GOOD POINT...
MAN, WHAT HAPPENED TO YOU? DID YOU, LIKE, FALL OUT OF A PLANE OR SOMETHING?
...WHO THE HELL FALLS OUT OF A PLANE?

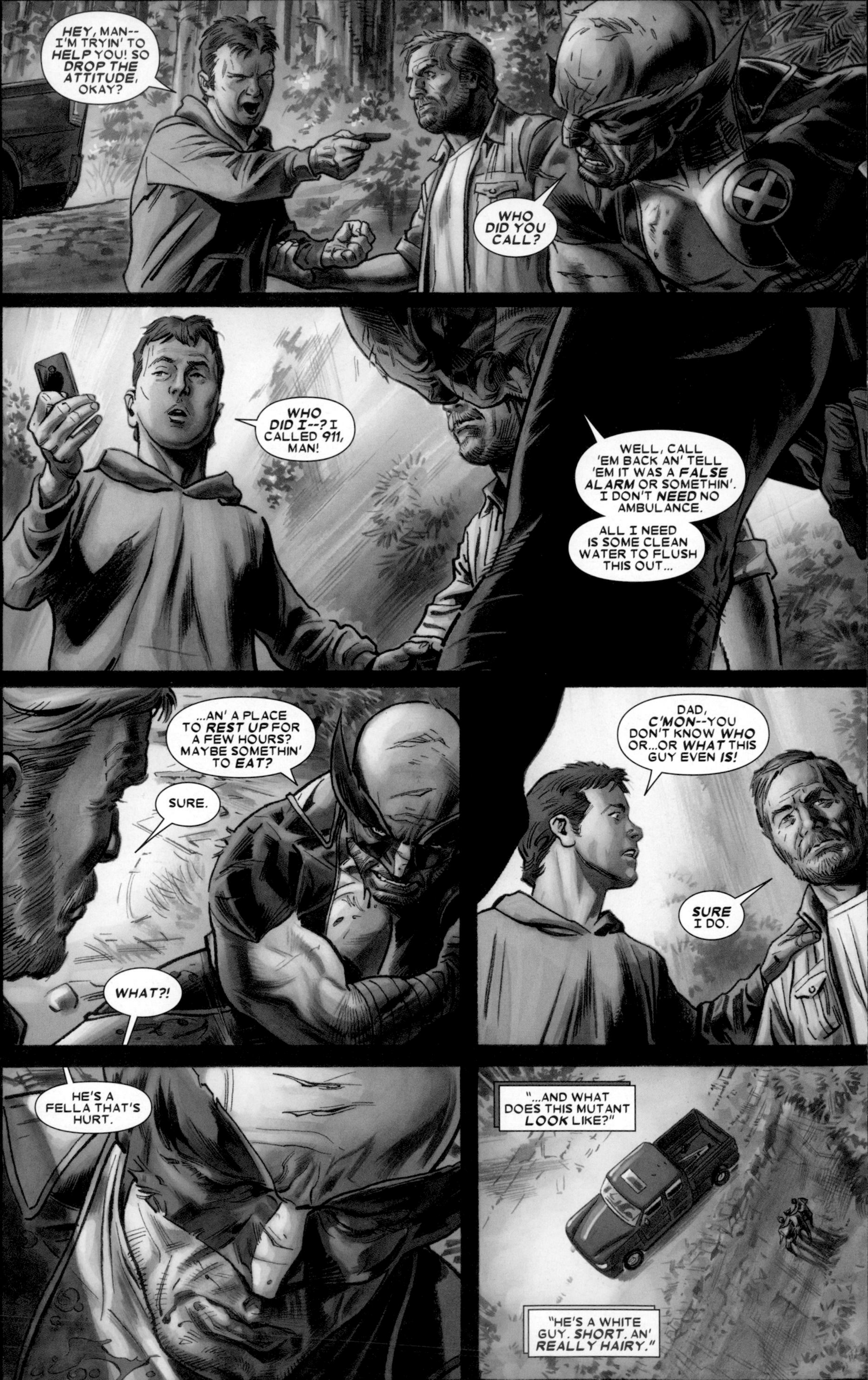
HEY, MAN-- I'M TRYIN' TO HELP YOU! SO DROP THE ATTITUDE, OKAY?
WHO DID YOU CALL?
WHO DID I--? I CALLED 911, MAN!
WELL, CALL 'EM BACK AN' TELL 'EM IT WAS A FALSE ALARM OR SOMETHIN'. I DON'T NEED NO AMBULANCE.
ALL I NEED IS SOME CLEAN WATER TO FLUSH THIS OUT...
...AN' A PLACE TO REST UP FOR A FEW HOURS? MAYBE SOMETHIN' TO EAT?
SURE.
WHAT?!
DAD, C'MON--YOU DON'T KNOW WHO OR...OR WHAT THIS GUY EVEN IS!
SURE I DO.
HE'S A FELLA THAT'S HURT.
"...AND WHAT DOES THIS MUTANT LOOK LIKE?"
"HE'S A WHITE GUY. SHORT. AN' REALLY HAIRY."

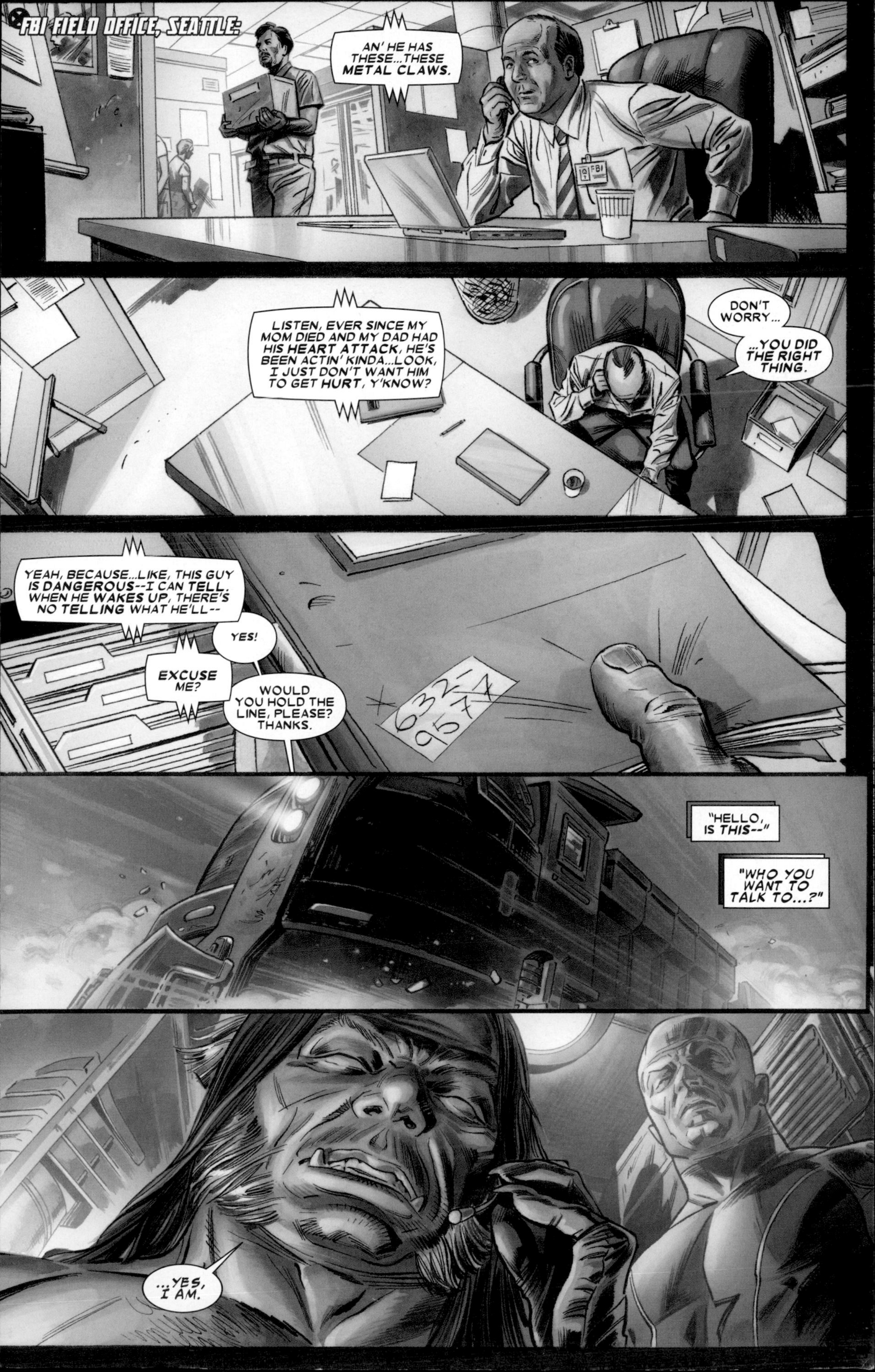
FBI FIELD OFFICE, SEATTLE:
AN' HE HAS THESE...THESE METAL CLAWS.
LISTEN, EVER SINCE MY MOM DIED AND MY DAD HAD HIS HEART ATTACK, HE'S BEEN ACTIN' KINDA...LOOK, I JUST DON'T WANT HIM TO GET HURT, Y'KNOW?
DON'T WORRY...
...YOU DID THE RIGHT THING.
YEAH, BECAUSE...LIKE, THIS GUY IS DANGEROUS--I CAN TELL. WHEN HE WAKES UP, THERE'S NO TELLING WHAT HE'LL--
YES!
EXCUSE ME?
WOULD YOU HOLD THE LINE, PLEASE? THANKS.
632-9577
"HELLO, IS THIS--"
"WHO YOU WANT TO TALK TO...?"
...YES, I AM.

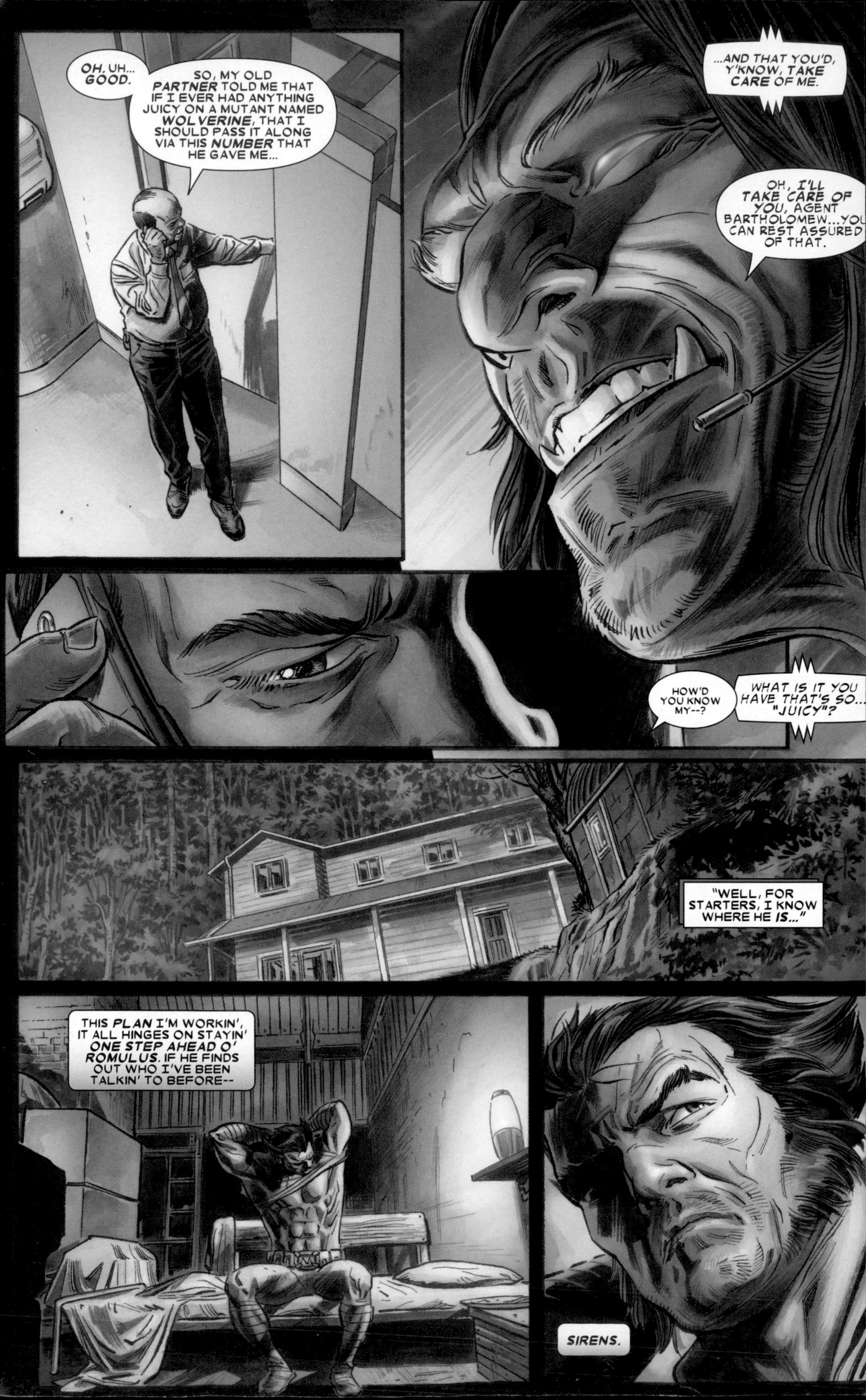

OH, UH... GOOD.
SO, MY OLD PARTNER TOLD ME THAT IF I EVER HAD ANYTHING JUICY ON A MUTANT NAMED WOLVERINE, THAT I SHOULD PASS IT ALONG VIA THIS NUMBER THAT HE GAVE ME...
...AND THAT YOU'D, Y'KNOW, TAKE CARE OF ME.
OH, I'LL TAKE CARE OF YOU, AGENT BARTHOLOMEW...YOU CAN REST ASSURED OF THAT.
HOW'D YOU KNOW MY--?
WHAT IS IT YOU HAVE THAT'S SO... "JUICY"?
"WELL, FOR STARTERS, I KNOW WHERE HE IS..."
THIS PLAN I'M WORKIN', IT ALL HINGES ON STAYIN' ONE STEP AHEAD O' ROMULUS. IF HE FINDS OUT WHO I'VE BEEN TALKIN' TO BEFORE--
SIRENS.

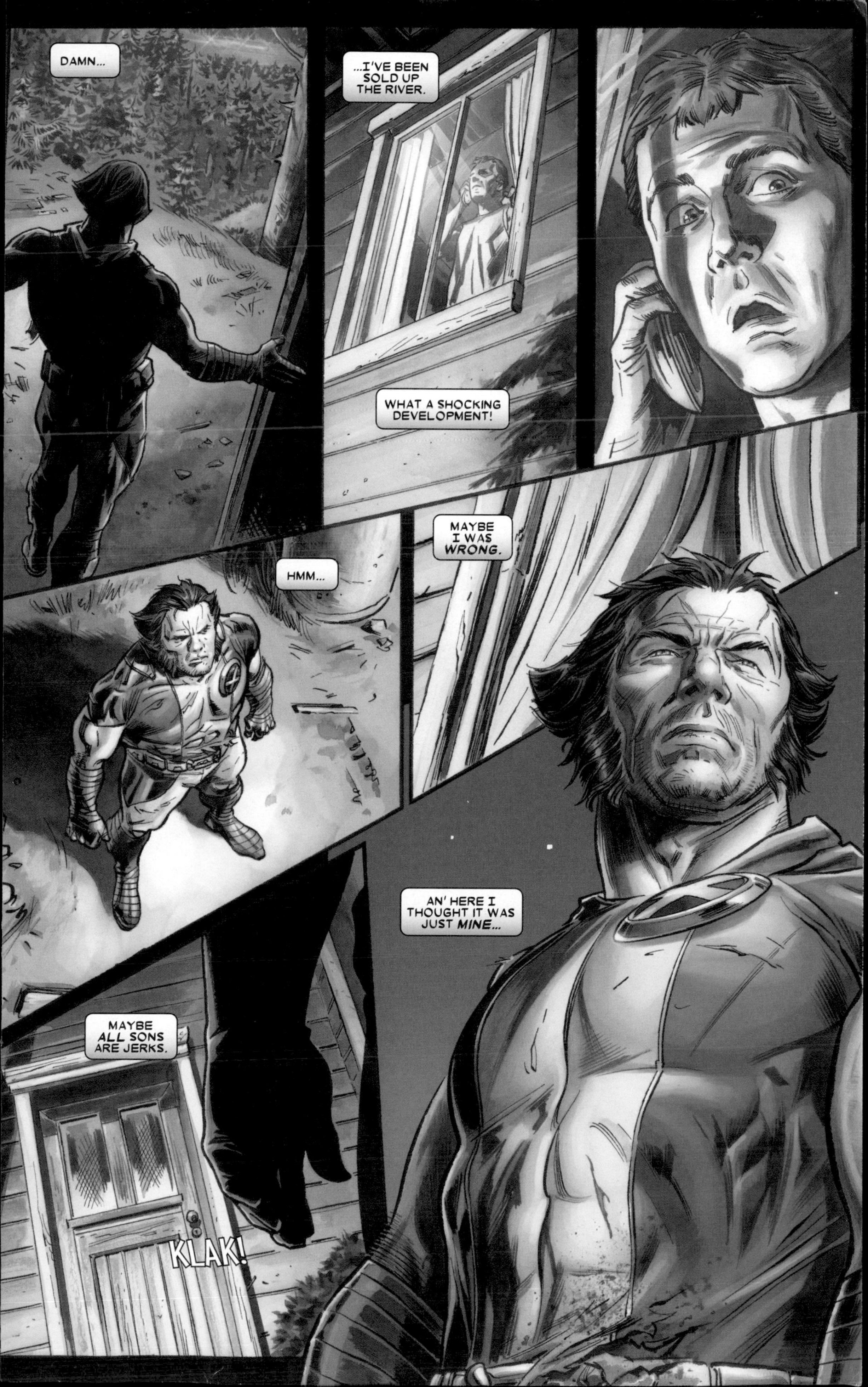
DAMN...
...I'VE BEEN SOLD UP THE RIVER.
WHAT A SHOCKING DEVELOPMENT!
HMM...
MAYBE I WAS WRONG.
AN' HERE I THOUGHT IT WAS JUST MINE...
MAYBE ALL SONS ARE JERKS.
KLAK!

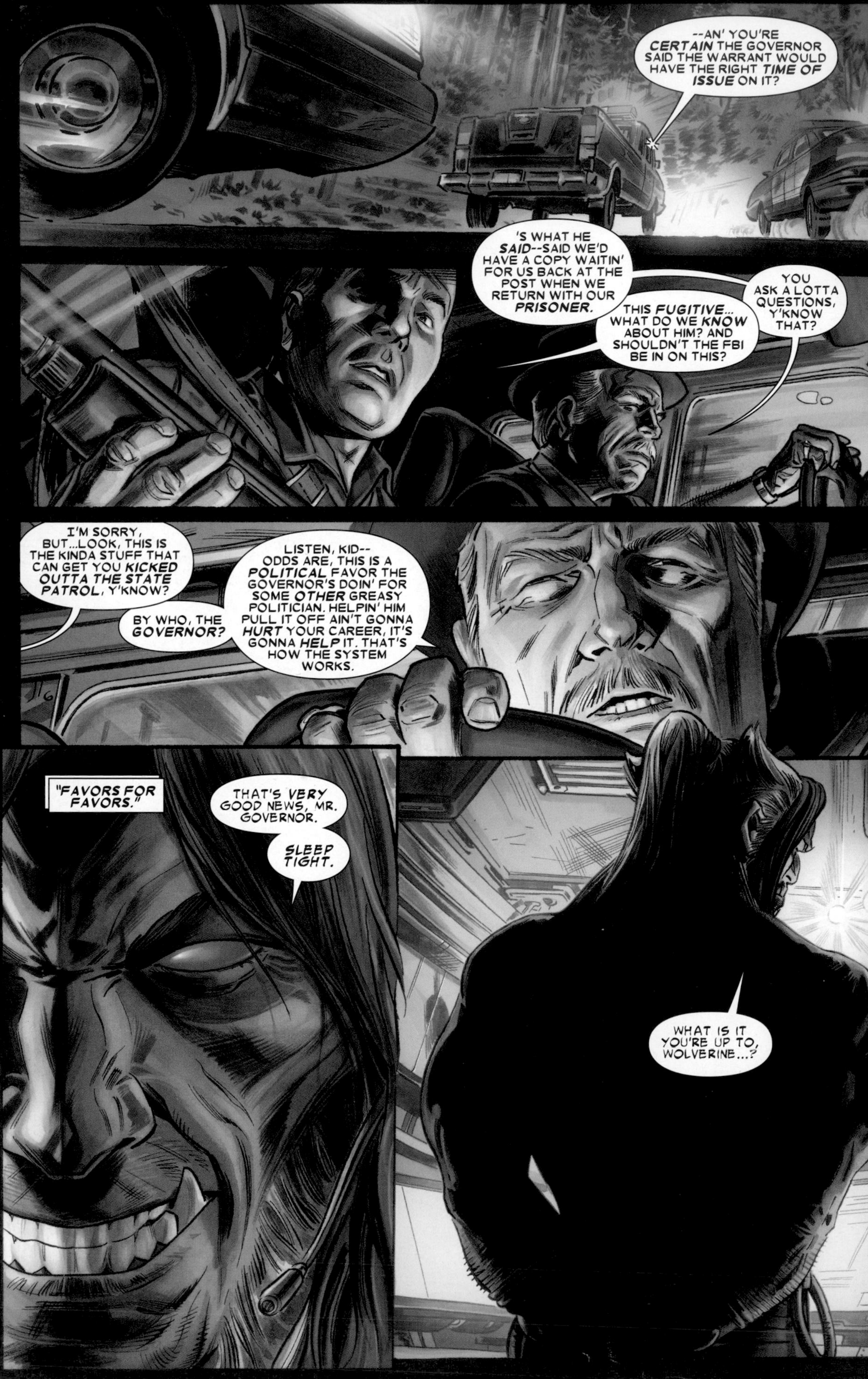
--AN' YOU'RE CERTAIN THE GOVERNOR SAID THE WARRANT WOULD HAVE THE RIGHT TIME OF ISSUE ON IT?
'S WHAT HE SAID--SAID WE'D HAVE A COPY WAITIN' FOR US BACK AT THE POST WHEN WE RETURN WITH OUR PRISONER.
THIS FUGITIVE... WHAT DO WE KNOW ABOUT HIM? AND SHOULDN'T THE FBI BE IN ON THIS?
YOU ASK A LOTTA QUESTIONS, Y'KNOW THAT?
I'M SORRY, BUT...LOOK, THIS IS THE KINDA STUFF THAT CAN GET YOU KICKED OUTTA THE STATE PATROL, Y'KNOW?
BY WHO, THE GOVERNOR?
LISTEN, KID-- ODDS ARE, THIS IS A POLITICAL FAVOR THE GOVERNOR'S DOIN' FOR SOME OTHER GREASY POLITICIAN. HELPIN' HIM PULL IT OFF AIN'T GONNA HURT YOUR CAREER, IT'S GONNA HELP IT. THAT'S HOW THE SYSTEM WORKS.
"FAVORS FOR FAVORS."
THAT'S VERY GOOD NEWS, MR. GOVERNOR.
SLEEP TIGHT.
WHAT IS IT YOU'RE UP TO, WOLVERINE...?

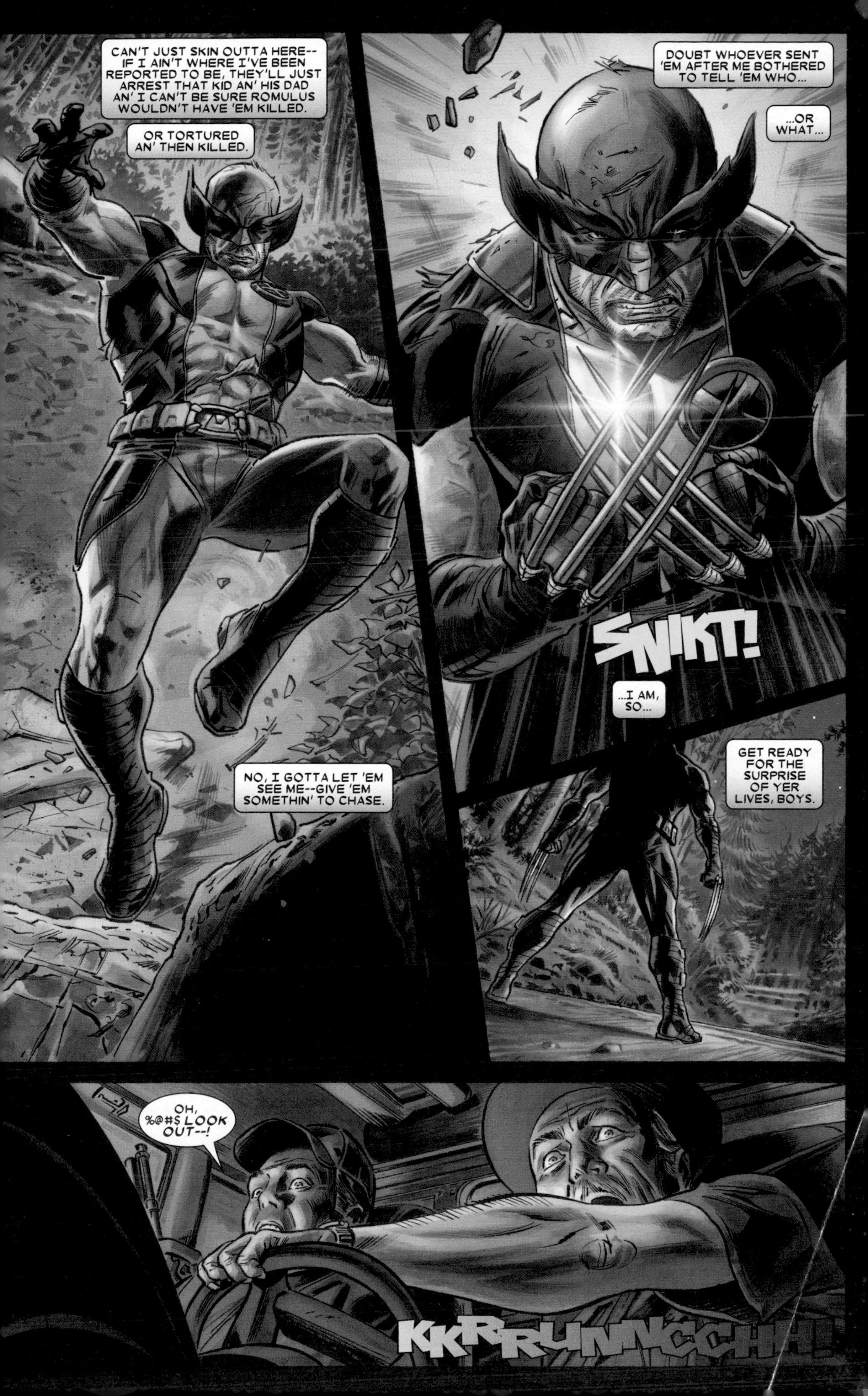
CAN'T JUST SKIN OUTTA HERE-- IF I AIN'T WHERE I'VE BEEN REPORTED TO BE, THEY'LL JUST ARREST THAT KID AN' HIS DAD AN' I CAN'T BE SURE ROMULUS WOULDN'T HAVE 'EM KILLED.
OR TORTURED AN' THEN KILLED.
NO, I GOTTA LET 'EM SEE ME--GIVE 'EM SOMETHIN' TO CHASE.
DOUBT WHOEVER SENT 'EM AFTER ME BOTHERED TO TELL 'EM WHO...
...OR WHAT...
SNIKT!
...I AM, SO...
GET READY FOR THE SURPRISE OF YER LIVES, BOYS.
OH, %@#$ LOOK OUT--!
KKRRRUNNCCHH!

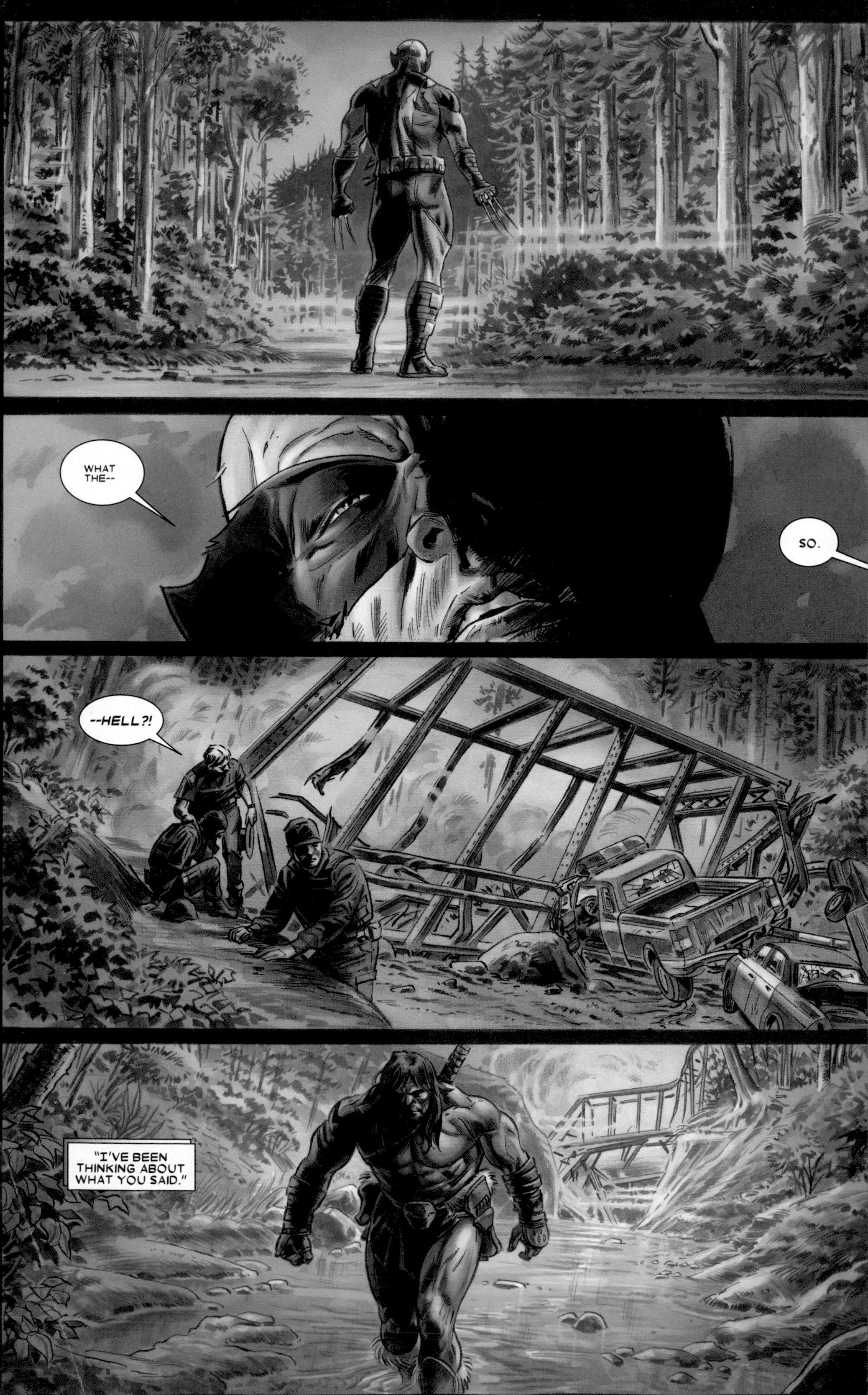
WHAT THE--
SO.
--HELL?!
"I'VE BEEN THINKING ABOUT WHAT YOU SAID."

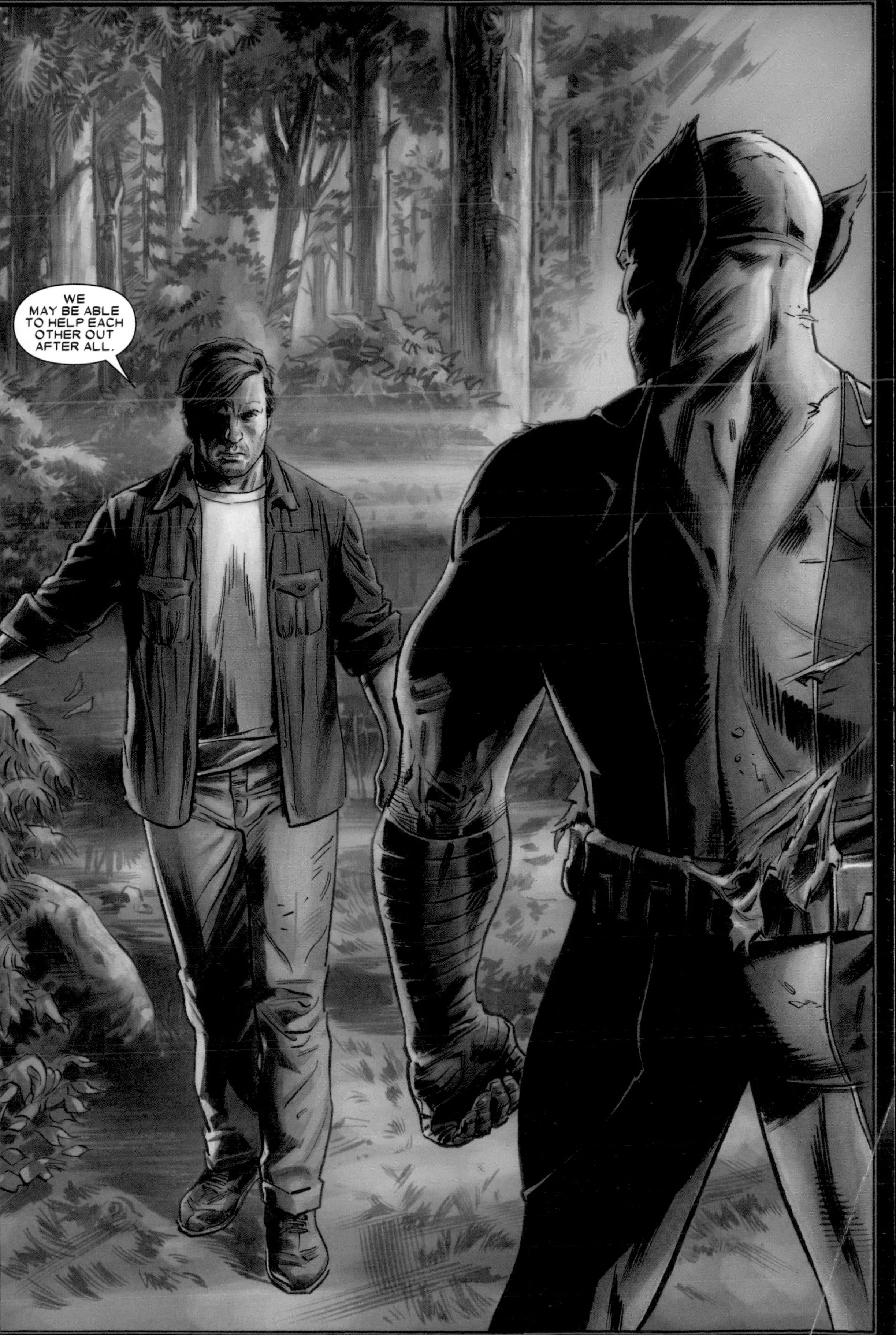
WE MAY BE ABLE TO HELP EACH OTHER OUT AFTER ALL.

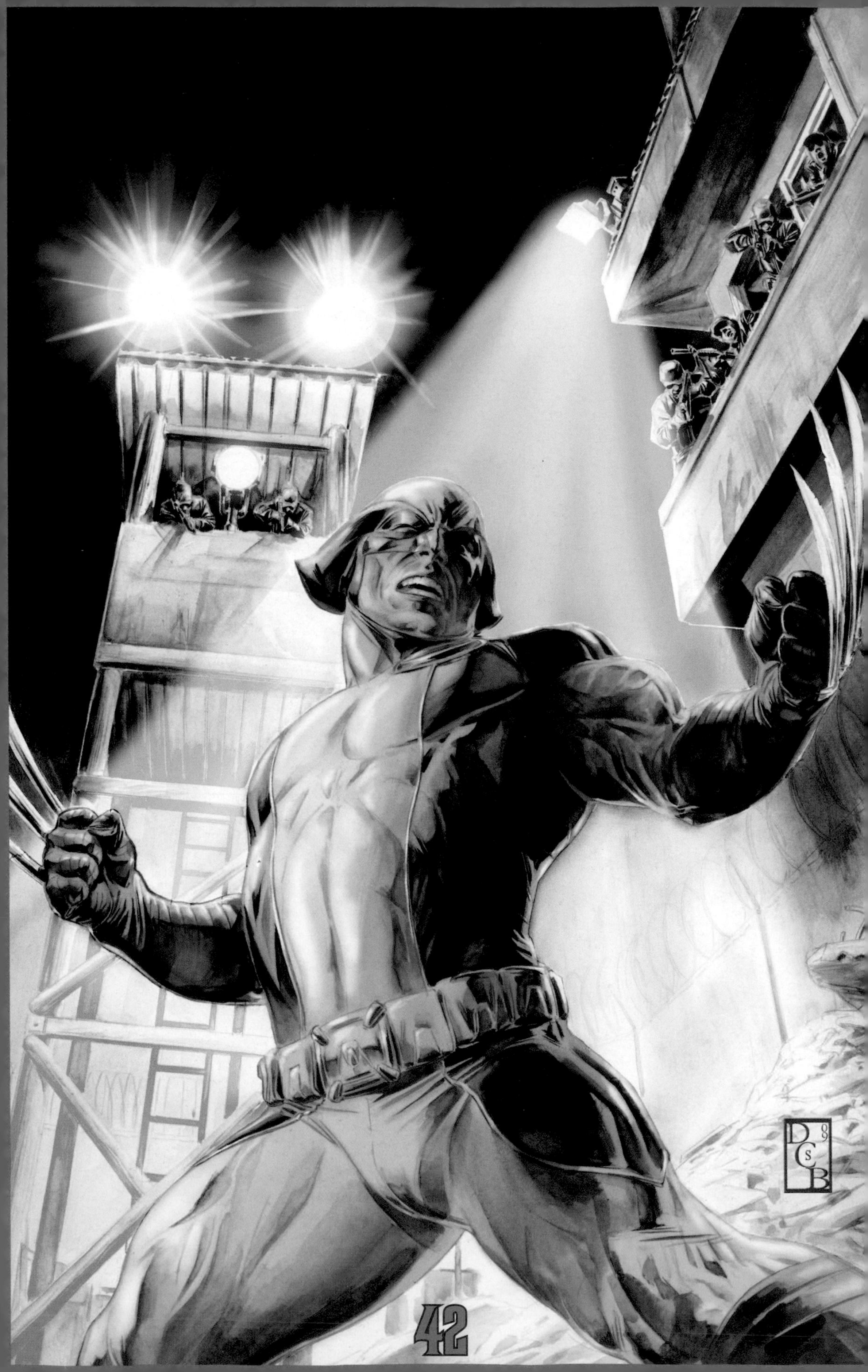
42

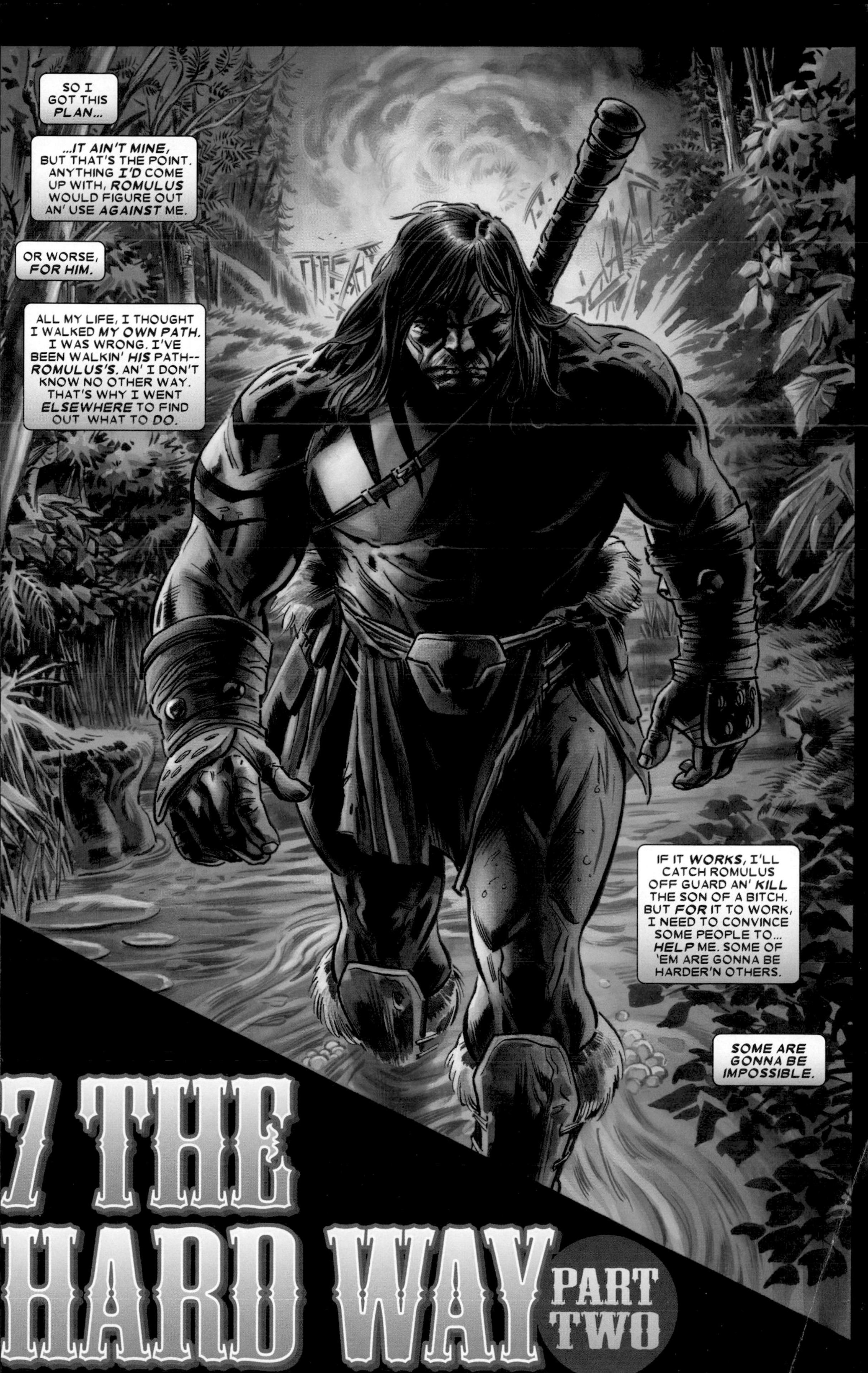
SO I GOT THIS PLAN...
...IT AIN'T MINE, BUT THAT'S THE POINT. ANYTHING I'D COME UP WITH, ROMULUS WOULD FIGURE OUT AN' USE AGAINST ME.
OR WORSE, FOR HIM.
ALL MY LIFE, I THOUGHT I WALKED MY OWN PATH. I WAS WRONG. I'VE BEEN WALKIN' HIS PATH-- ROMULUS'S. AN' I DON'T KNOW NO OTHER WAY. THAT'S WHY I WENT ELSEWHERE TO FIND OUT WHAT TO DO.
IF IT WORKS, I'LL CATCH ROMULUS OFF GUARD AN' KILL THE SON OF A BITCH. BUT FOR IT TO WORK, I NEED TO CONVINCE SOME PEOPLE TO... HELP ME. SOME OF 'EM ARE GONNA BE HARDER'N OTHERS.
SOME ARE GONNA BE IMPOSSIBLE.
7 THE HARD WAY PART TWO

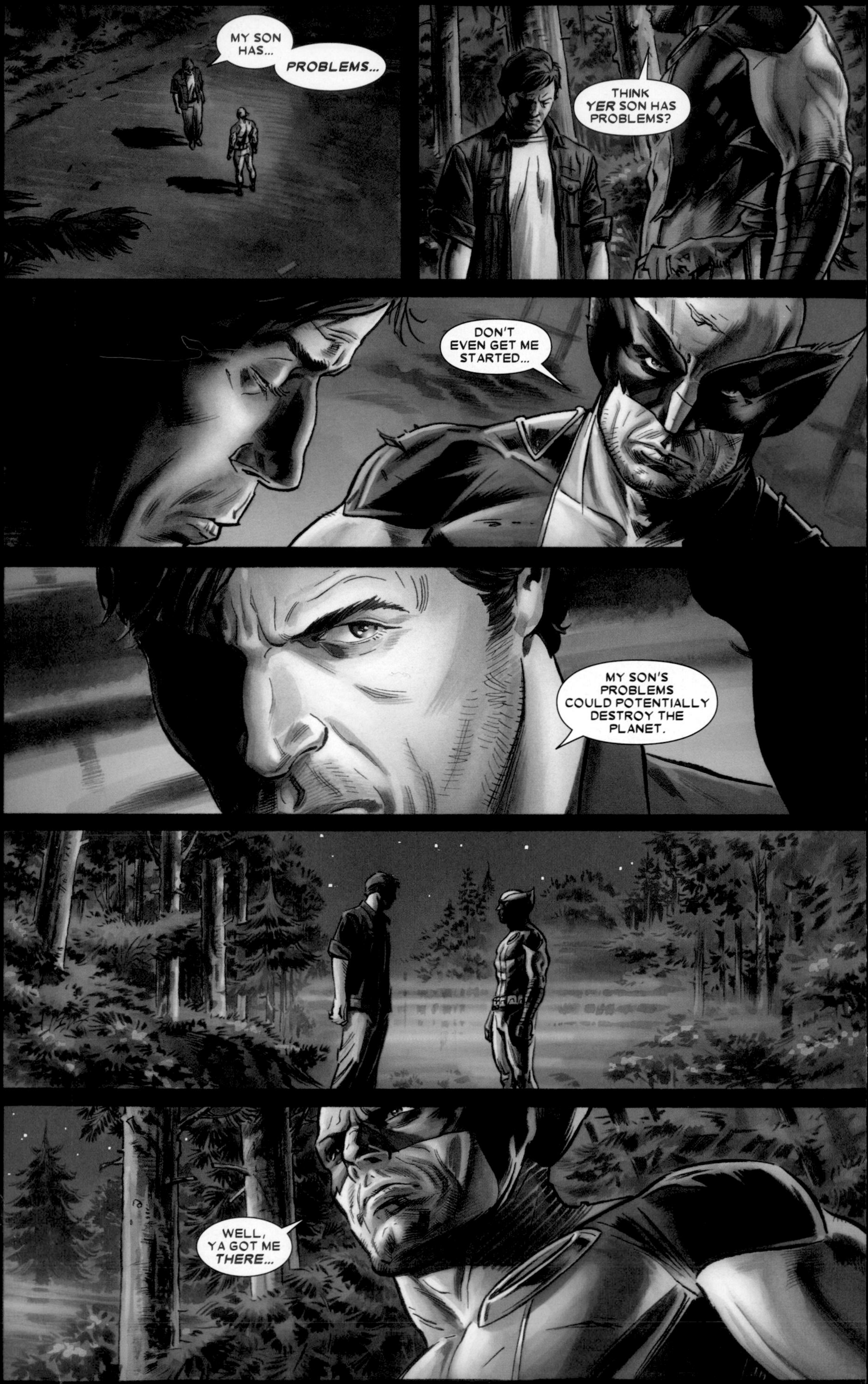
MY SON HAS... PROBLEMS...
THINK YER SON HAS PROBLEMS?
DON'T EVEN GET ME STARTED...
MY SON'S PROBLEMS COULD POTENTIALLY DESTROY THE PLANET.
WELL, YA GOT ME THERE...

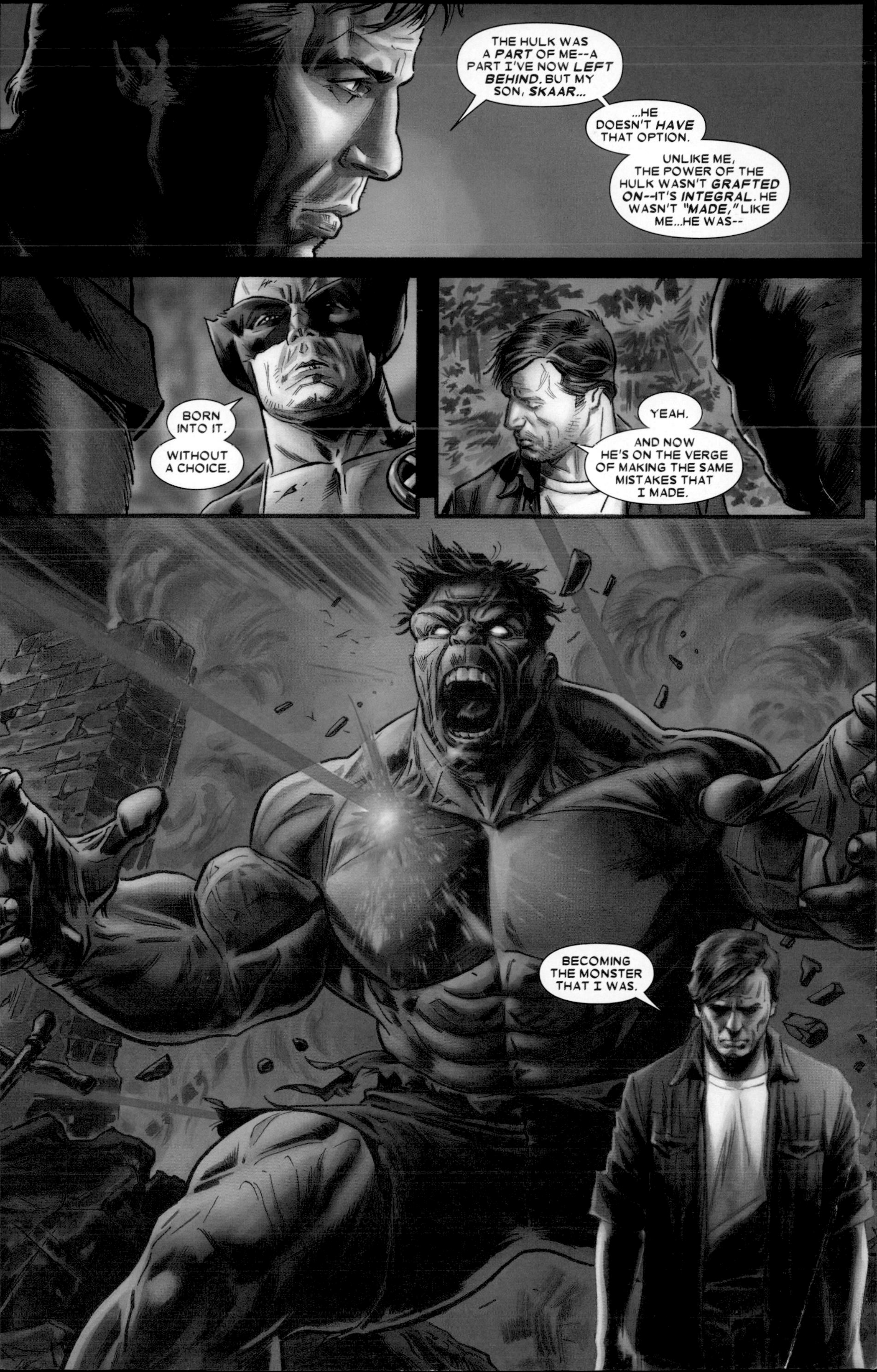
THE HULK WAS A PART OF ME--A PART I'VE NOW LEFT BEHIND. BUT MY SON, SKAAR...
...HE DOESN'T HAVE THAT OPTION.
UNLIKE ME, THE POWER OF THE HULK WASN'T GRAFTED ON--IT'S INTEGRAL. HE WASN'T "MADE," LIKE ME...HE WAS--
BORN INTO IT.
WITHOUT A CHOICE.
YEAH.
AND NOW HE'S ON THE VERGE OF MAKING THE SAME MISTAKES THAT I MADE.
BECOMING THE MONSTER THAT I WAS.

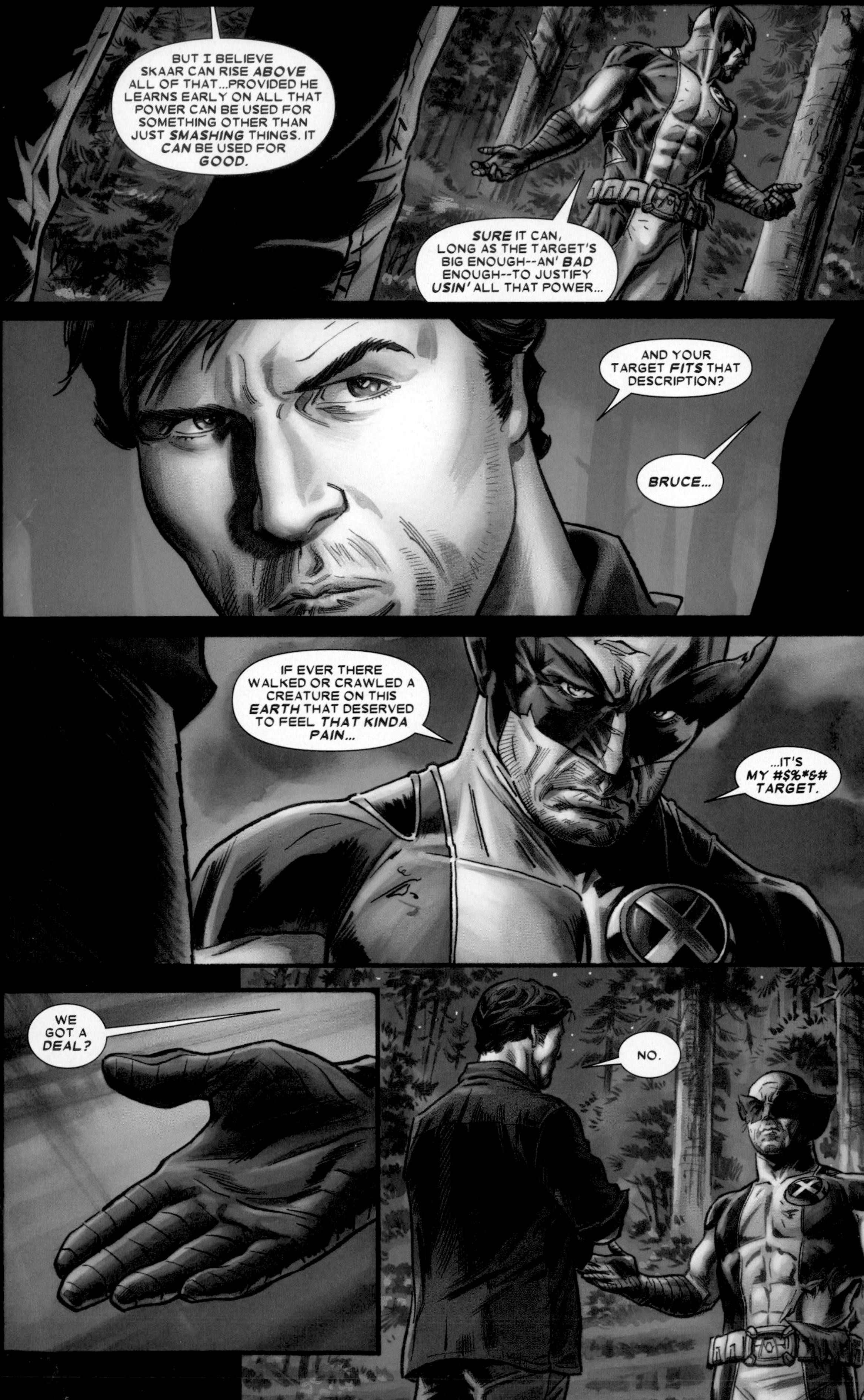
BUT I BELIEVE SKAAR CAN RISE ABOVE ALL OF THAT...PROVIDED HE LEARNS EARLY ON ALL THAT POWER CAN BE USED FOR SOMETHING OTHER THAN JUST SMASHING THINGS. IT CAN BE USED FOR GOOD.
SURE IT CAN, LONG AS THE TARGET'S BIG ENOUGH--AN' BAD ENOUGH--TO JUSTIFY USIN' ALL THAT POWER...
AND YOUR TARGET FITS THAT DESCRIPTION?
BRUCE...
IF EVER THERE WALKED OR CRAWLED A CREATURE ON THIS EARTH THAT DESERVED TO FEEL THAT KINDA PAIN...
...IT'S MY #$%*&# TARGET.
WE GOT A DEAL?
NO.

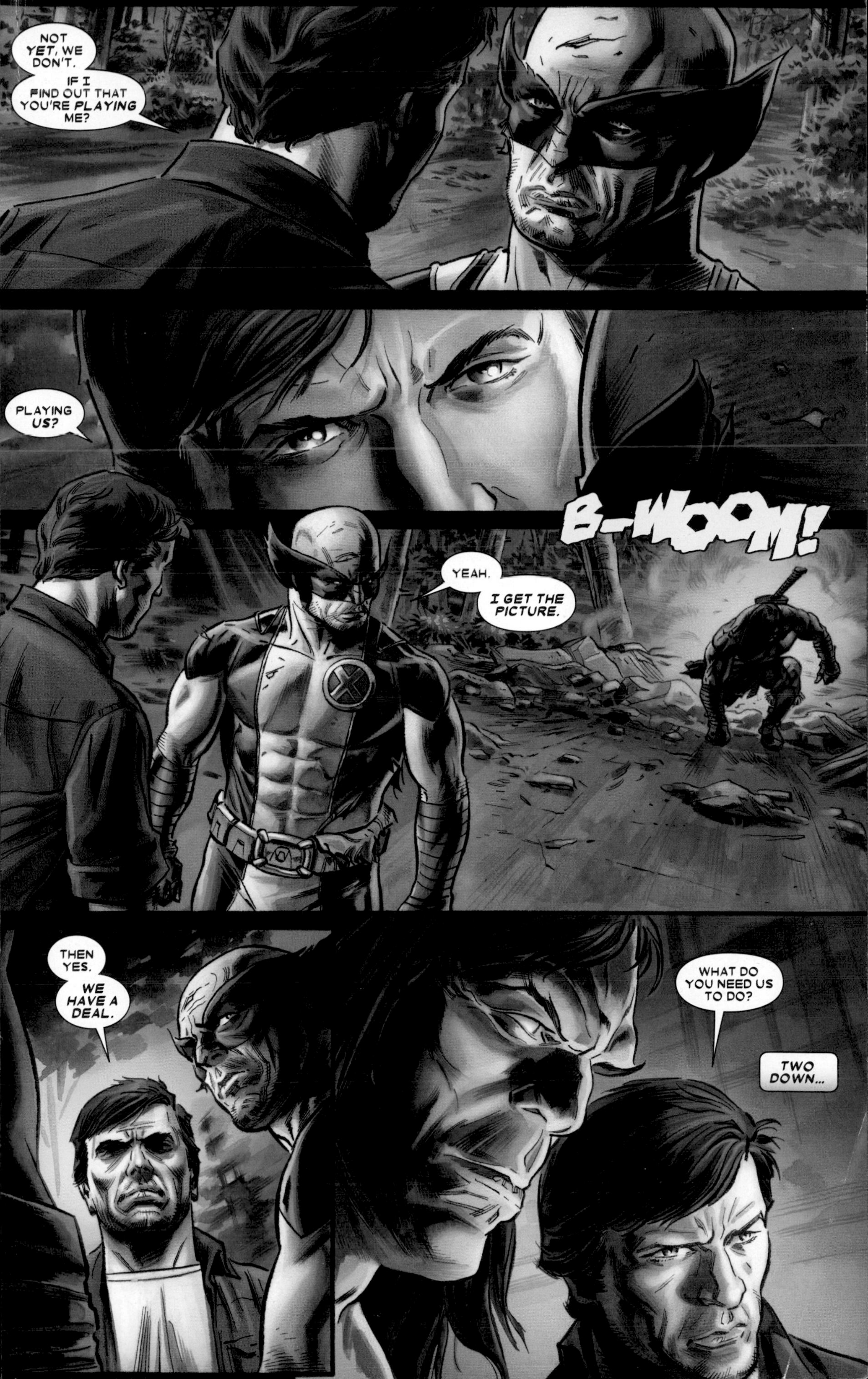
NOT YET, WE DON'T.
IF I FIND OUT THAT YOU'RE PLAYING ME?
PLAYING US?
B-WOOM!
YEAH.
I GET THE PICTURE.
THEN YES.
WE HAVE A DEAL.
WHAT DO YOU NEED US TO DO?
TWO DOWN...

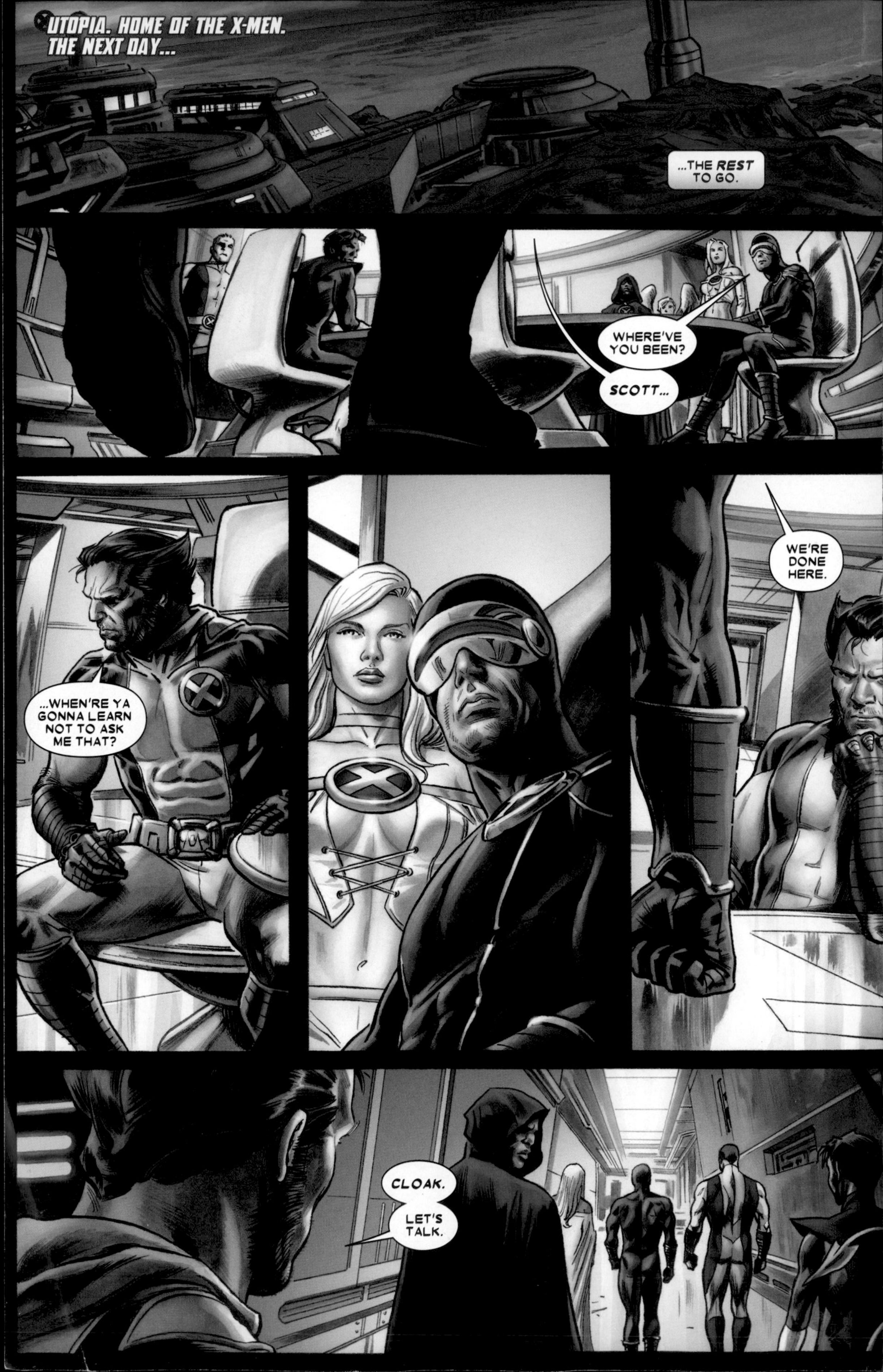
UTOPIA. HOME OF THE X-MEN.
THE NEXT DAY...
...THE REST TO GO.
WHERE'VE YOU BEEN?
SCOTT...
...WHEN'RE YA GONNA LEARN NOT TO ASK ME THAT?
WE'RE DONE HERE.
CLOAK.
LET'S TALK.

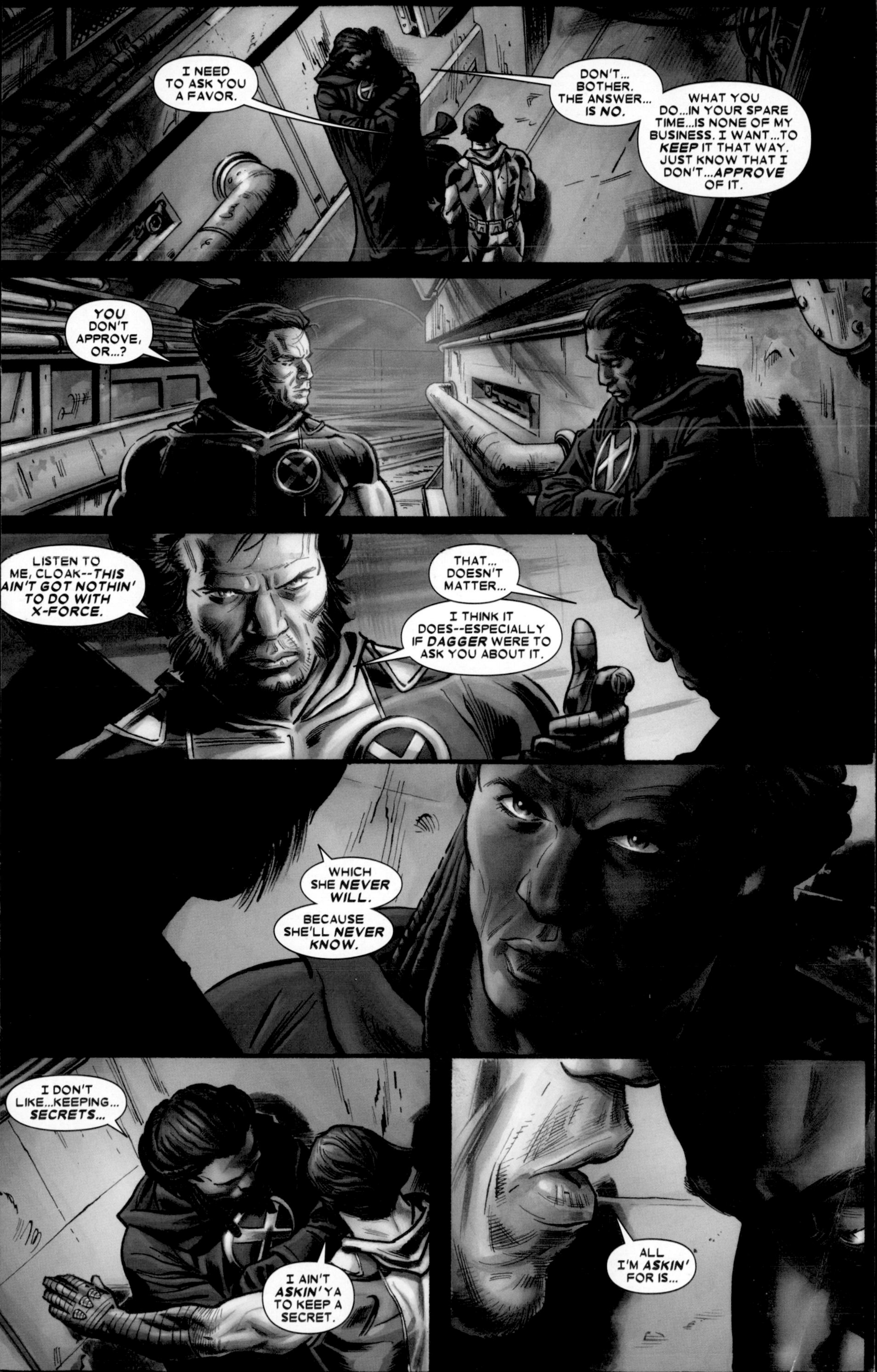
I NEED TO ASK YOU A FAVOR.
DON'T... BOTHER. THE ANSWER... IS *NO.*
WHAT YOU DO...IN YOUR SPARE TIME...IS NONE OF MY BUSINESS. I WANT...TO *KEEP* IT THAT WAY. JUST KNOW THAT I DON'T...*APPROVE* OF IT.
YOU DON'T APPROVE, OR...?
LISTEN TO ME, CLOAK--*THIS AIN'T GOT NOTHIN' TO DO WITH X-FORCE.*
THAT... DOESN'T MATTER...
I THINK IT DOES--ESPECIALLY IF *DAGGER* WERE TO ASK YOU ABOUT IT.
WHICH SHE *NEVER WILL.*
BECAUSE SHE'LL *NEVER KNOW.*
I DON'T LIKE...KEEPING... *SECRETS...*
I AIN'T *ASKIN'* YA TO KEEP A SECRET.
ALL I'M *ASKIN'* FOR IS...

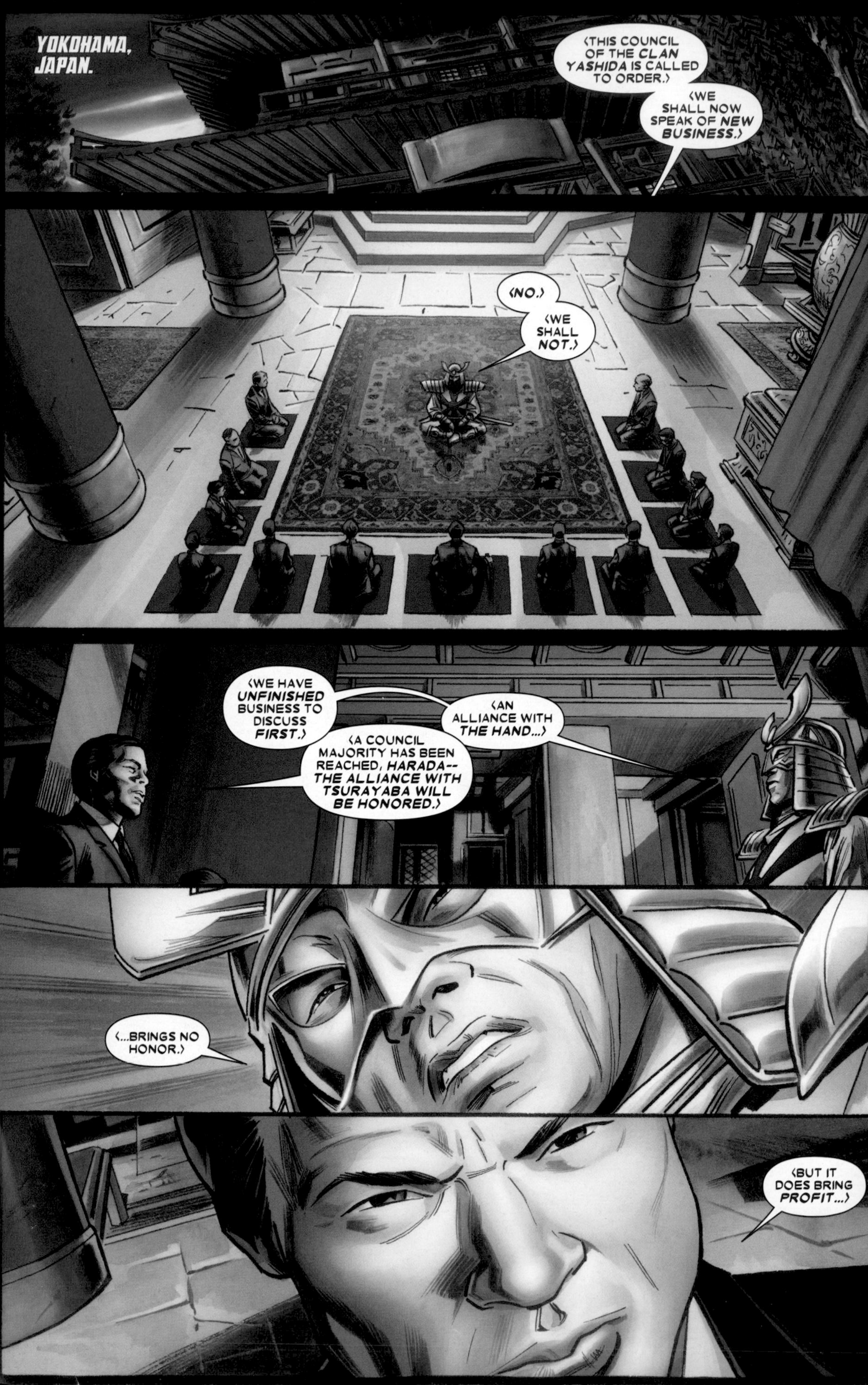
YOKOHAMA, JAPAN.
‹THIS COUNCIL OF THE CLAN YASHIDA IS CALLED TO ORDER.›
‹WE SHALL NOW SPEAK OF NEW BUSINESS.›
‹NO.›
‹WE SHALL NOT.›
‹WE HAVE UNFINISHED BUSINESS TO DISCUSS FIRST.›
‹AN ALLIANCE WITH THE HAND...›
‹A COUNCIL MAJORITY HAS BEEN REACHED, HARADA-- THE ALLIANCE WITH TSURAYABA WILL BE HONORED.›
‹...BRINGS NO HONOR.›
‹BUT IT DOES BRING PROFIT...›

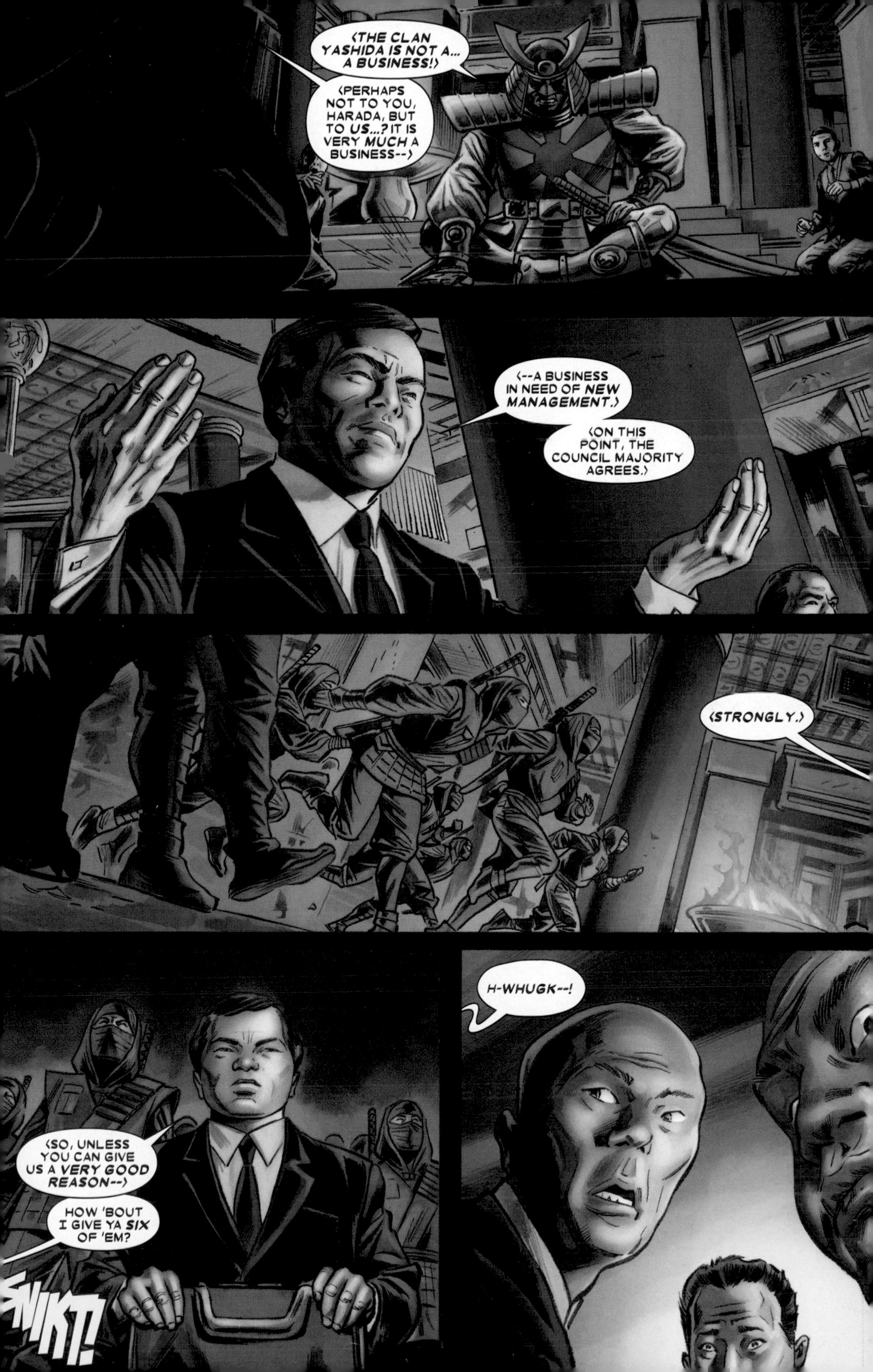

‹THE CLAN YASHIDA IS NOT A... A BUSINESS!›
‹PERHAPS NOT TO YOU, HARADA, BUT TO US...? IT IS VERY MUCH A BUSINESS--›
‹--A BUSINESS IN NEED OF NEW MANAGEMENT.›
‹ON THIS POINT, THE COUNCIL MAJORITY AGREES.›
‹STRONGLY.›
‹SO, UNLESS YOU CAN GIVE US A VERY GOOD REASON--›
HOW 'BOUT I GIVE YA SIX OF 'EM?
SNIKT!
H-WHUGK--!

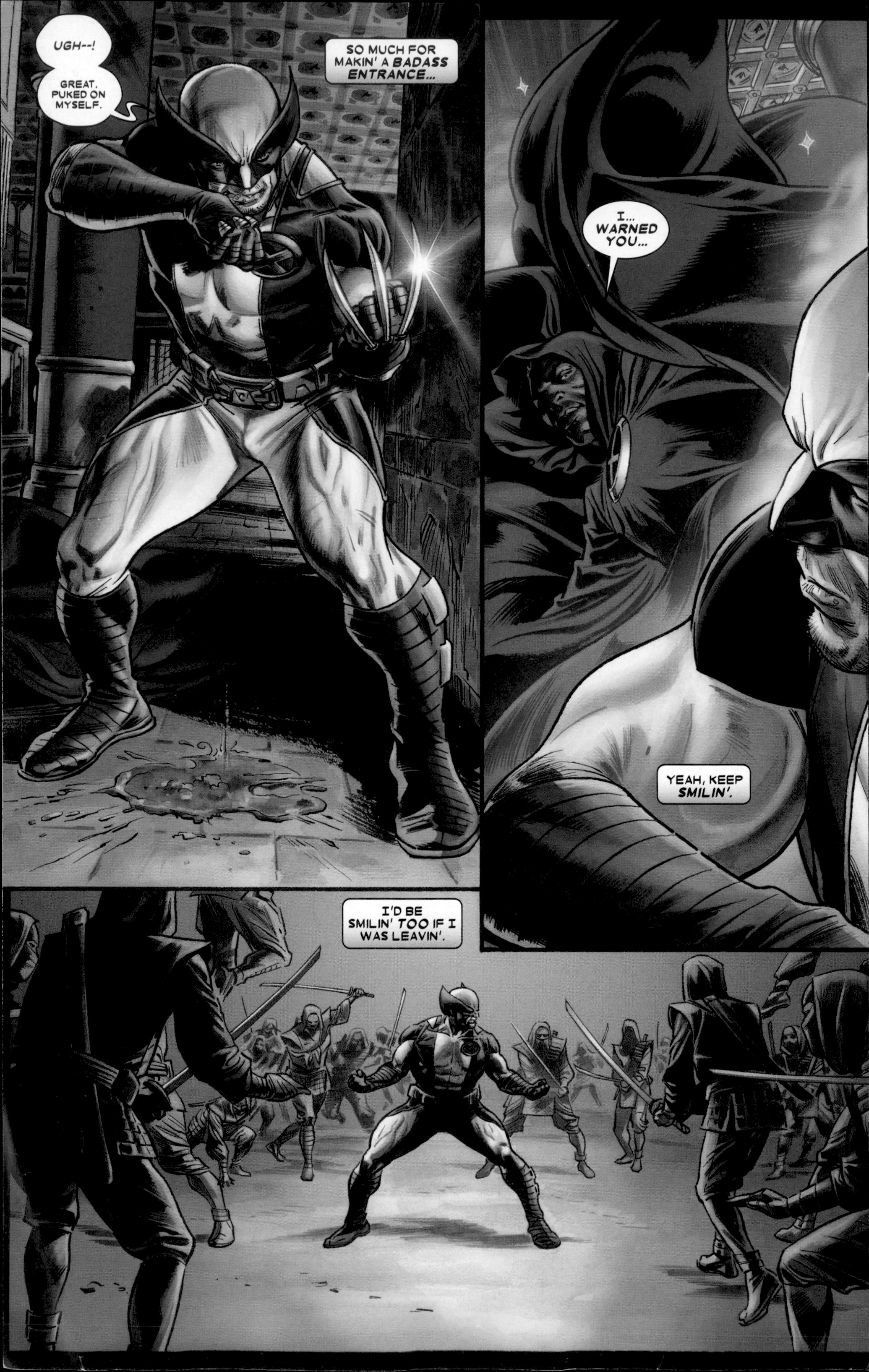
UGH--!
GREAT. PUKED ON MYSELF.
SO MUCH FOR MAKIN' A BADASS ENTRANCE...
I... WARNED YOU...
YEAH, KEEP SMILIN'.
I'D BE SMILIN' TOO IF I WAS LEAVIN'.

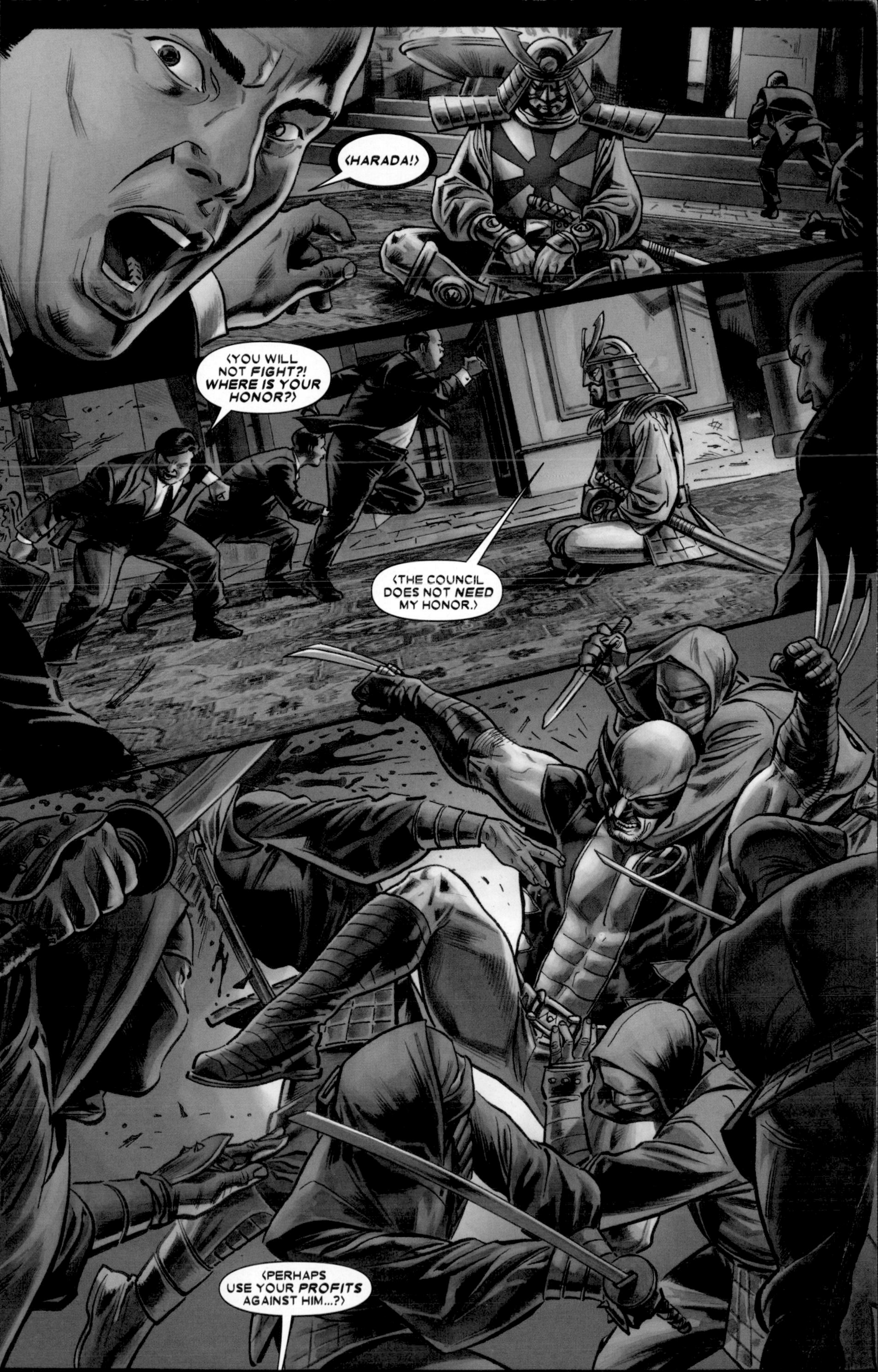
‹HARADA!›
‹YOU WILL NOT FIGHT?! WHERE IS YOUR HONOR?›
‹THE COUNCIL DOES NOT NEED MY HONOR.›
‹PERHAPS USE YOUR PROFITS AGAINST HIM...?›

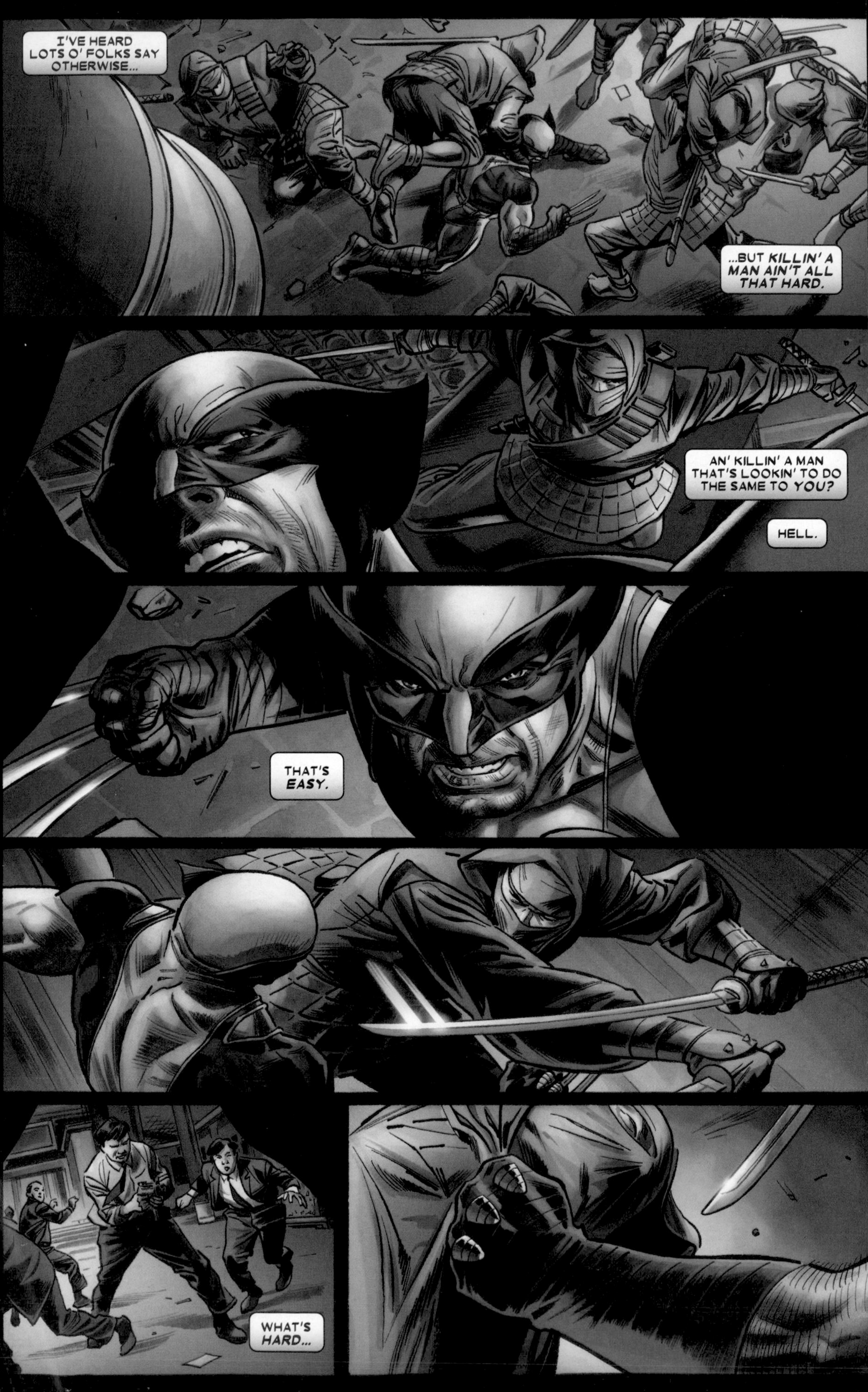
I'VE HEARD LOTS O' FOLKS SAY OTHERWISE...
...BUT KILLIN' A MAN AIN'T ALL THAT HARD.
AN' KILLIN' A MAN THAT'S LOOKIN' TO DO THE SAME TO YOU?
HELL.
THAT'S EASY.
WHAT'S HARD...

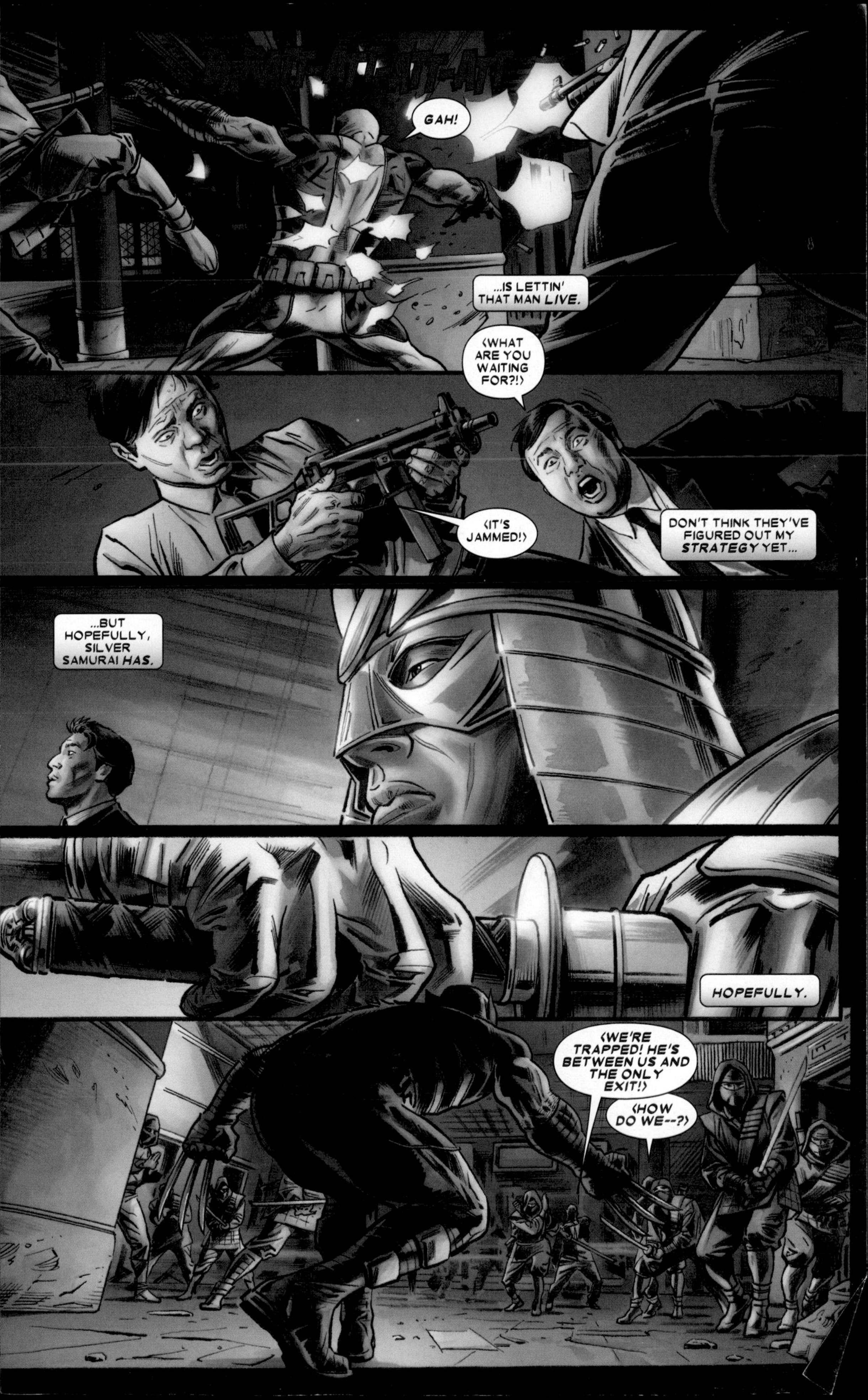
GAH!
...IS LETTIN' THAT MAN LIVE.
‹WHAT ARE YOU WAITING FOR?!›
‹IT'S JAMMED!›
DON'T THINK THEY'VE FIGURED OUT MY STRATEGY YET...
...BUT HOPEFULLY, SILVER SAMURAI HAS.
HOPEFULLY.
‹WE'RE TRAPPED! HE'S BETWEEN US AND THE ONLY EXIT!›
‹HOW DO WE--?›

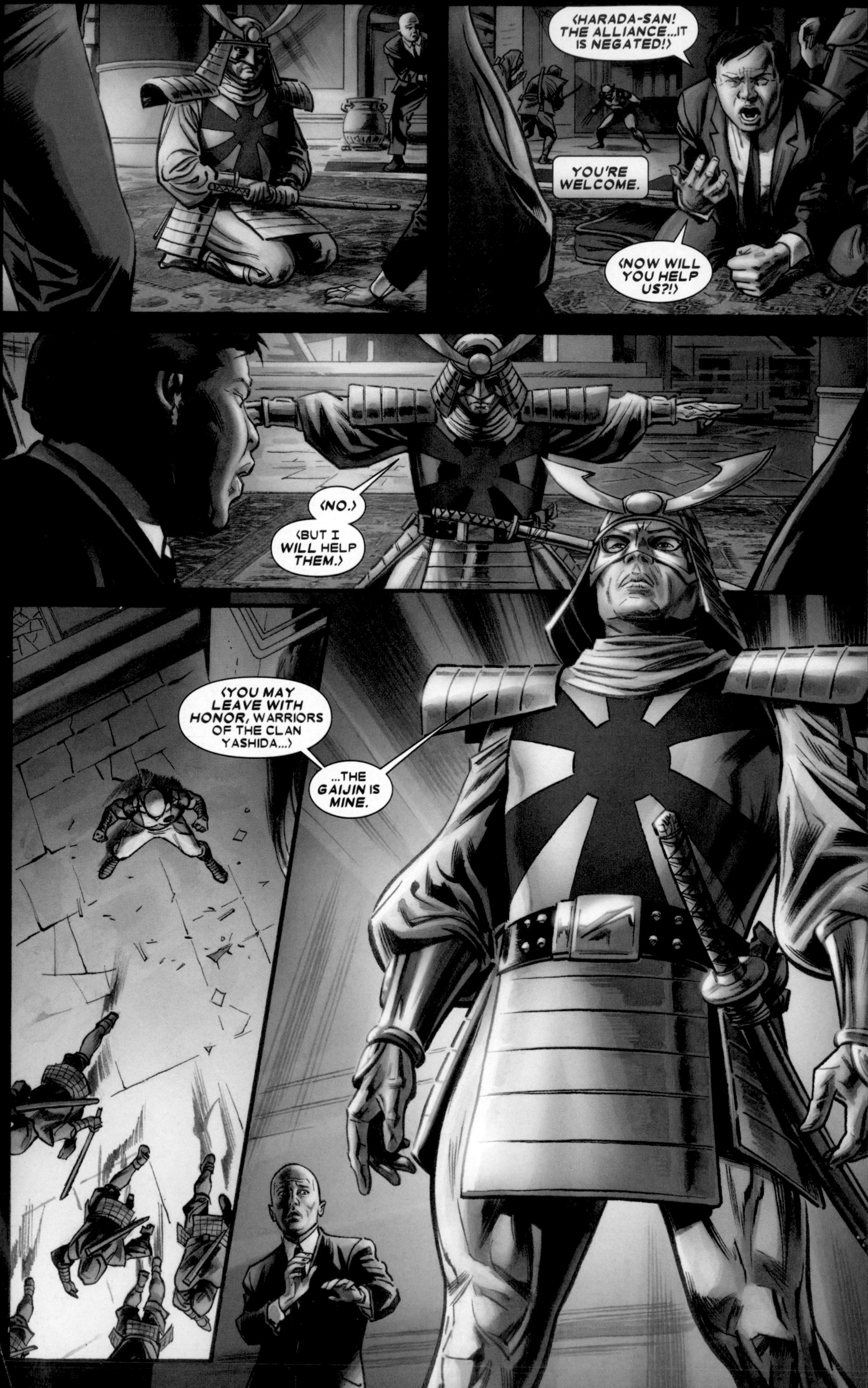
‹HARADA-SAN! THE ALLIANCE...IT IS NEGATED!›
YOU'RE WELCOME.
‹NOW WILL YOU HELP US?!›
‹NO.›
‹BUT I WILL HELP THEM.›
‹YOU MAY LEAVE WITH HONOR, WARRIORS OF THE CLAN YASHIDA...›
...THE GAIJIN IS MINE.

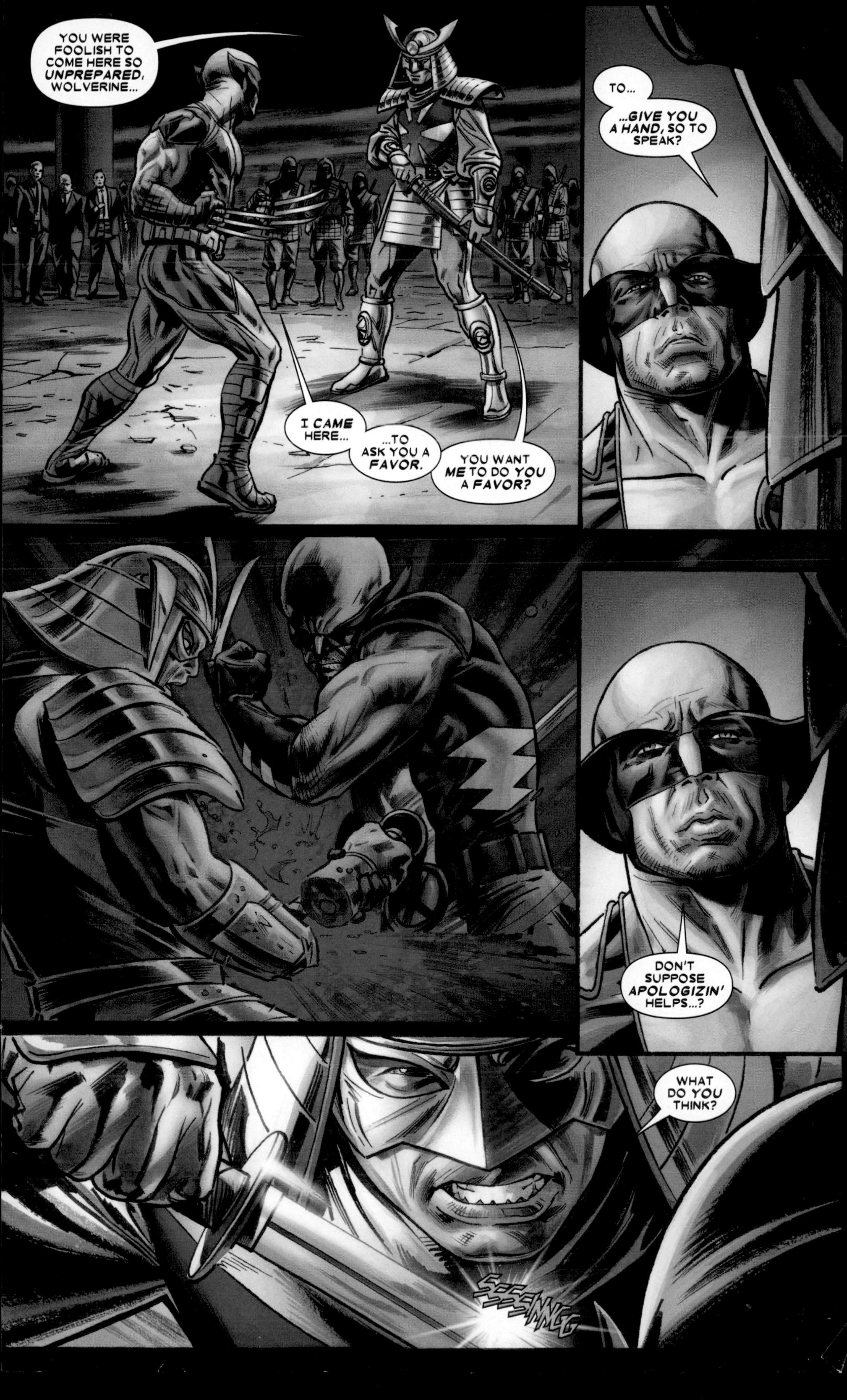
YOU WERE FOOLISH TO COME HERE SO UNPREPARED, WOLVERINE...
I CAME HERE...
...TO ASK YOU A FAVOR.
YOU WANT ME TO DO YOU A FAVOR?
TO...
...GIVE YOU A HAND, SO TO SPEAK?
DON'T SUPPOSE APOLOGIZIN' HELPS...?
WHAT DO YOU THINK?
SSSSNNGG

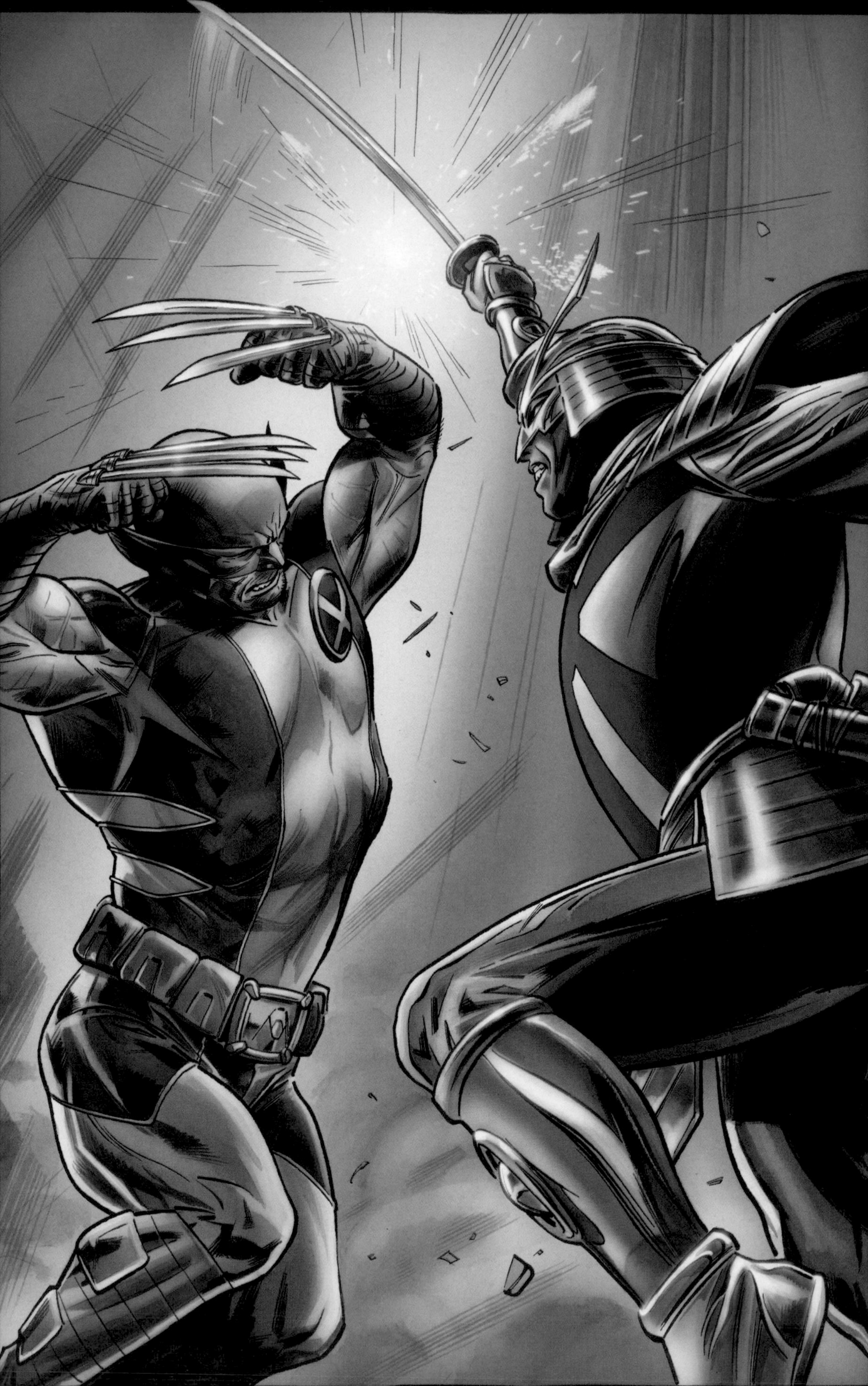

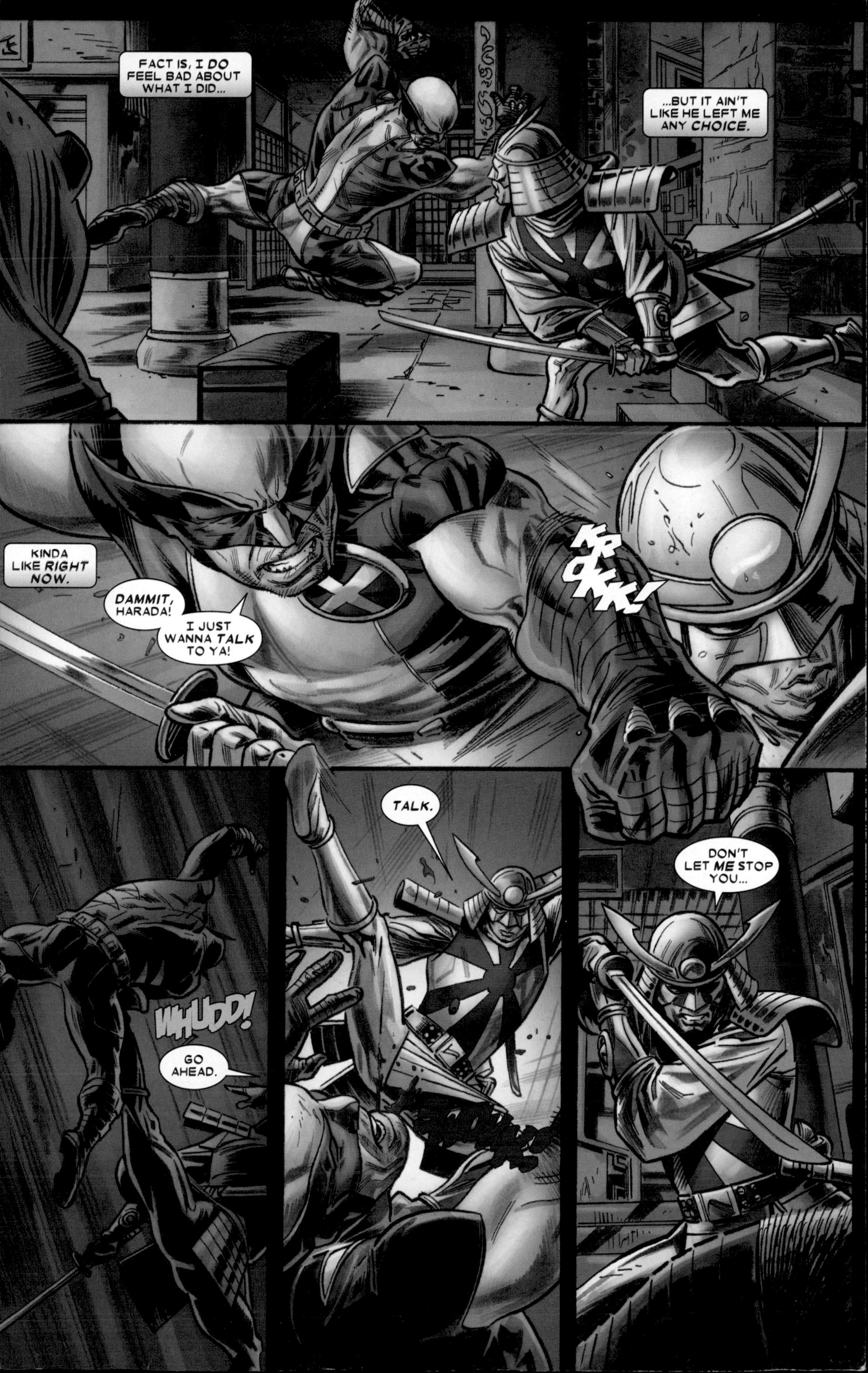
FACT IS, I DO FEEL BAD ABOUT WHAT I DID...
...BUT IT AIN'T LIKE HE LEFT ME ANY CHOICE.
KINDA LIKE RIGHT NOW.
DAMMIT, HARADA!
I JUST WANNA TALK TO YA!
KROKK!
WHUDD!
GO AHEAD.
TALK.
DON'T LET ME STOP YOU...

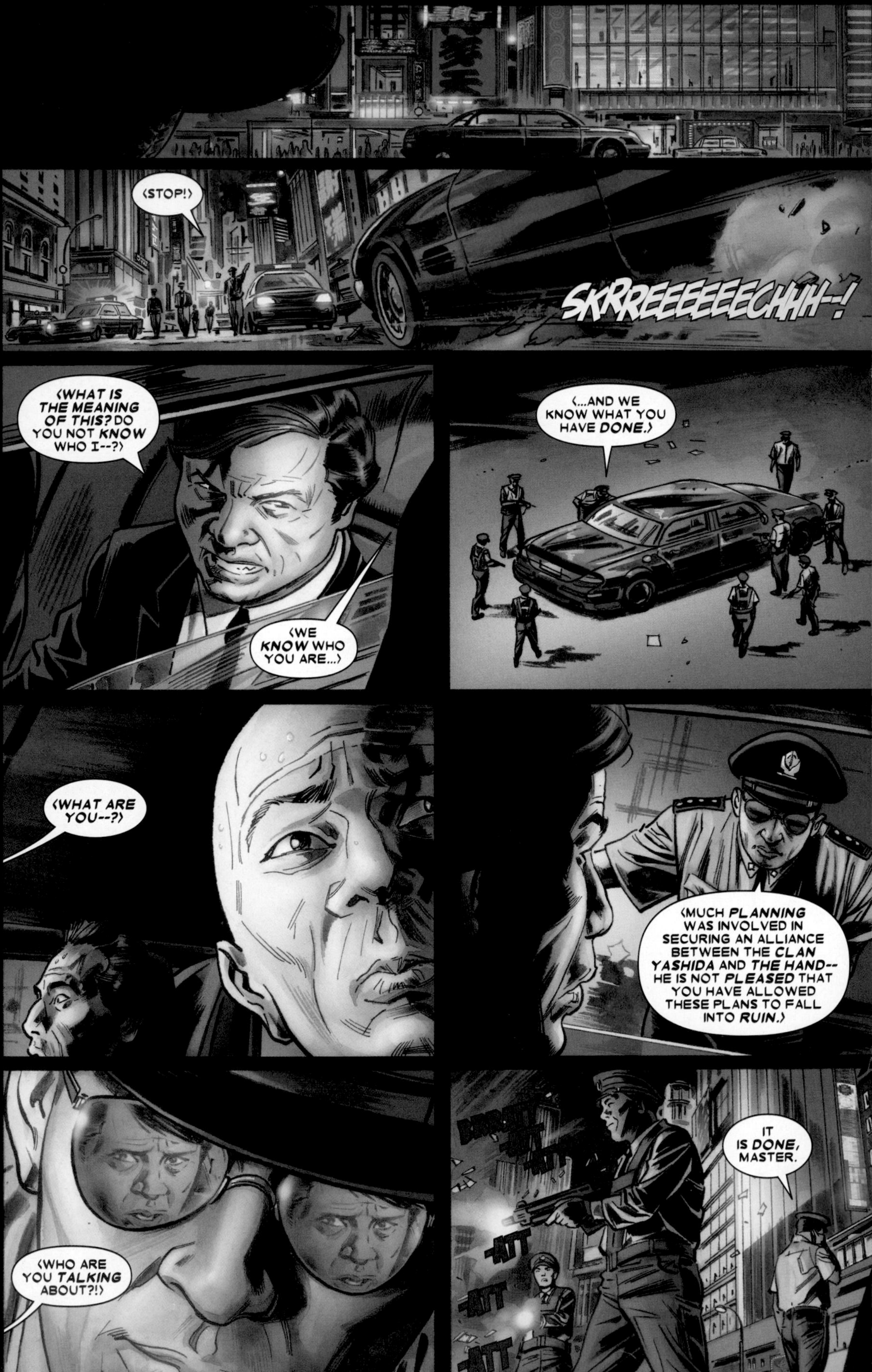
‹STOP!›
SKRREEEEEEECHHH--!
‹WHAT IS THE MEANING OF THIS? DO YOU NOT KNOW WHO I--?›
‹WE KNOW WHO YOU ARE...›
‹...AND WE KNOW WHAT YOU HAVE DONE.›
‹WHAT ARE YOU--?›
‹MUCH PLANNING WAS INVOLVED IN SECURING AN ALLIANCE BETWEEN THE CLAN YASHIDA AND THE HAND-- HE IS NOT PLEASED THAT YOU HAVE ALLOWED THESE PLANS TO FALL INTO RUIN.›
‹WHO ARE YOU TALKING ABOUT?!›
IT IS DONE, MASTER.

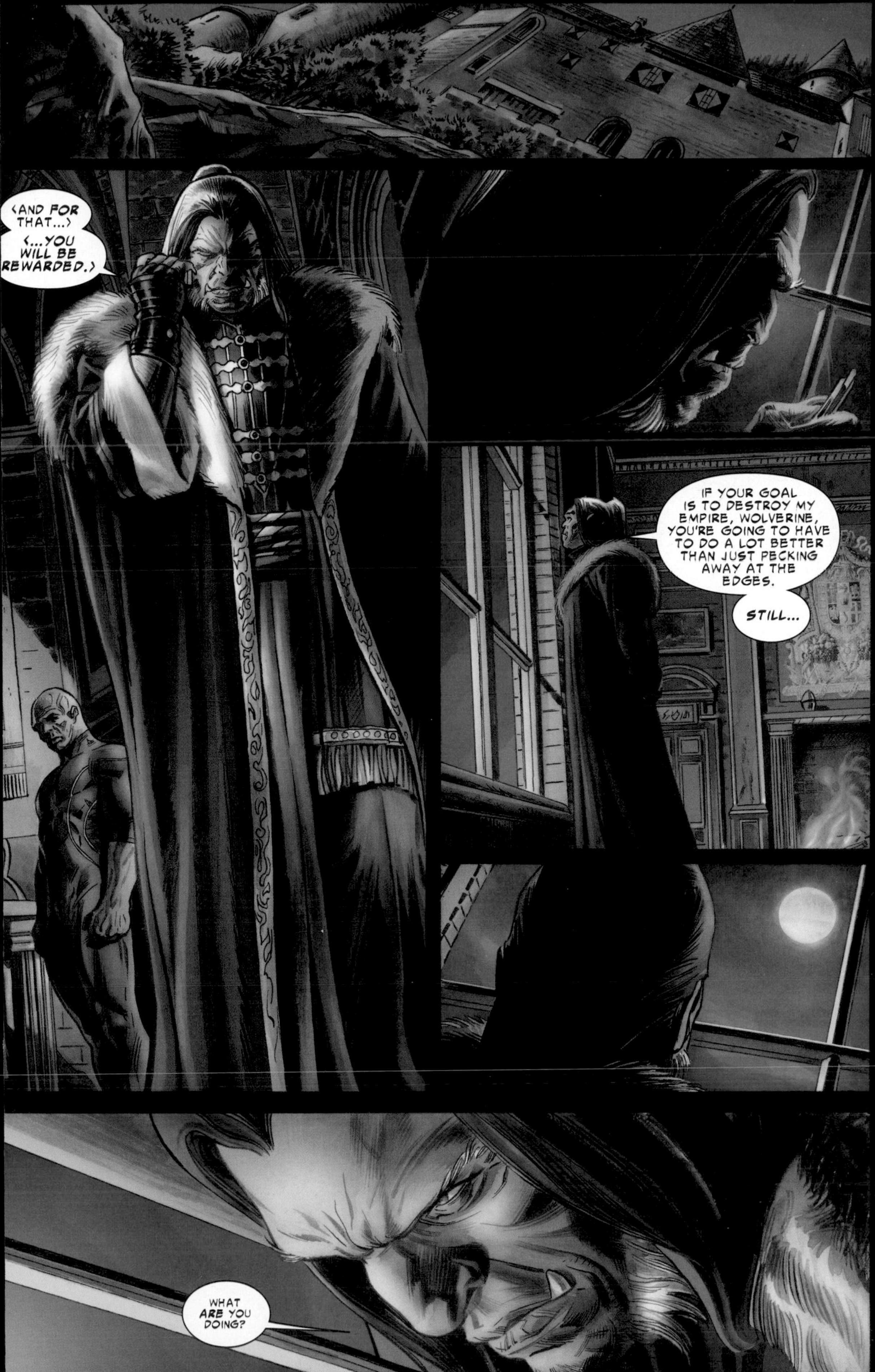

<AND FOR THAT...>
<...YOU WILL BE REWARDED.>
IF YOUR GOAL IS TO DESTROY MY EMPIRE, WOLVERINE, YOU'RE GOING TO HAVE TO DO A LOT BETTER THAN JUST PECKING AWAY AT THE EDGES.
STILL...
WHAT ARE YOU DOING?

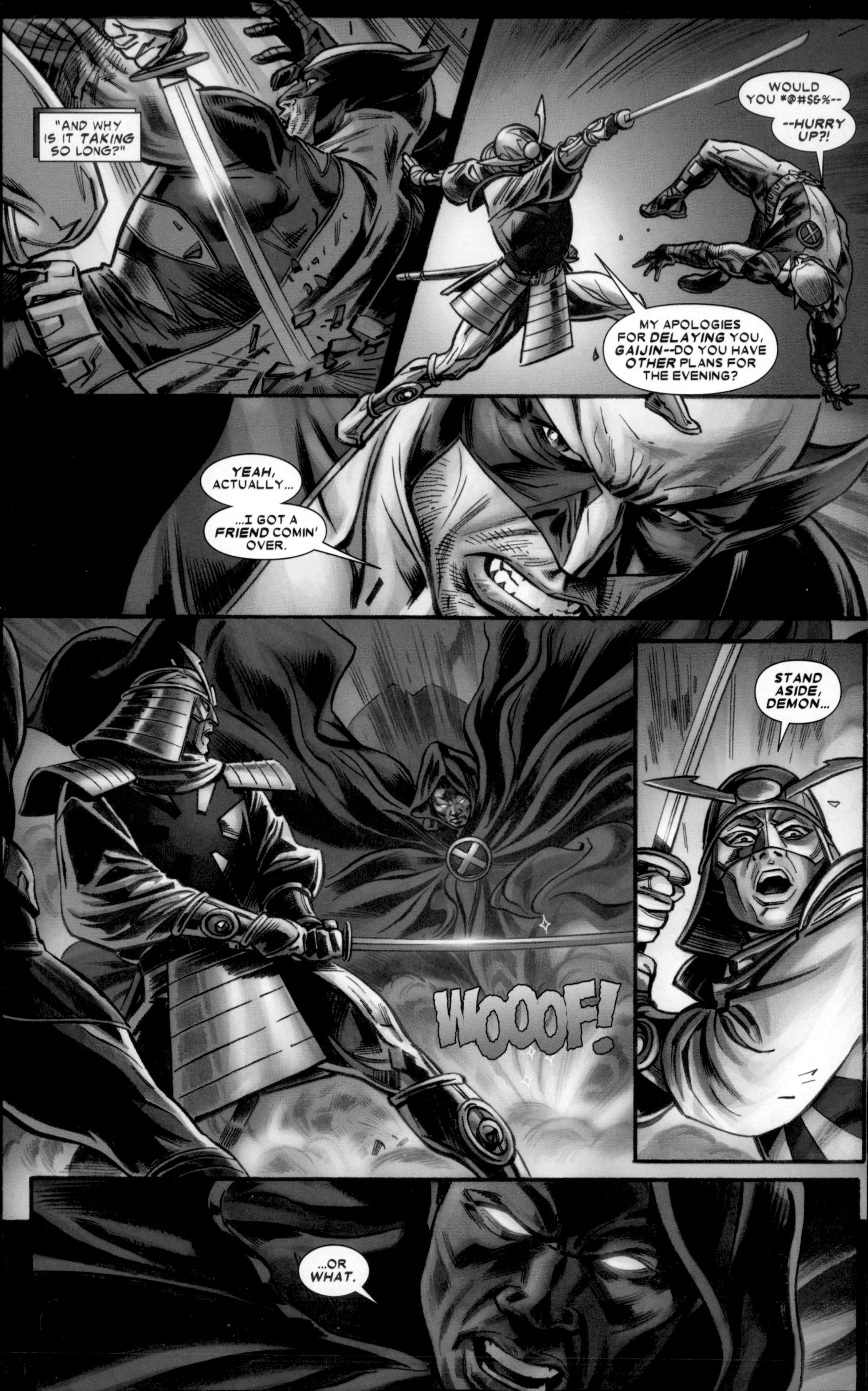
"AND WHY IS IT TAKING SO LONG?"
WOULD YOU *@#$&%--
--HURRY UP?!
MY APOLOGIES FOR DELAYING YOU, GAIJIN--DO YOU HAVE OTHER PLANS FOR THE EVENING?
YEAH, ACTUALLY...
...I GOT A FRIEND COMIN' OVER.
STAND ASIDE, DEMON...
WOOOF!
...OR WHAT.

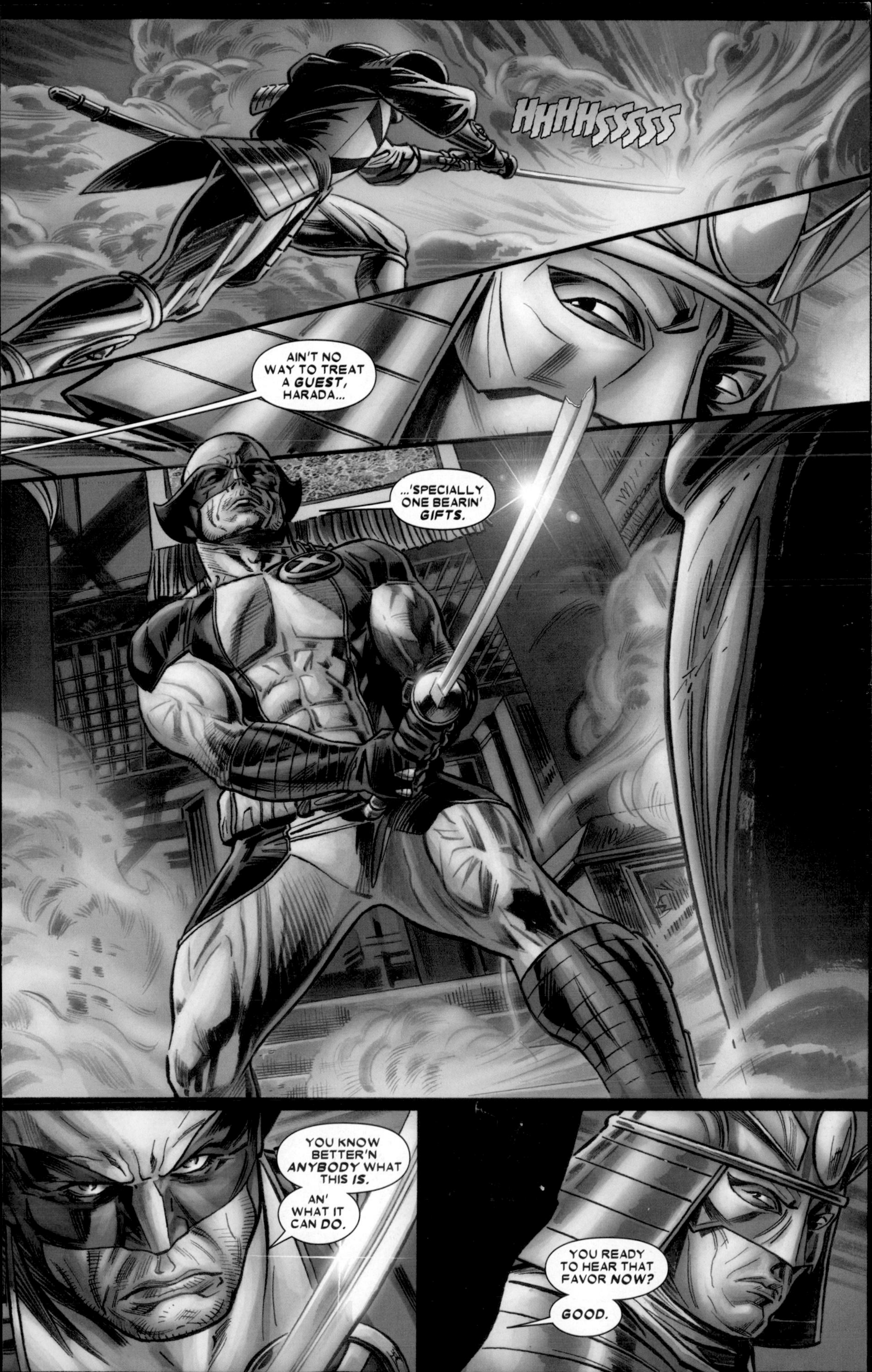
HHHHSSSSSS
AIN'T NO WAY TO TREAT A GUEST, HARADA...
...'SPECIALLY ONE BEARIN' GIFTS.
YOU KNOW BETTER'N ANYBODY WHAT THIS IS.
AN' WHAT IT CAN DO.
YOU READY TO HEAR THAT FAVOR NOW?
GOOD.

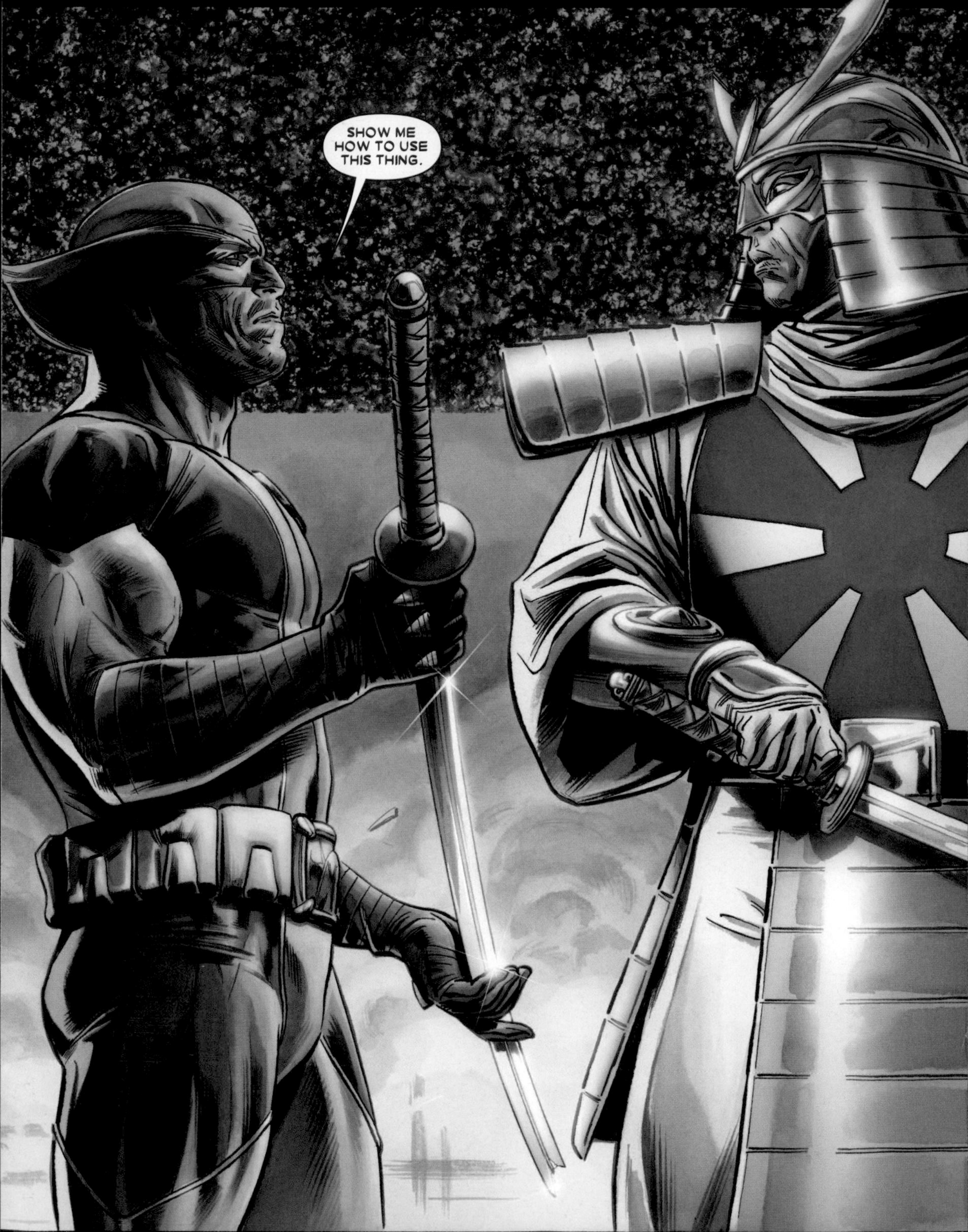
SHOW ME HOW TO USE THIS THING.

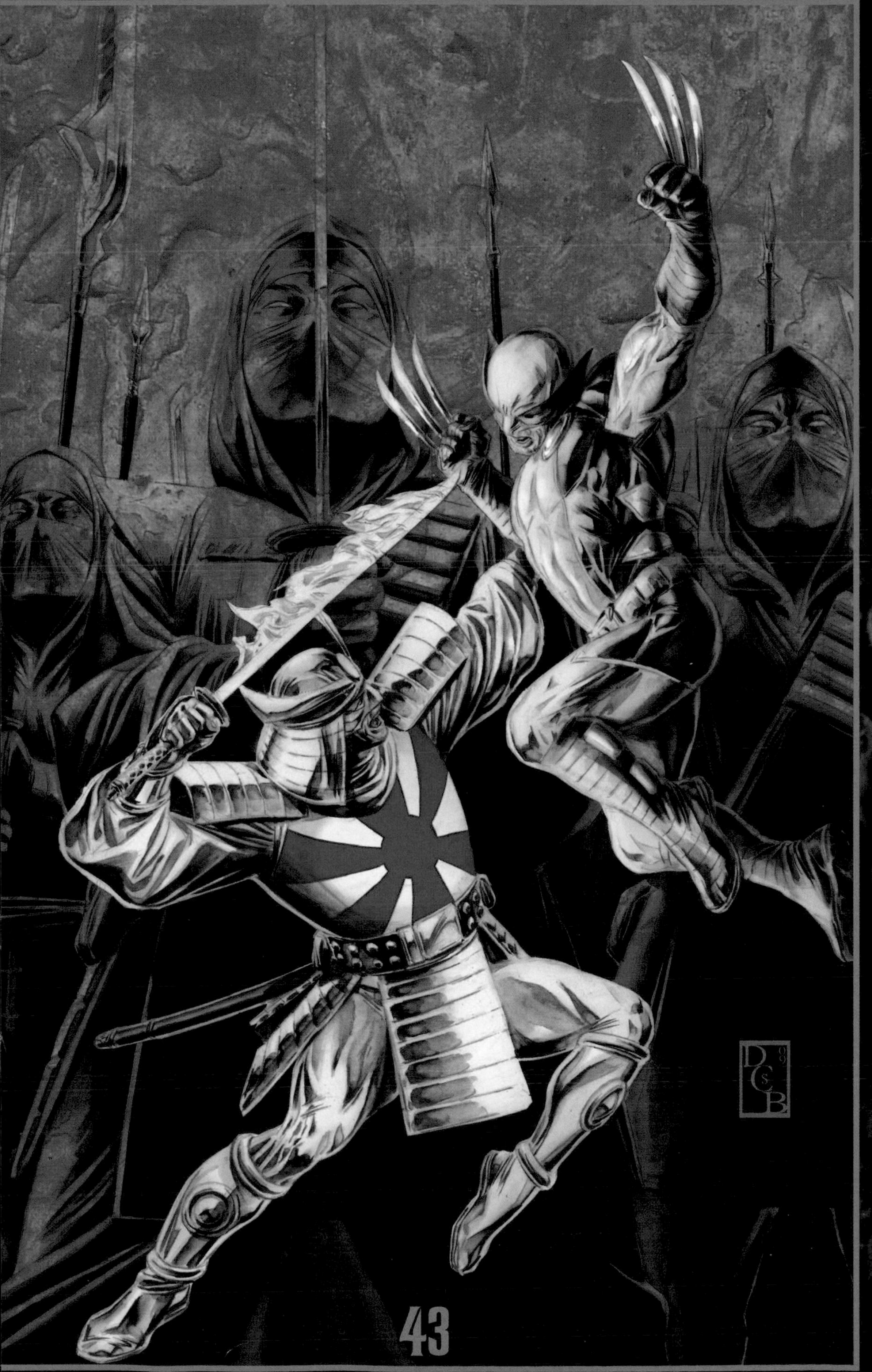
43

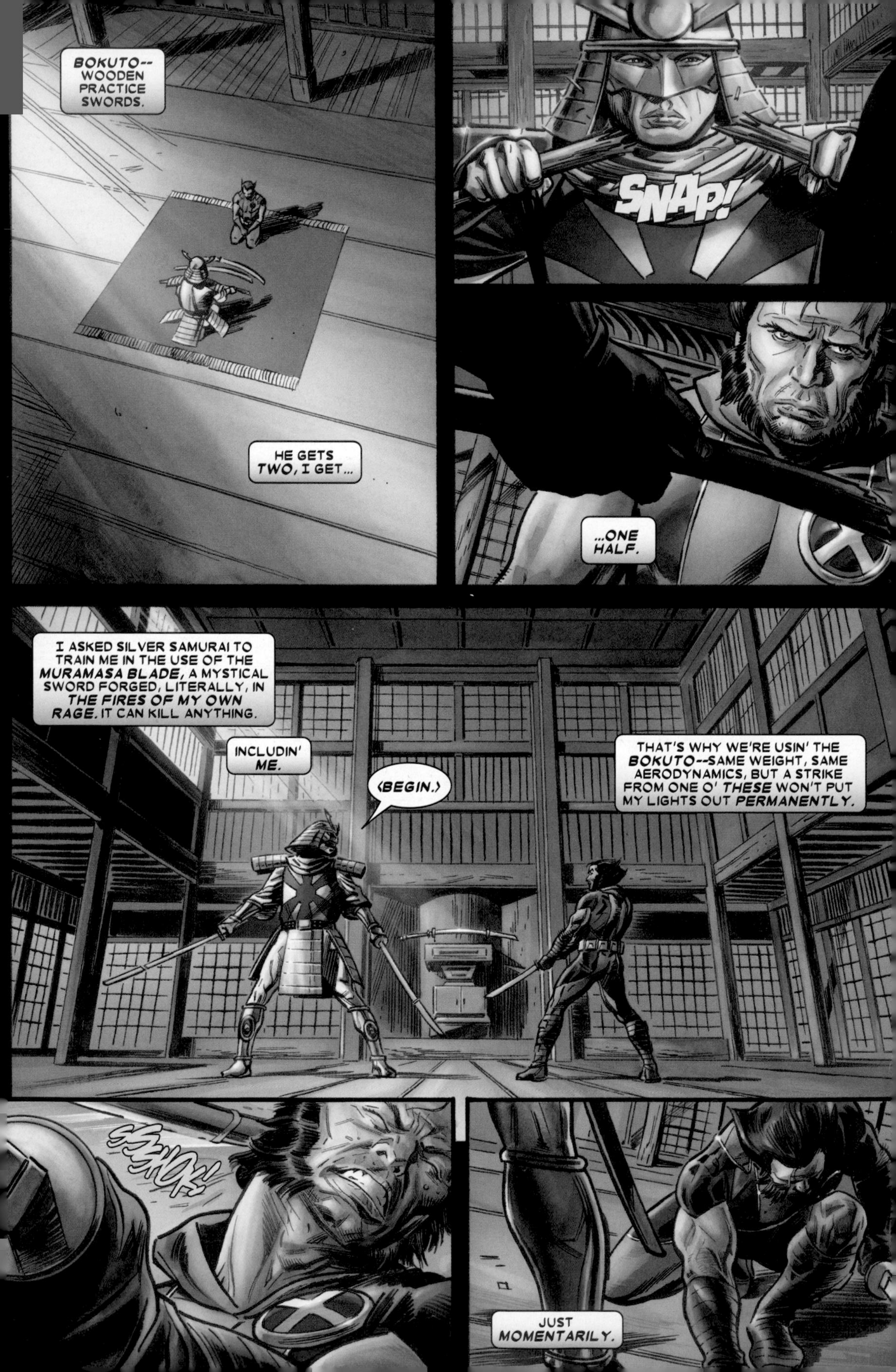

BOKUTO--WOODEN PRACTICE SWORDS.
SNAP!
HE GETS TWO, I GET...
...ONE HALF.
I ASKED SILVER SAMURAI TO TRAIN ME IN THE USE OF THE MURAMASA BLADE, A MYSTICAL SWORD FORGED, LITERALLY, IN THE FIRES OF MY OWN RAGE. IT CAN KILL ANYTHING.
INCLUDIN' ME.
<BEGIN.>
THAT'S WHY WE'RE USIN' THE BOKUTO--SAME WEIGHT, SAME AERODYNAMICS, BUT A STRIKE FROM ONE O' THESE WON'T PUT MY LIGHTS OUT PERMANENTLY.
JUST MOMENTARILY.

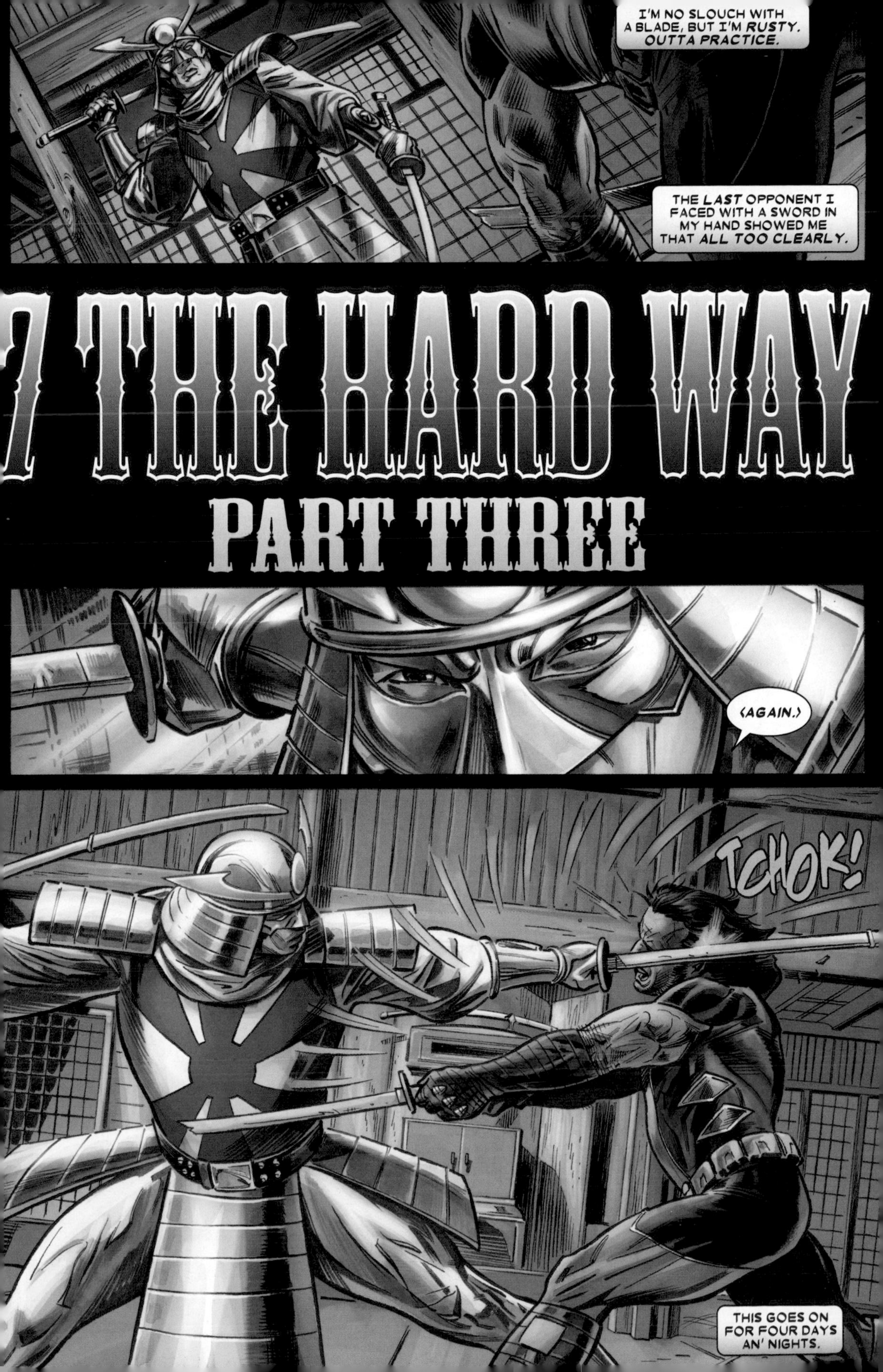

I'M NO SLOUCH WITH A BLADE, BUT I'M *RUSTY.* *OUTTA PRACTICE.*
THE *LAST* OPPONENT I FACED WITH A SWORD IN MY HAND SHOWED ME THAT *ALL TOO CLEARLY.*
7 THE HARD WAY
PART THREE
‹AGAIN.›
TCHOK!
THIS GOES ON FOR FOUR DAYS AN' NIGHTS.

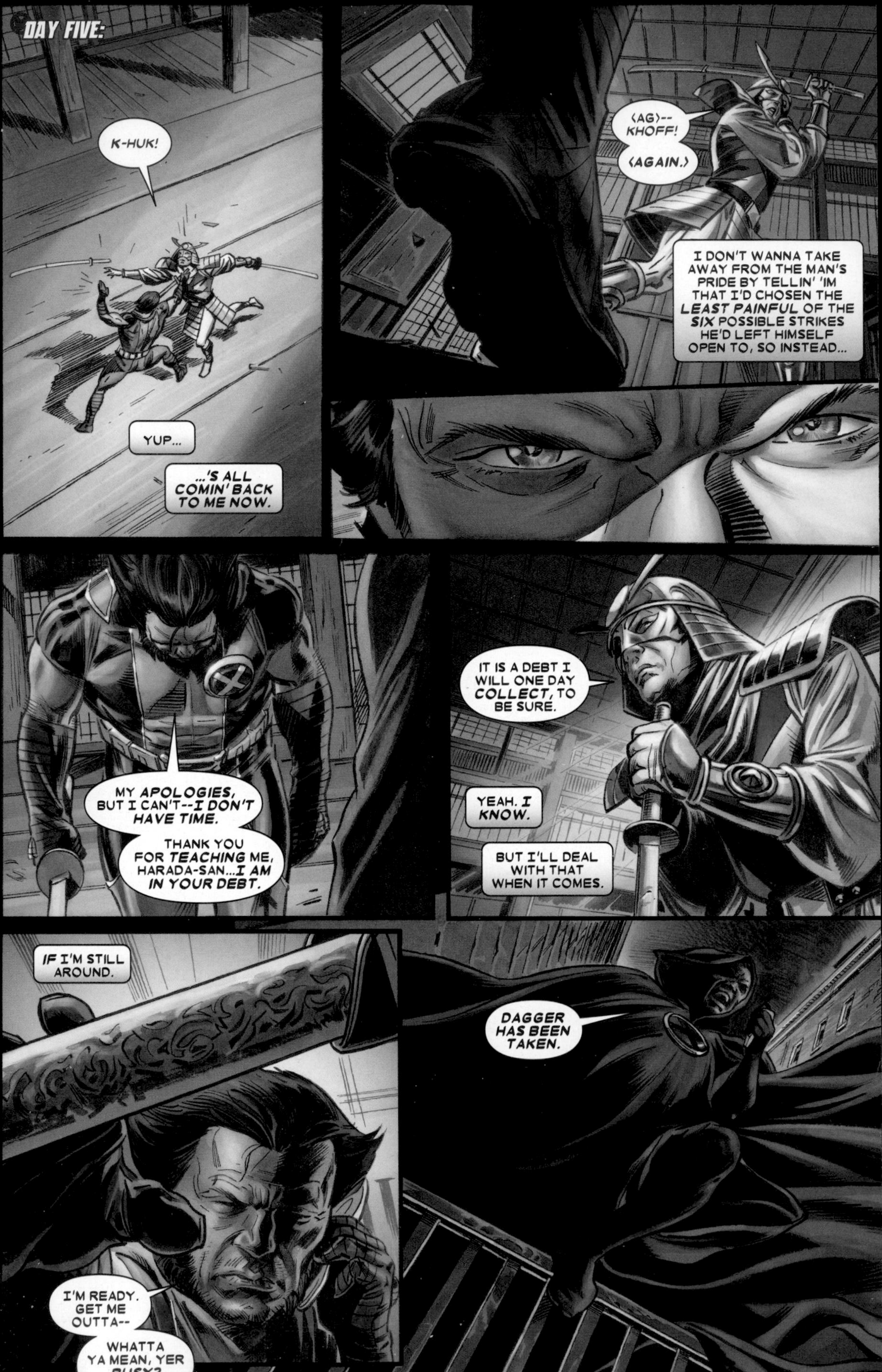
DAY FIVE:
K-HUK!
YUP...
...'S ALL COMIN' BACK TO ME NOW.
‹AG›--KHOFF!
‹AGAIN.›
I DON'T WANNA TAKE AWAY FROM THE MAN'S PRIDE BY TELLIN' 'IM THAT I'D CHOSEN THE LEAST PAINFUL OF THE SIX POSSIBLE STRIKES HE'D LEFT HIMSELF OPEN TO, SO INSTEAD...
MY APOLOGIES, BUT I CAN'T--I DON'T HAVE TIME.
THANK YOU FOR TEACHING ME, HARADA-SAN...I AM IN YOUR DEBT.
IT IS A DEBT I WILL ONE DAY COLLECT, TO BE SURE.
YEAH. I KNOW.
BUT I'LL DEAL WITH THAT WHEN IT COMES.
IF I'M STILL AROUND.
I'M READY. GET ME OUTTA--
WHATTA YA MEAN, YER BUSY? WHAT--?
DAGGER HAS BEEN TAKEN.

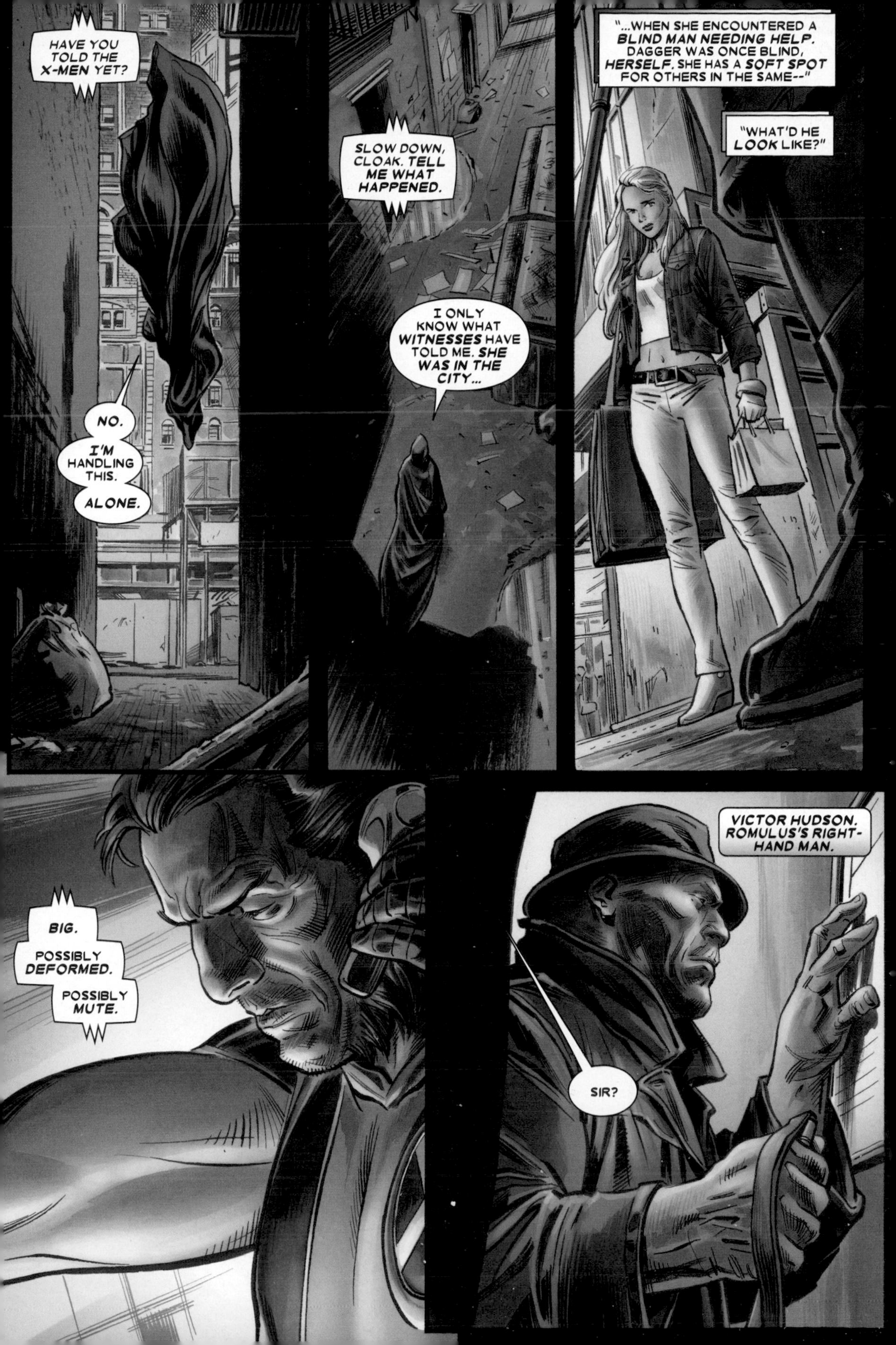
HAVE YOU TOLD THE X-MEN YET?
NO.
I'M HANDLING THIS.
ALONE.
SLOW DOWN, CLOAK. TELL ME WHAT HAPPENED.
I ONLY KNOW WHAT WITNESSES HAVE TOLD ME. SHE WAS IN THE CITY...
"...WHEN SHE ENCOUNTERED A BLIND MAN NEEDING HELP. DAGGER WAS ONCE BLIND, HERSELF. SHE HAS A SOFT SPOT FOR OTHERS IN THE SAME--"
"WHAT'D HE LOOK LIKE?"
BIG.
POSSIBLY DEFORMED.
POSSIBLY MUTE.
VICTOR HUDSON. ROMULUS'S RIGHT-HAND MAN.
SIR?

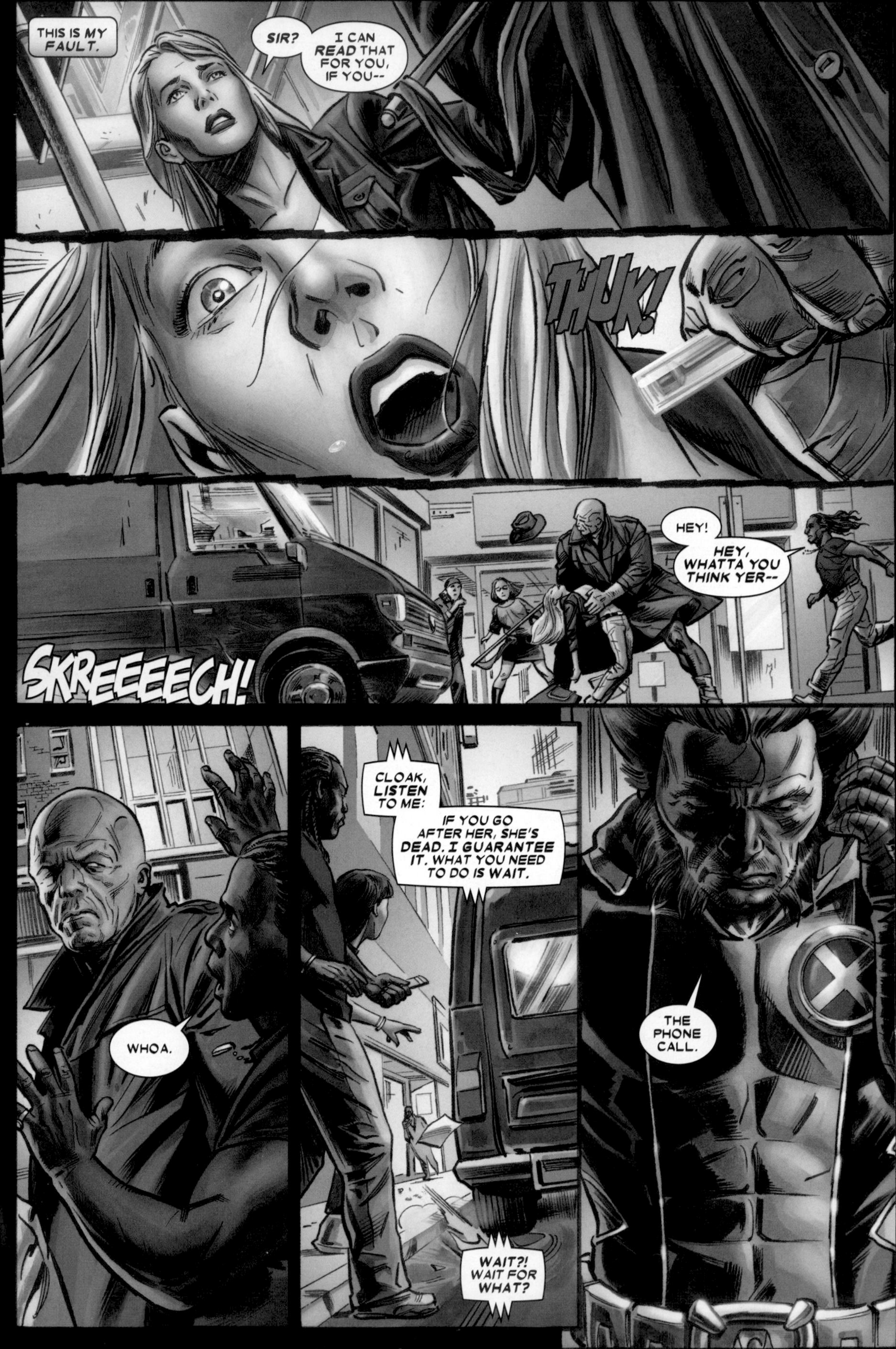

THIS IS MY FAULT.
SIR?
I CAN READ THAT FOR YOU, IF YOU--
THUK!
HEY!
HEY, WHATTA YOU THINK YER--
SKREEEEECH!
WHOA.
CLOAK, LISTEN TO ME:
IF YOU GO AFTER HER, SHE'S DEAD. I GUARANTEE IT. WHAT YOU NEED TO DO IS WAIT.
WAIT?! WAIT FOR WHAT?
THE PHONE CALL.

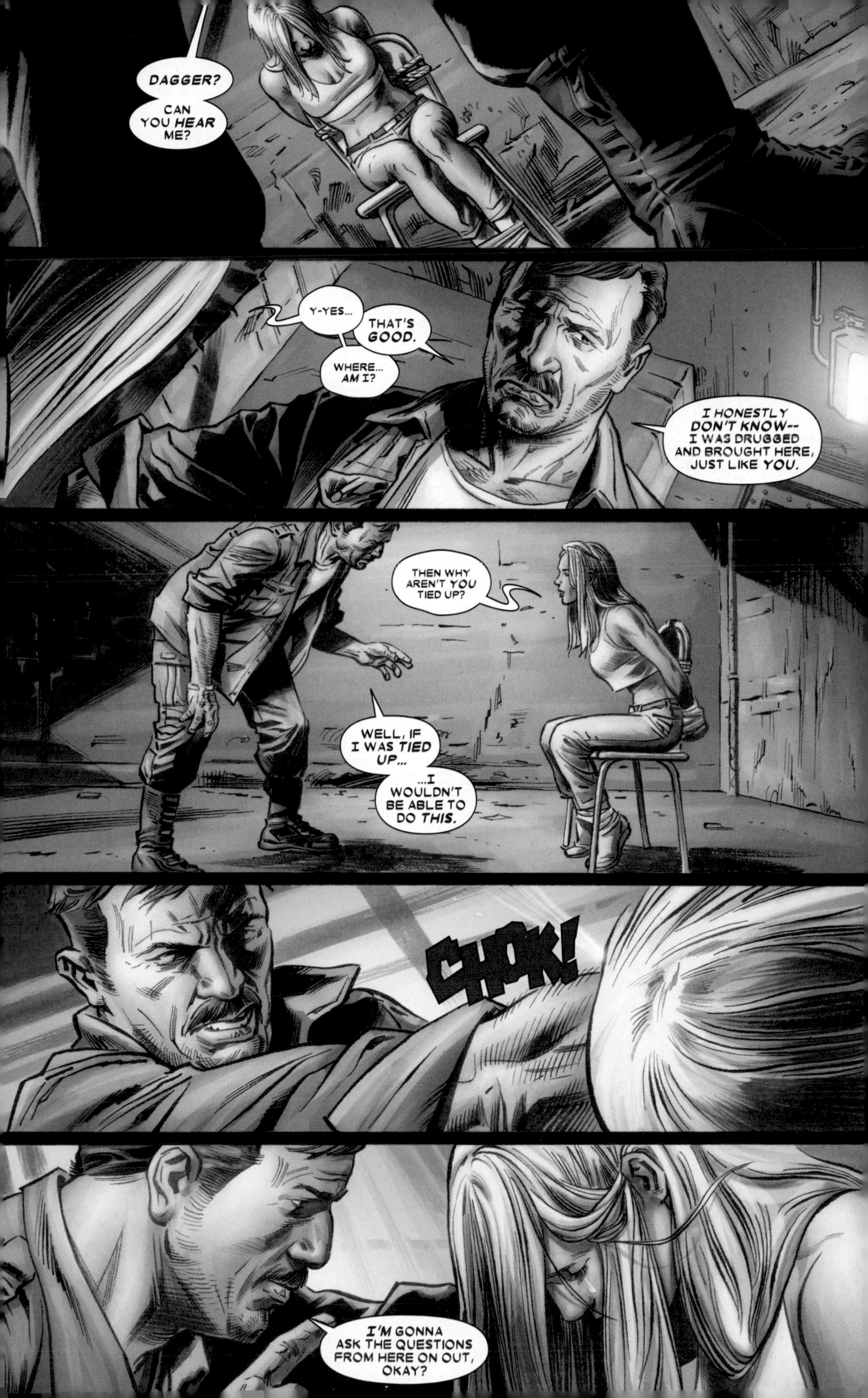
DAGGER?
CAN YOU HEAR ME?
Y-YES...
THAT'S GOOD.
WHERE... AM I?
I HONESTLY DON'T KNOW-- I WAS DRUGGED AND BROUGHT HERE, JUST LIKE YOU.
THEN WHY AREN'T YOU TIED UP?
WELL, IF I WAS TIED UP...
...I WOULDN'T BE ABLE TO DO THIS.
CHOK!
I'M GONNA ASK THE QUESTIONS FROM HERE ON OUT, OKAY?

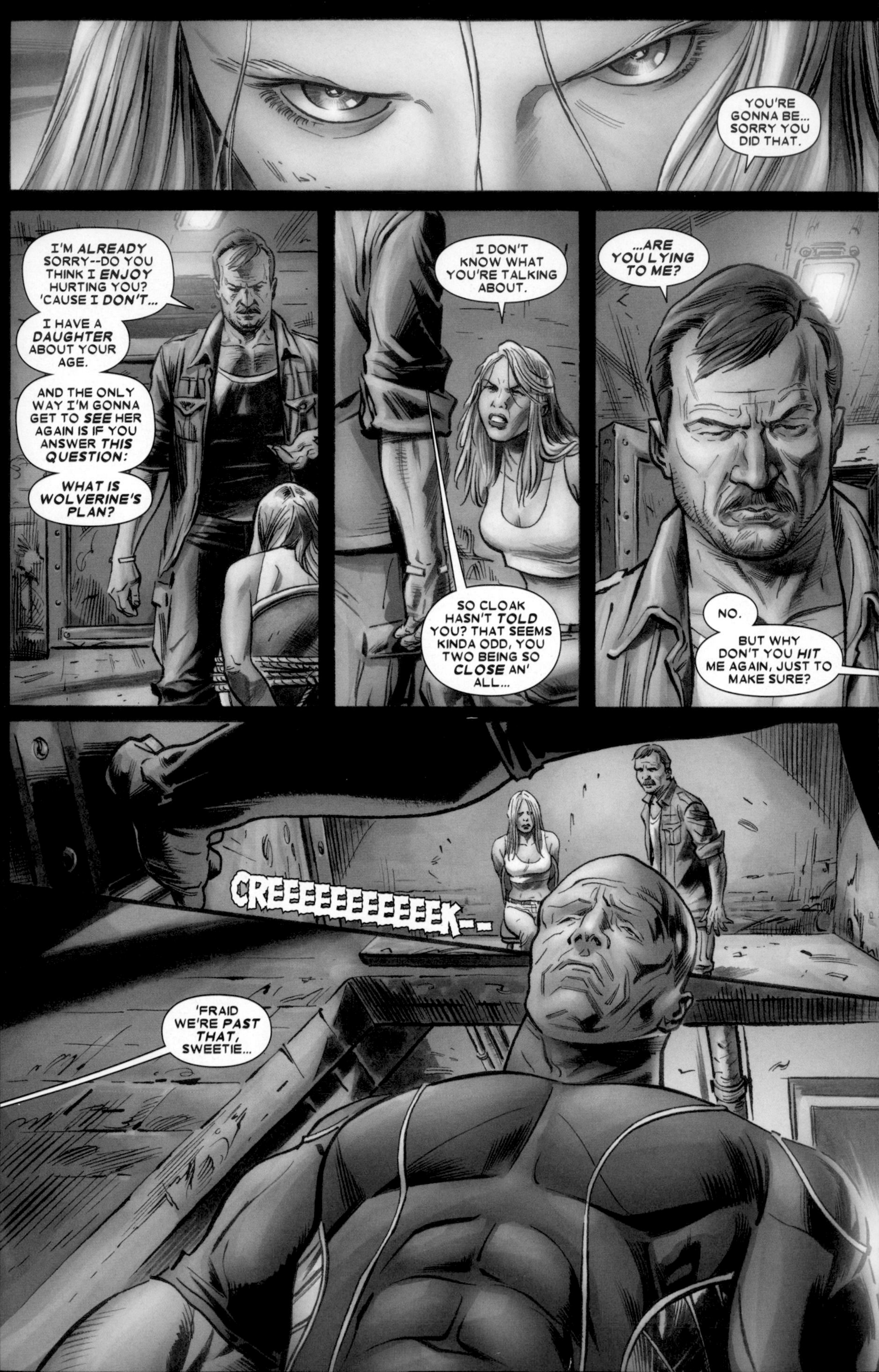
YOU'RE GONNA BE... SORRY YOU DID THAT.
I'M ALREADY SORRY--DO YOU THINK I ENJOY HURTING YOU? 'CAUSE I DON'T...
I HAVE A DAUGHTER ABOUT YOUR AGE.
AND THE ONLY WAY I'M GONNA GET TO SEE HER AGAIN IS IF YOU ANSWER THIS QUESTION:
WHAT IS WOLVERINE'S PLAN?
I DON'T KNOW WHAT YOU'RE TALKING ABOUT.
SO CLOAK HASN'T TOLD YOU? THAT SEEMS KINDA ODD, YOU TWO BEING SO CLOSE AN' ALL...
...ARE YOU LYING TO ME?
NO.
BUT WHY DON'T YOU HIT ME AGAIN, JUST TO MAKE SURE?
CREEEEEEEEEEEEK--
'FRAID WE'RE PAST THAT, SWEETIE...

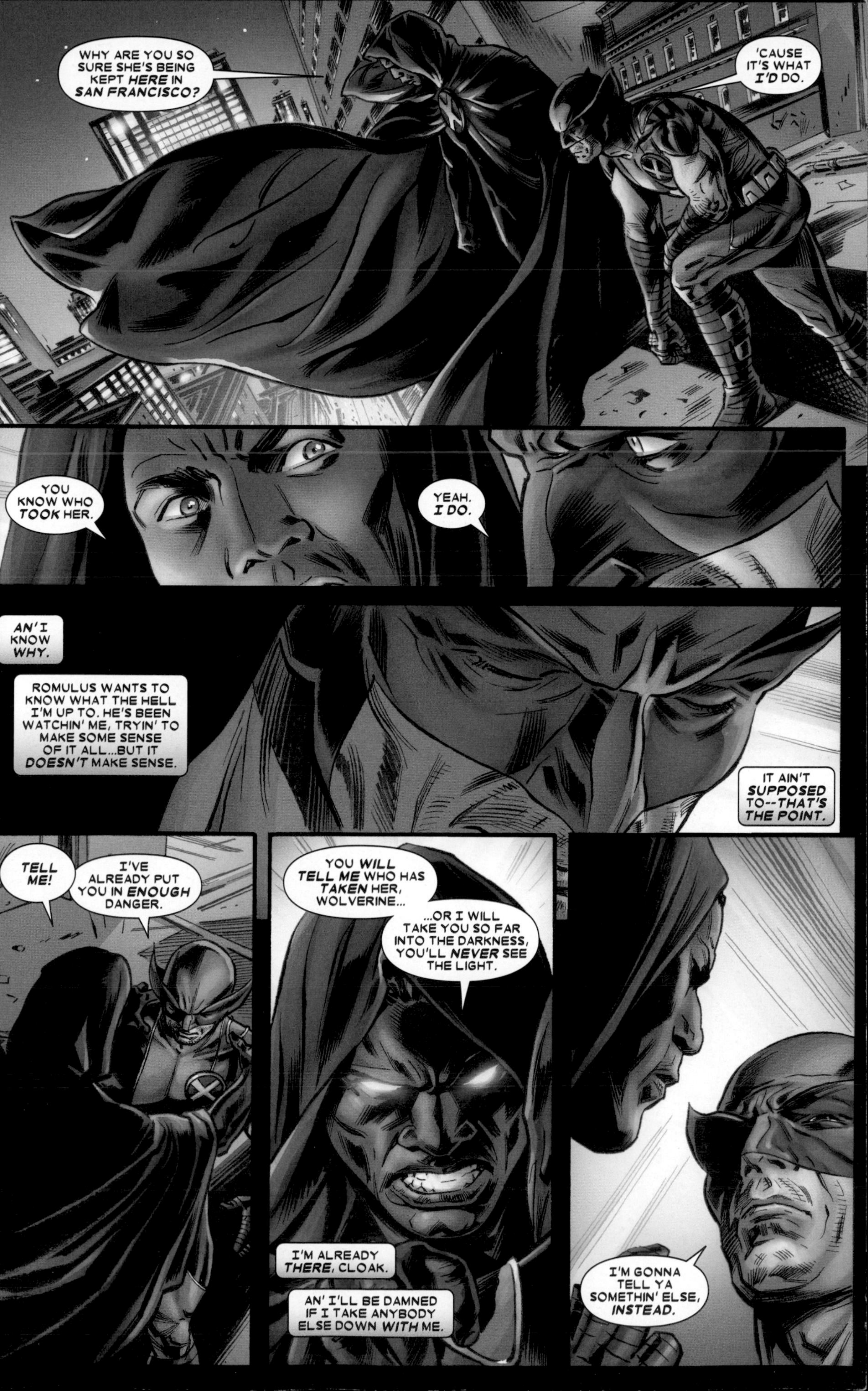
WHY ARE YOU SO SURE SHE'S BEING KEPT HERE IN SAN FRANCISCO?
'CAUSE IT'S WHAT I'D DO.
YOU KNOW WHO TOOK HER.
YEAH. I DO.
AN' I KNOW WHY.
ROMULUS WANTS TO KNOW WHAT THE HELL I'M UP TO. HE'S BEEN WATCHIN' ME, TRYIN' TO MAKE SOME SENSE OF IT ALL...BUT IT DOESN'T MAKE SENSE.
IT AIN'T SUPPOSED TO--THAT'S THE POINT.
TELL ME!
I'VE ALREADY PUT YOU IN ENOUGH DANGER.
YOU WILL TELL ME WHO HAS TAKEN HER, WOLVERINE...
...OR I WILL TAKE YOU SO FAR INTO THE DARKNESS, YOU'LL NEVER SEE THE LIGHT.
I'M ALREADY THERE, CLOAK.
AN' I'LL BE DAMNED IF I TAKE ANYBODY ELSE DOWN WITH ME.
I'M GONNA TELL YA SOMETHIN' ELSE, INSTEAD.

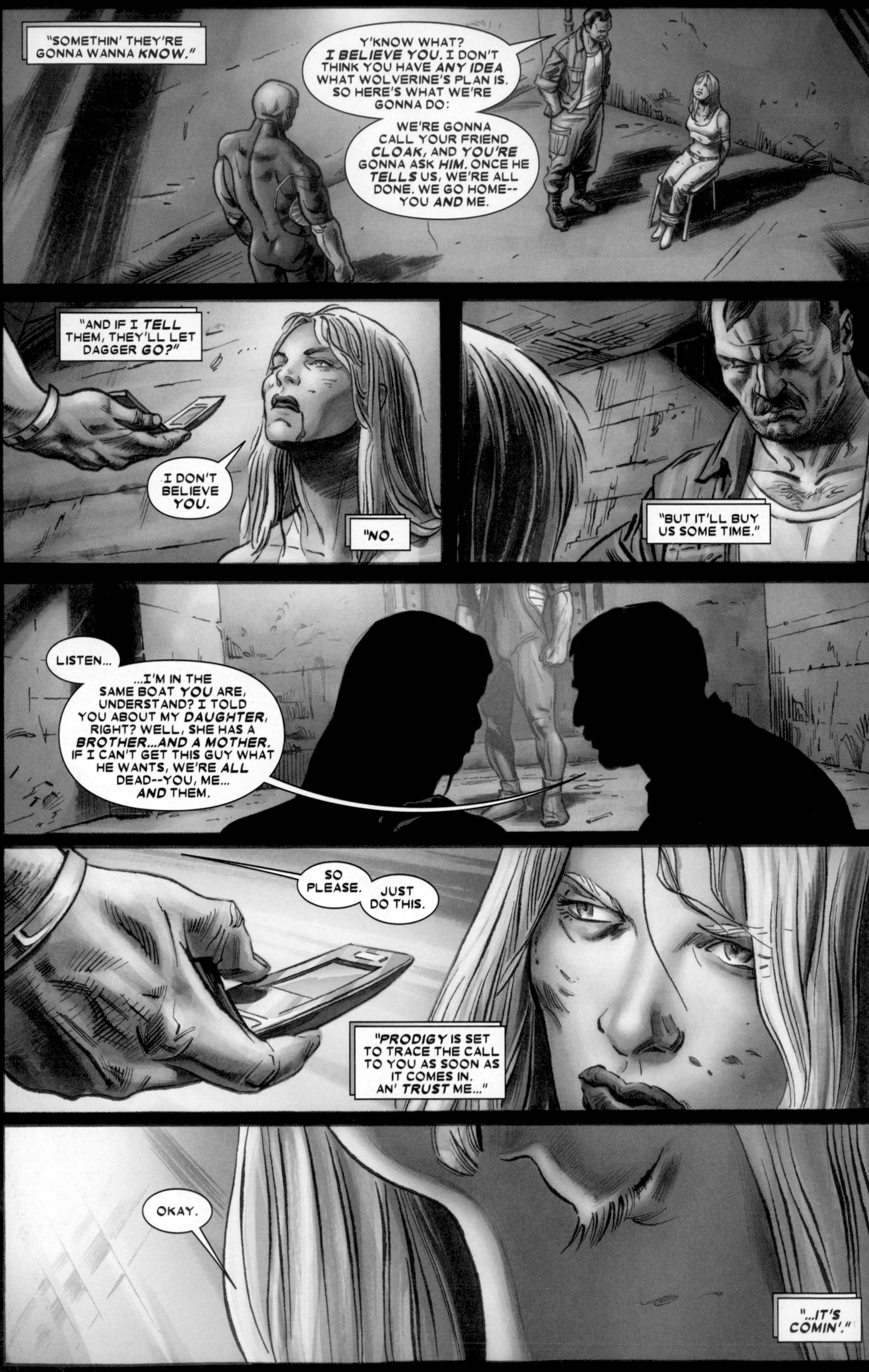
"SOMETHIN' THEY'RE GONNA WANNA KNOW."
Y'KNOW WHAT? I BELIEVE YOU. I DON'T THINK YOU HAVE ANY IDEA WHAT WOLVERINE'S PLAN IS. SO HERE'S WHAT WE'RE GONNA DO:
WE'RE GONNA CALL YOUR FRIEND CLOAK, AND YOU'RE GONNA ASK HIM. ONCE HE TELLS US, WE'RE ALL DONE. WE GO HOME-- YOU AND ME.
"AND IF I TELL THEM, THEY'LL LET DAGGER GO?"
I DON'T BELIEVE YOU.
"NO.
"BUT IT'LL BUY US SOME TIME."
LISTEN...
...I'M IN THE SAME BOAT YOU ARE, UNDERSTAND? I TOLD YOU ABOUT MY DAUGHTER, RIGHT? WELL, SHE HAS A BROTHER...AND A MOTHER. IF I CAN'T GET THIS GUY WHAT HE WANTS, WE'RE ALL DEAD--YOU, ME... AND THEM.
SO PLEASE.
JUST DO THIS.
"PRODIGY IS SET TO TRACE THE CALL TO YOU AS SOON AS IT COMES IN. AN' TRUST ME..."
OKAY.
"...IT'S COMIN'."

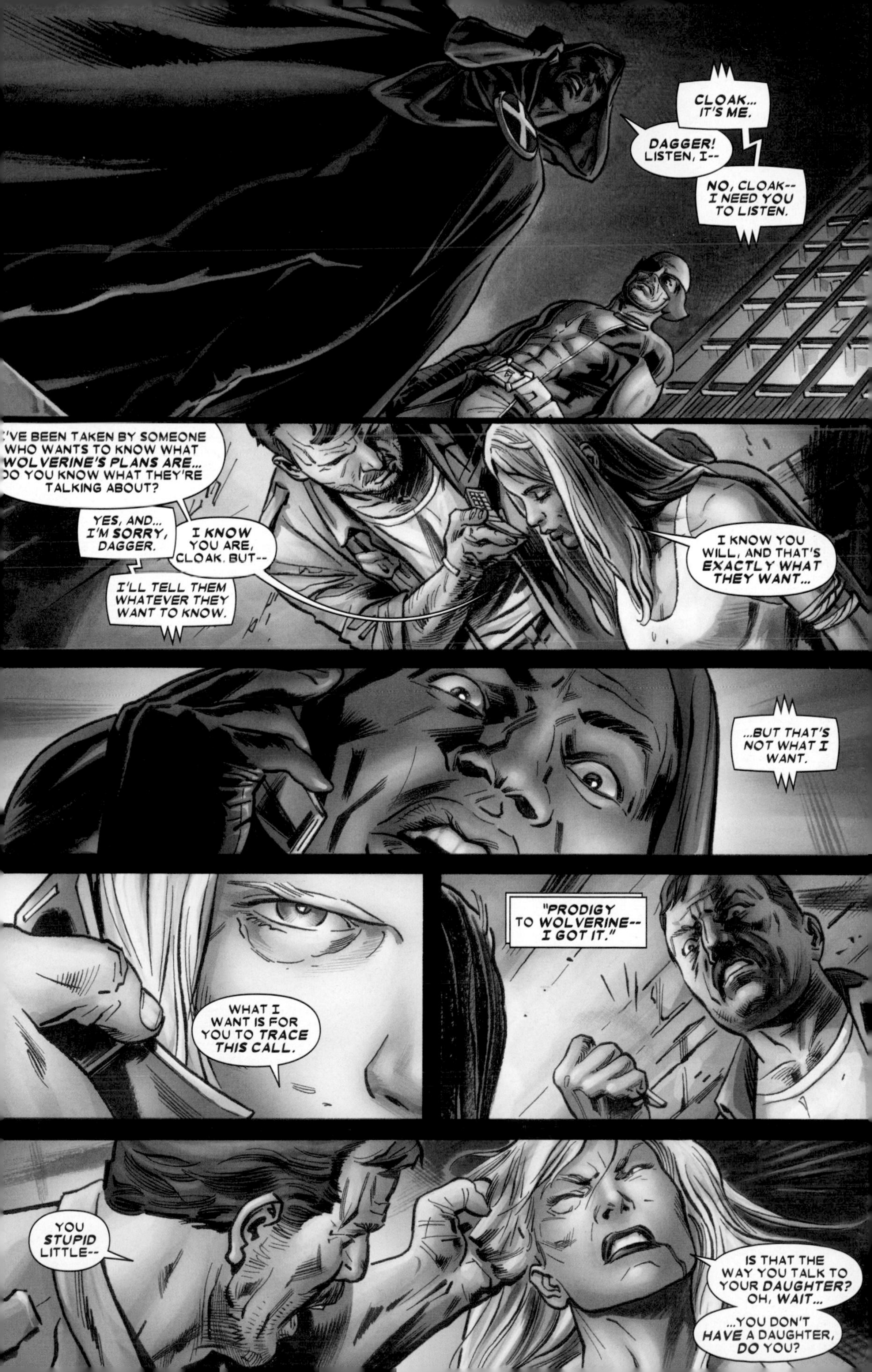
CLOAK... IT'S ME.
DAGGER! LISTEN, I--
NO, CLOAK-- I NEED YOU TO LISTEN.
I'VE BEEN TAKEN BY SOMEONE WHO WANTS TO KNOW WHAT WOLVERINE'S PLANS ARE... DO YOU KNOW WHAT THEY'RE TALKING ABOUT?
YES, AND... I'M SORRY, DAGGER.
I'LL TELL THEM WHATEVER THEY WANT TO KNOW.
I KNOW YOU ARE, CLOAK, BUT--
I KNOW YOU WILL, AND THAT'S EXACTLY WHAT THEY WANT...
...BUT THAT'S NOT WHAT I WANT.
WHAT I WANT IS FOR YOU TO TRACE THIS CALL.
"PRODIGY TO WOLVERINE-- I GOT IT."
YOU STUPID LITTLE--
IS THAT THE WAY YOU TALK TO YOUR DAUGHTER? OH, WAIT...
...YOU DON'T HAVE A DAUGHTER, DO YOU?

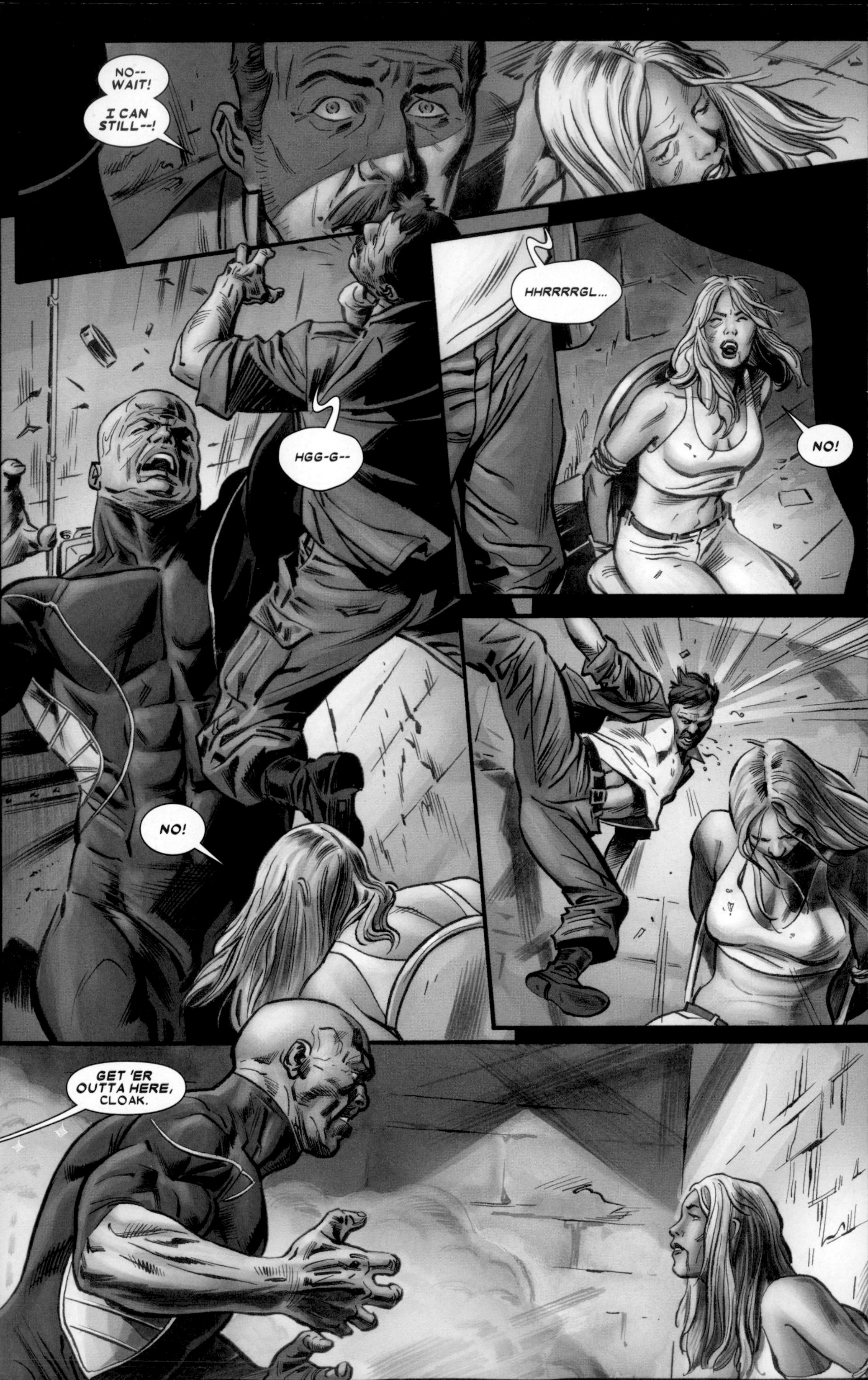
NO-- WAIT!
I CAN STILL--!
HHRRRRGL...
HGG-G--
NO!
NO!
GET 'ER OUTTA HERE, CLOAK.

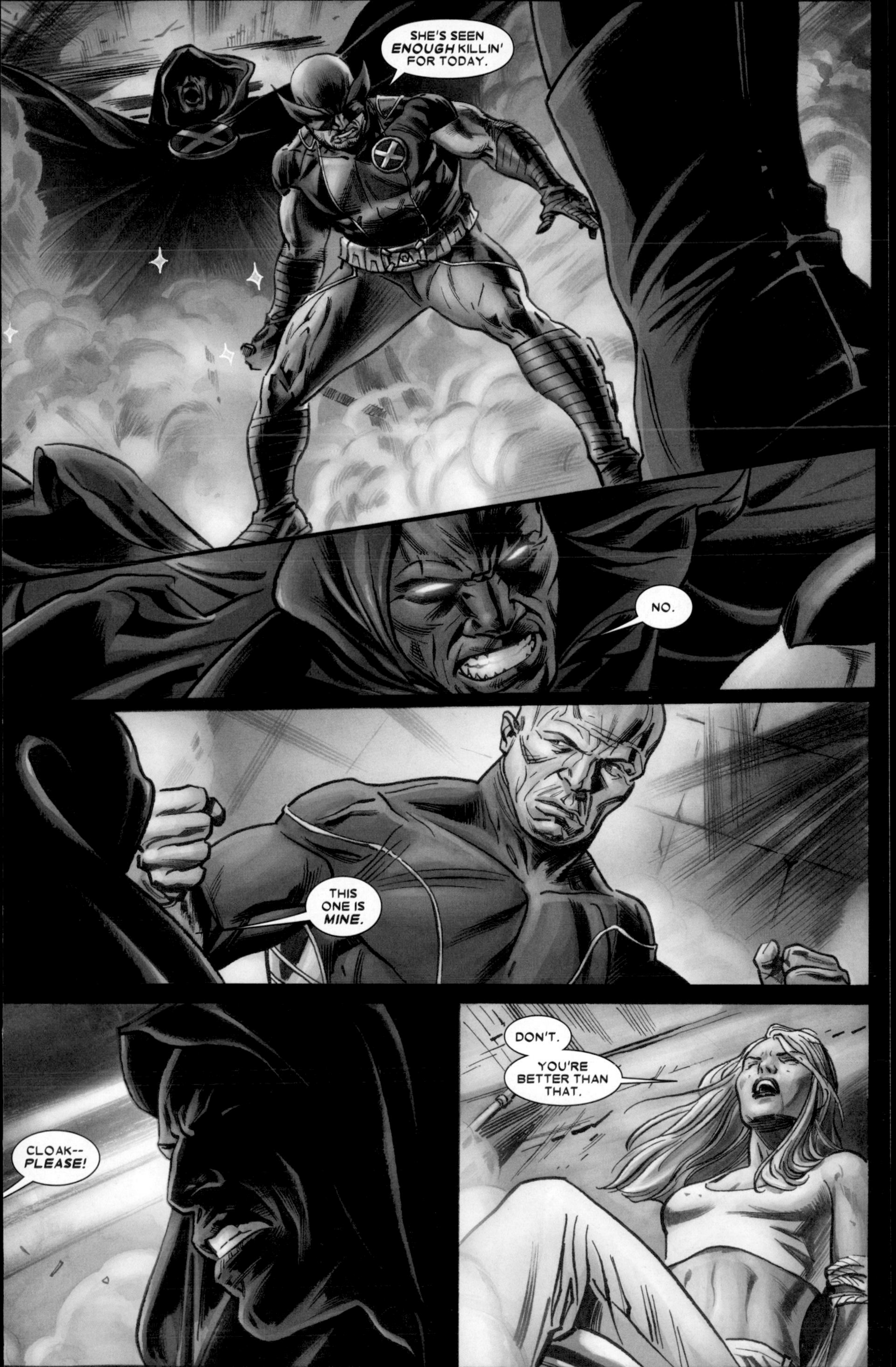
SHE'S SEEN ENOUGH KILLIN' FOR TODAY.
NO.
THIS ONE IS MINE.
CLOAK-- PLEASE!
DON'T.
YOU'RE BETTER THAN THAT.

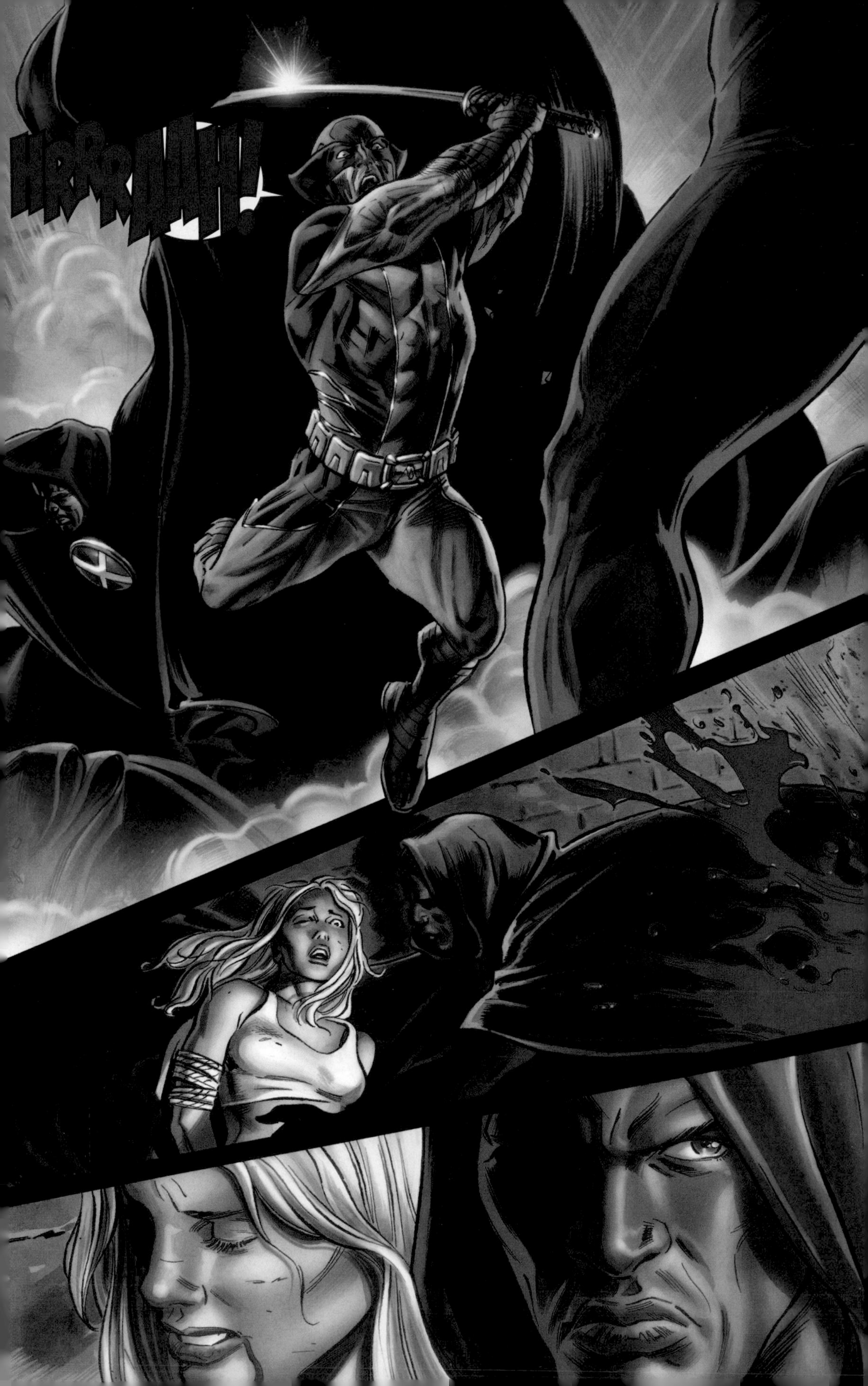
HRRRAAAH!

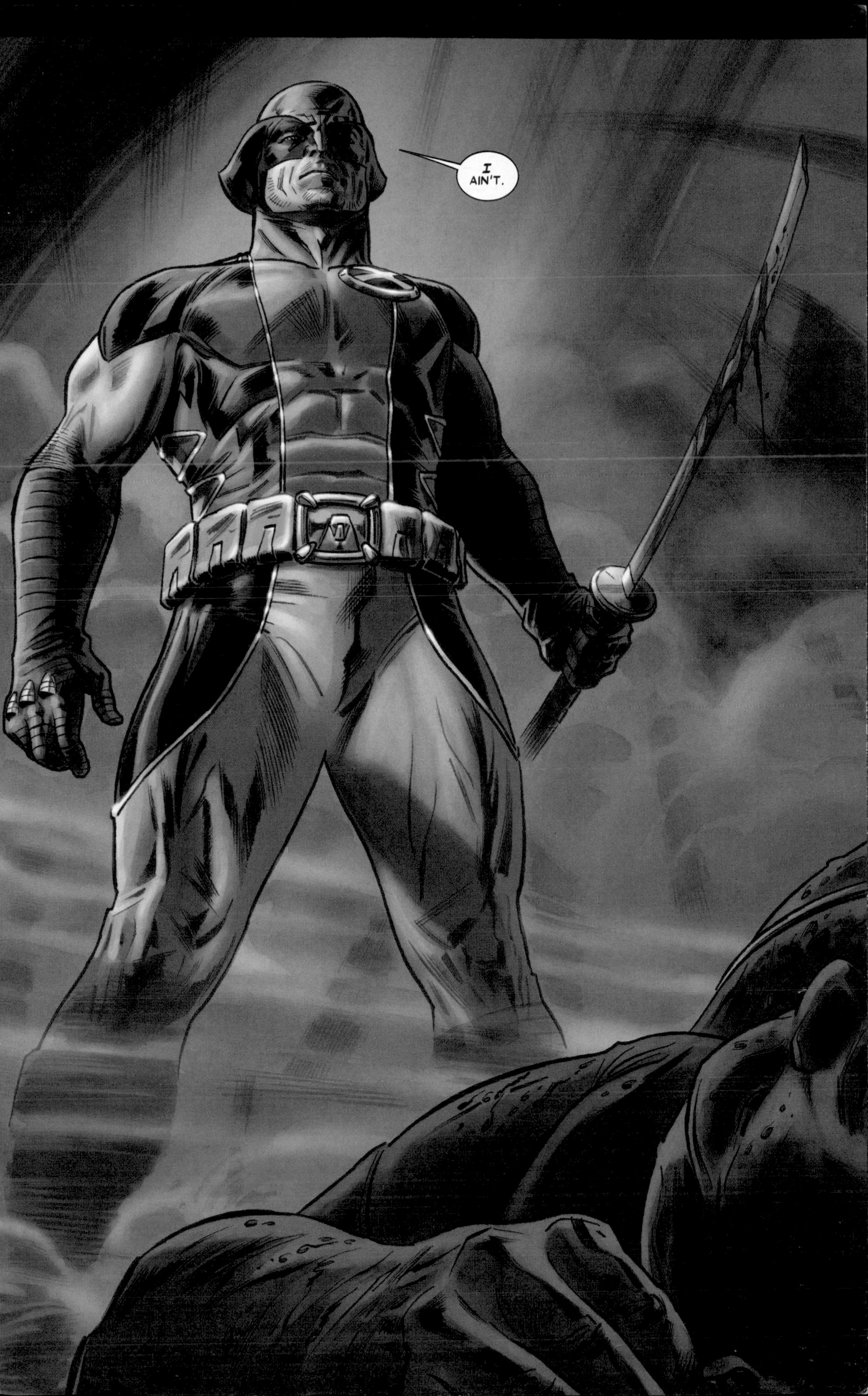
I AIN'T.

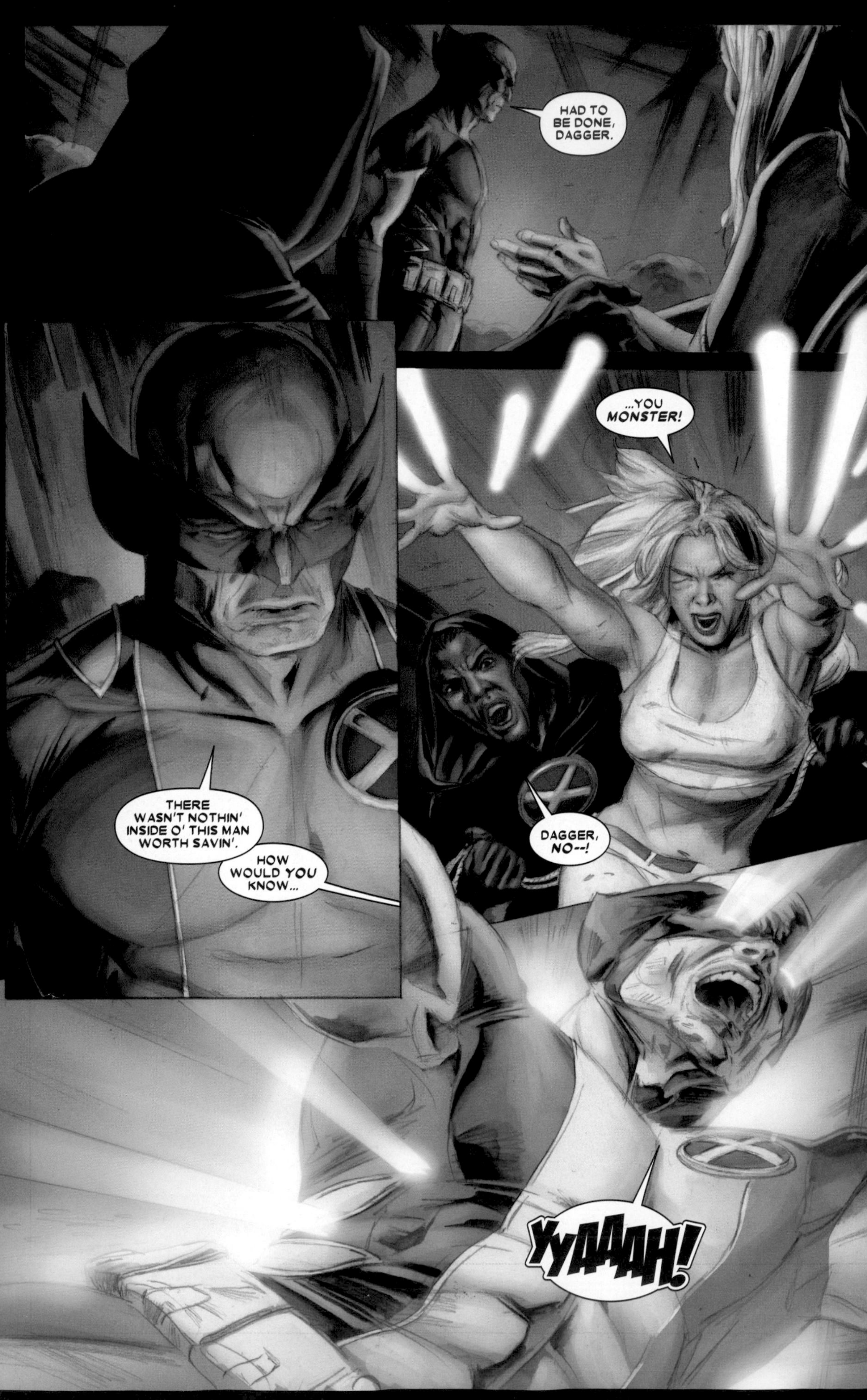
HAD TO BE DONE, DAGGER.
THERE WASN'T NOTHIN' INSIDE O' THIS MAN WORTH SAVIN'.
HOW WOULD YOU KNOW...
...YOU MONSTER!
DAGGER, NO--!
YYAAAH!

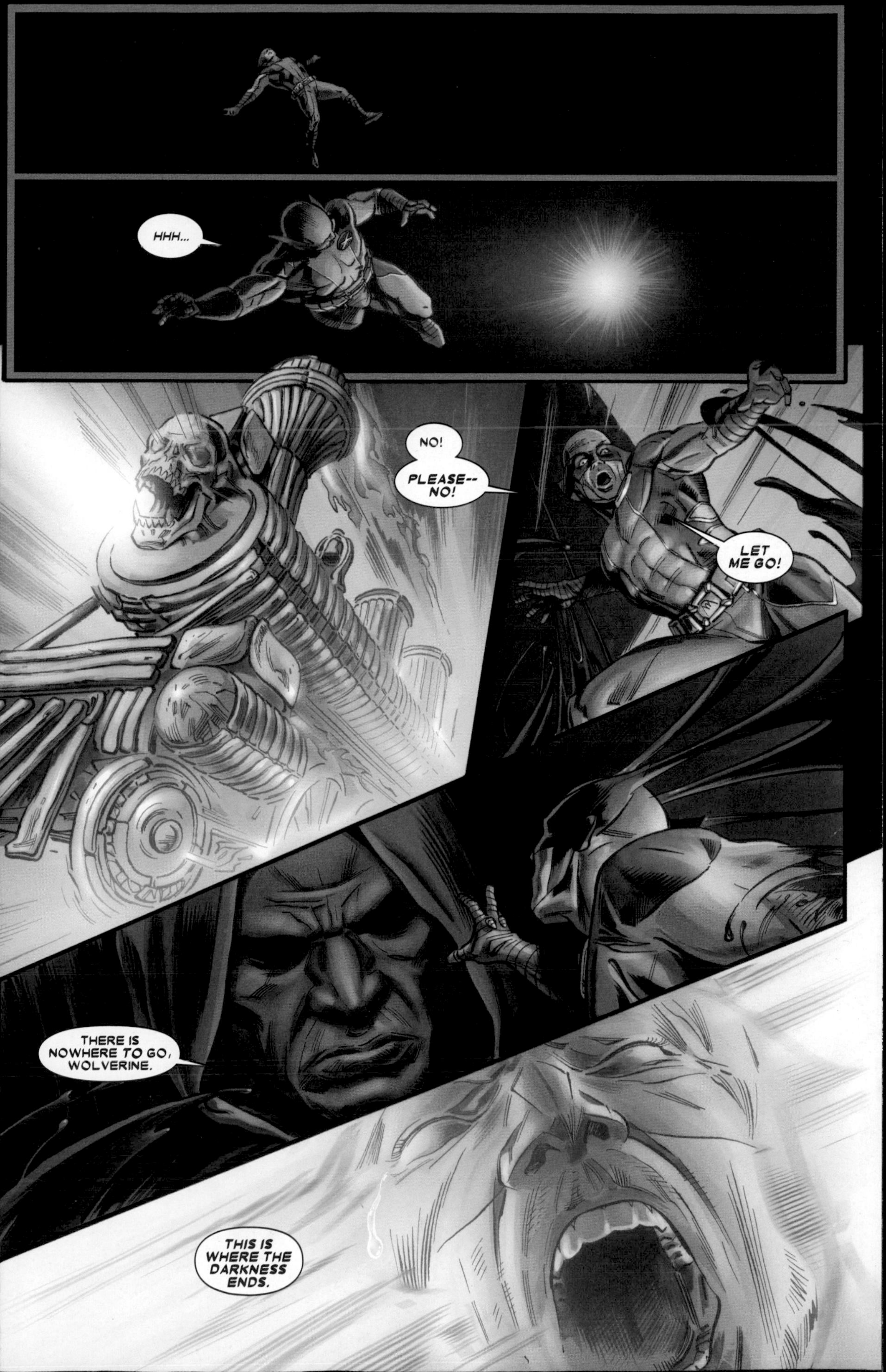
HHH...
NO!
PLEASE--
NO!
LET ME GO!
THERE IS NOWHERE TO GO, WOLVERINE.
THIS IS WHERE THE DARKNESS ENDS.

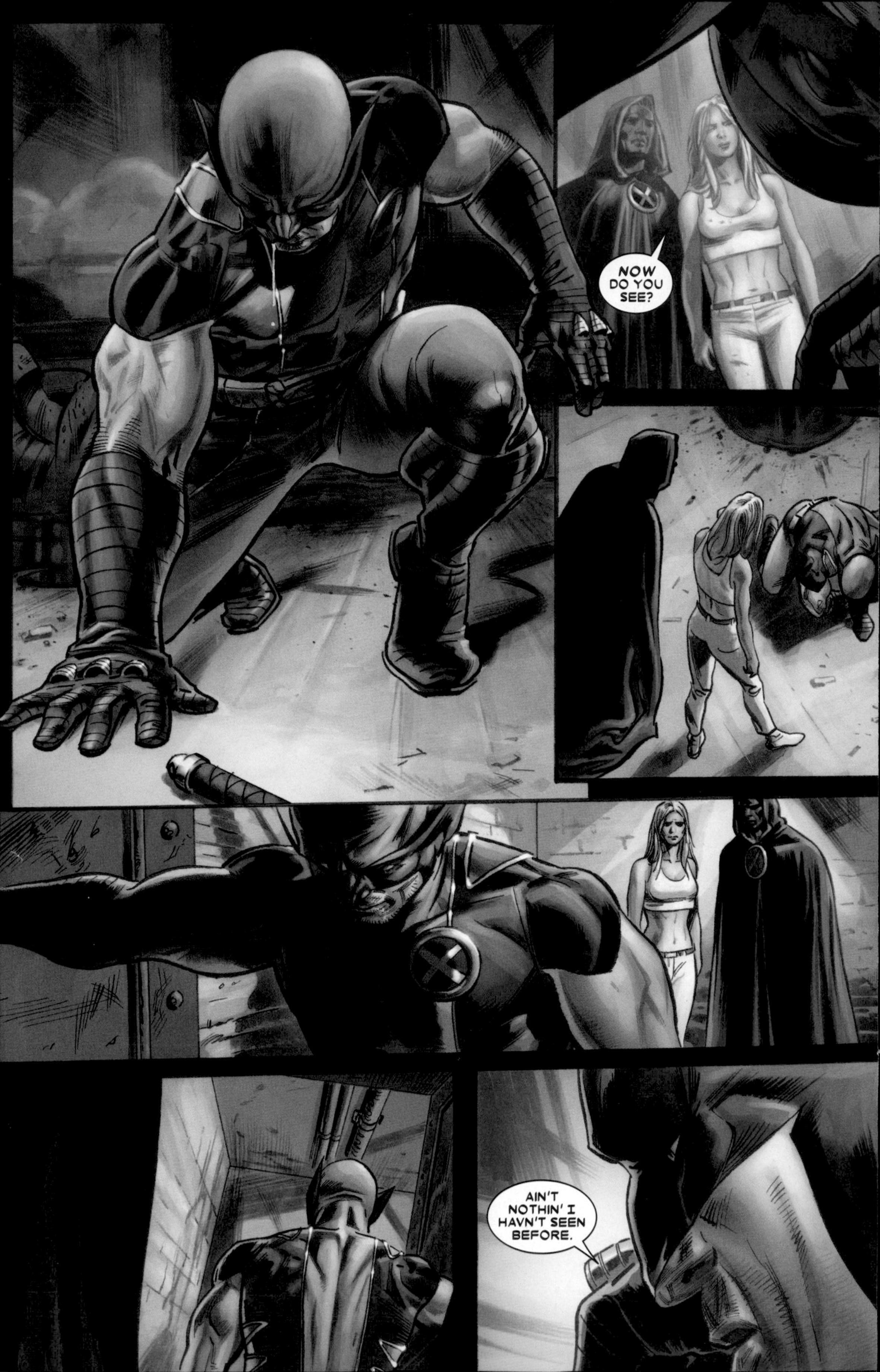
NOW DO YOU SEE?
AIN'T NOTHIN' I HAVN'T SEEN BEFORE.

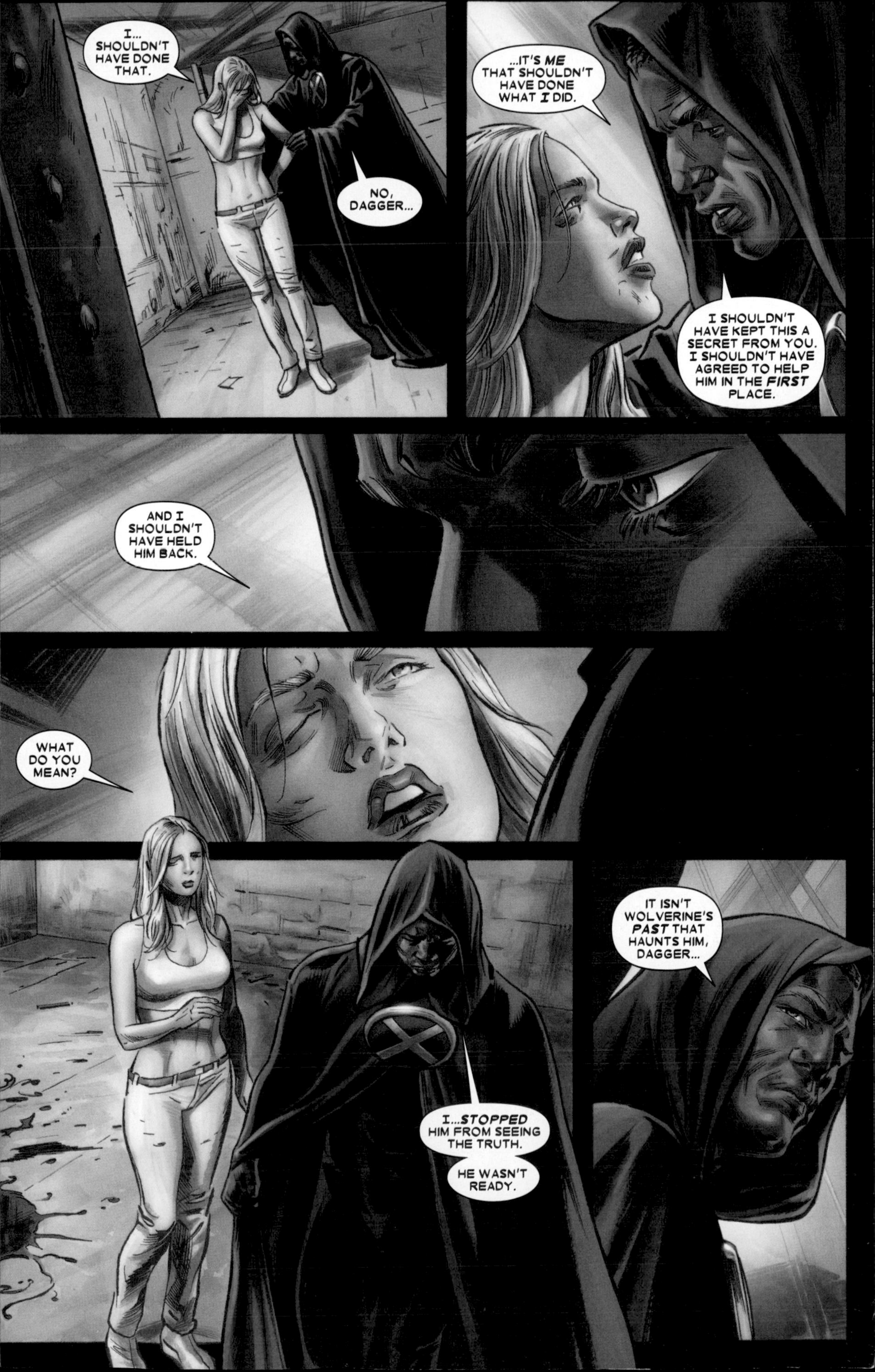
I... SHOULDN'T HAVE DONE THAT.
NO, DAGGER...
...IT'S ME THAT SHOULDN'T HAVE DONE WHAT I DID.
I SHOULDN'T HAVE KEPT THIS A SECRET FROM YOU. I SHOULDN'T HAVE AGREED TO HELP HIM IN THE FIRST PLACE.
AND I SHOULDN'T HAVE HELD HIM BACK.
WHAT DO YOU MEAN?
I...STOPPED HIM FROM SEEING THE TRUTH.
HE WASN'T READY.
IT ISN'T WOLVERINE'S PAST THAT HAUNTS HIM, DAGGER...

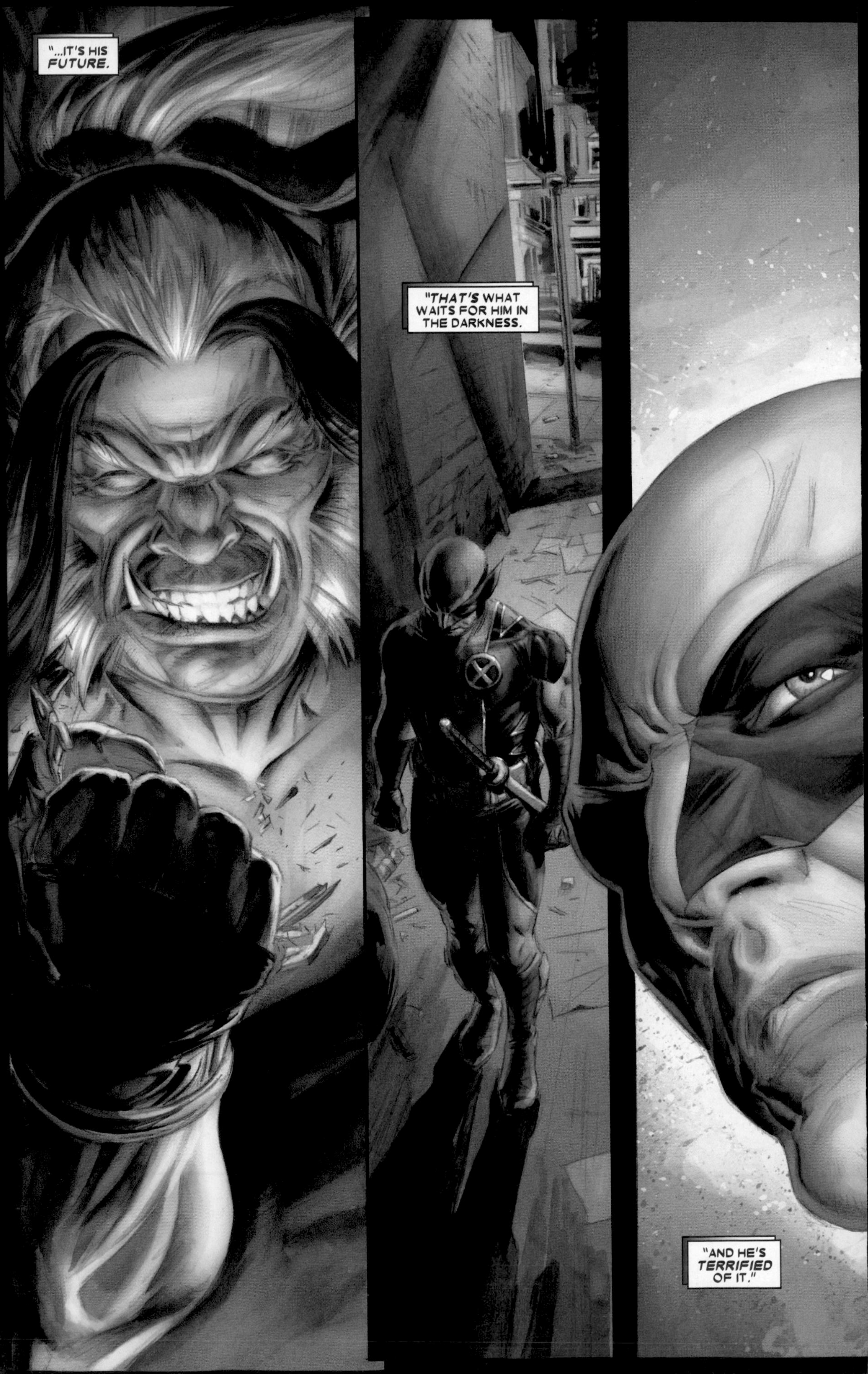
"...IT'S HIS FUTURE.
"THAT'S WHAT WAITS FOR HIM IN THE DARKNESS.
"AND HE'S TERRIFIED OF IT."

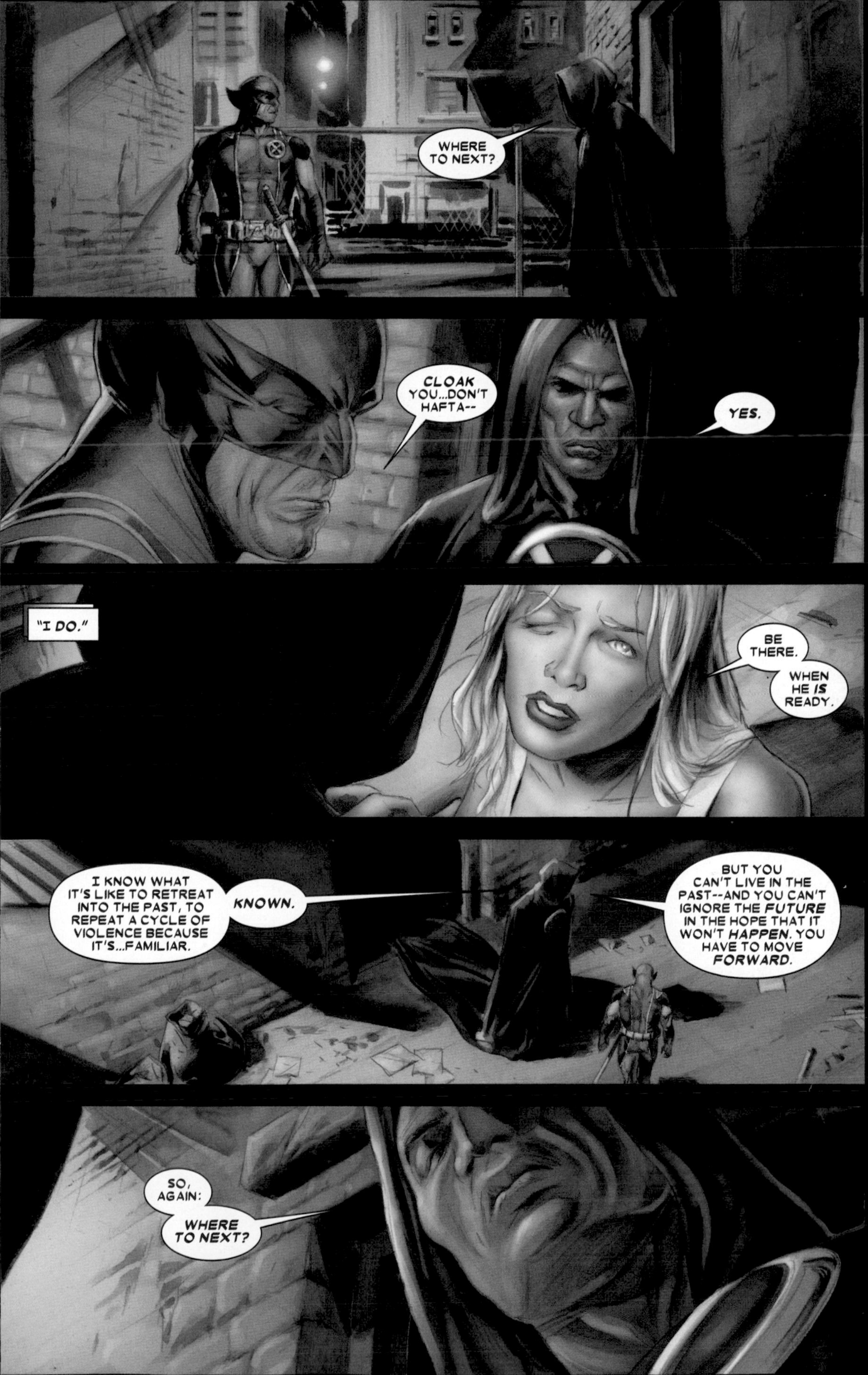
WHERE TO NEXT?
CLOAK YOU...DON'T HAFTA--
YES.
"I DO."
BE THERE.
WHEN HE IS READY.
I KNOW WHAT IT'S LIKE TO RETREAT INTO THE PAST, TO REPEAT A CYCLE OF VIOLENCE BECAUSE IT'S...FAMILIAR.
KNOWN.
BUT YOU CAN'T LIVE IN THE PAST--AND YOU CAN'T IGNORE THE FUTURE IN THE HOPE THAT IT WON'T HAPPEN. YOU HAVE TO MOVE FORWARD.
SO, AGAIN:
WHERE TO NEXT?

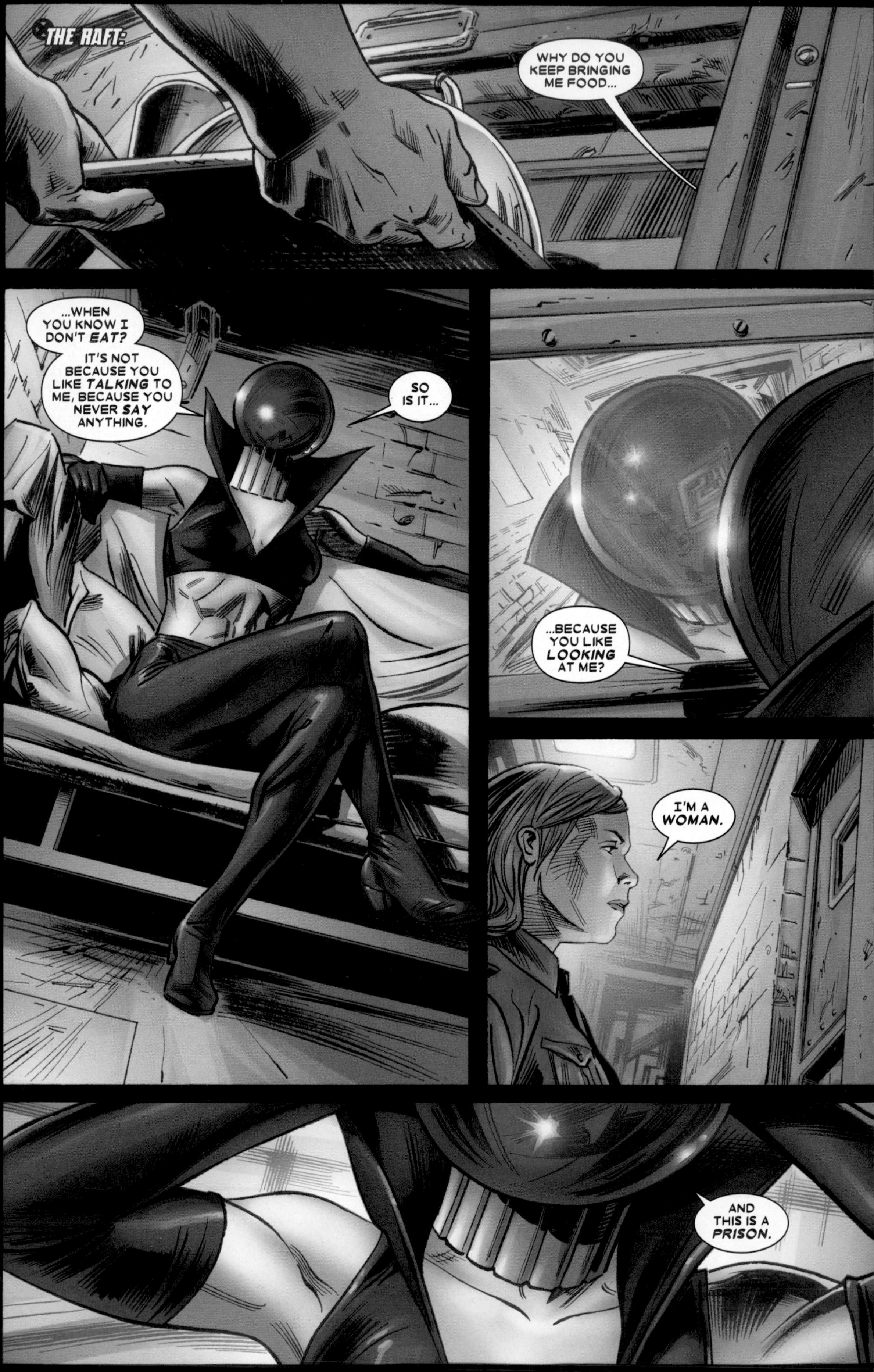
THE RAFT:
WHY DO YOU KEEP BRINGING ME FOOD...
...WHEN YOU KNOW I DON'T EAT?
IT'S NOT BECAUSE YOU LIKE TALKING TO ME, BECAUSE YOU NEVER SAY ANYTHING.
SO IS IT...
...BECAUSE YOU LIKE LOOKING AT ME?
I'M A WOMAN.
AND THIS IS A PRISON.

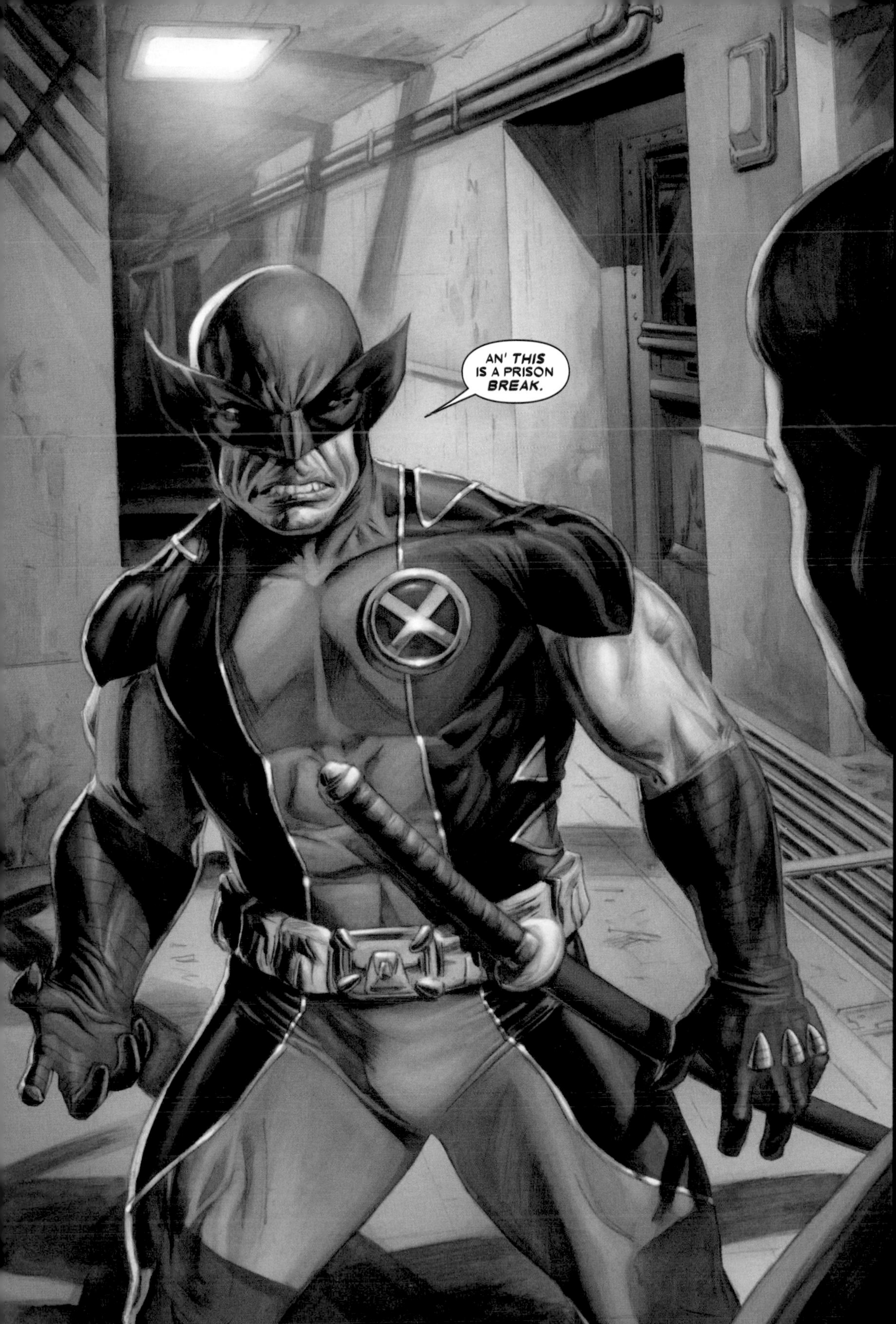
AN' THIS IS A PRISON BREAK.

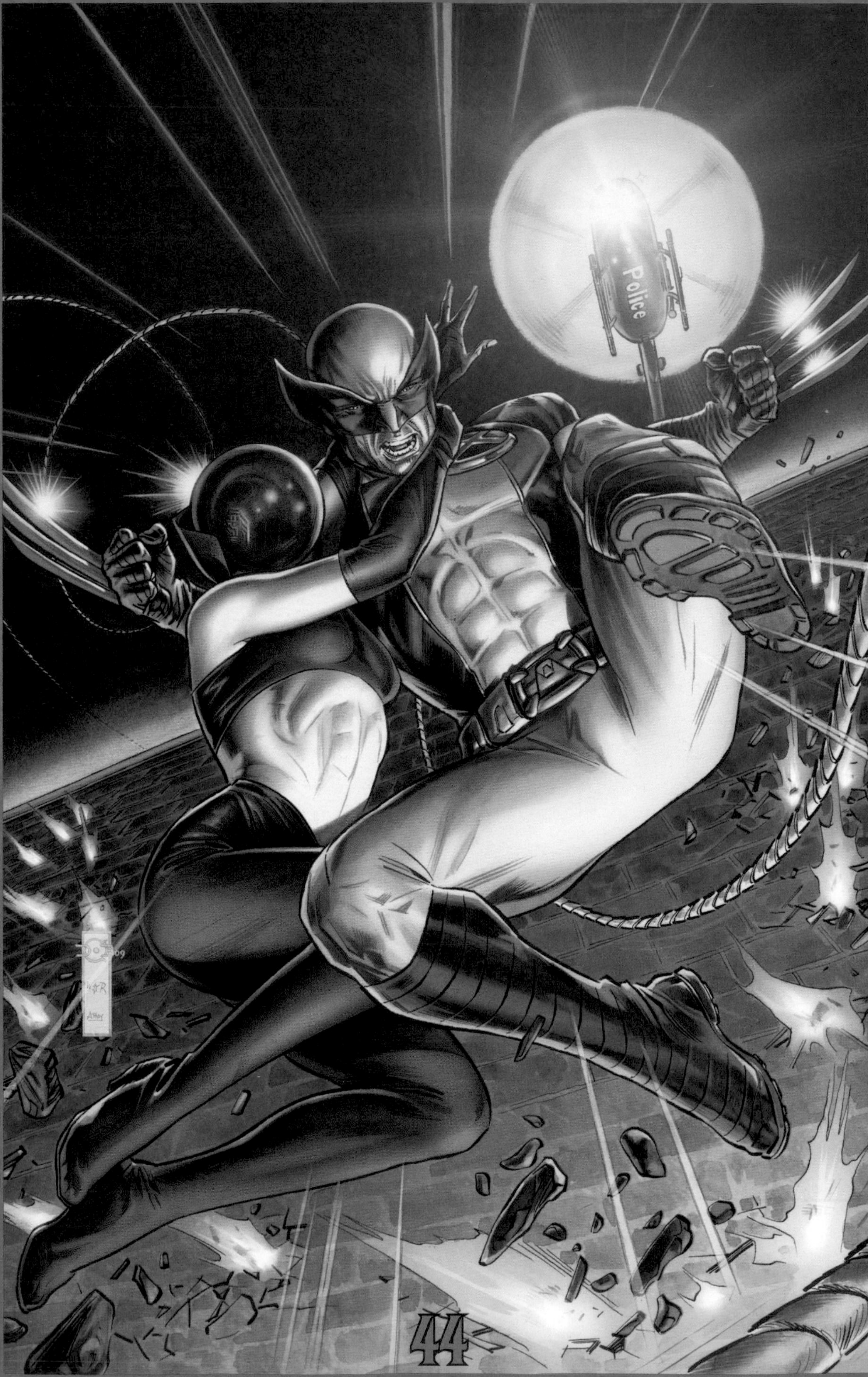
Police

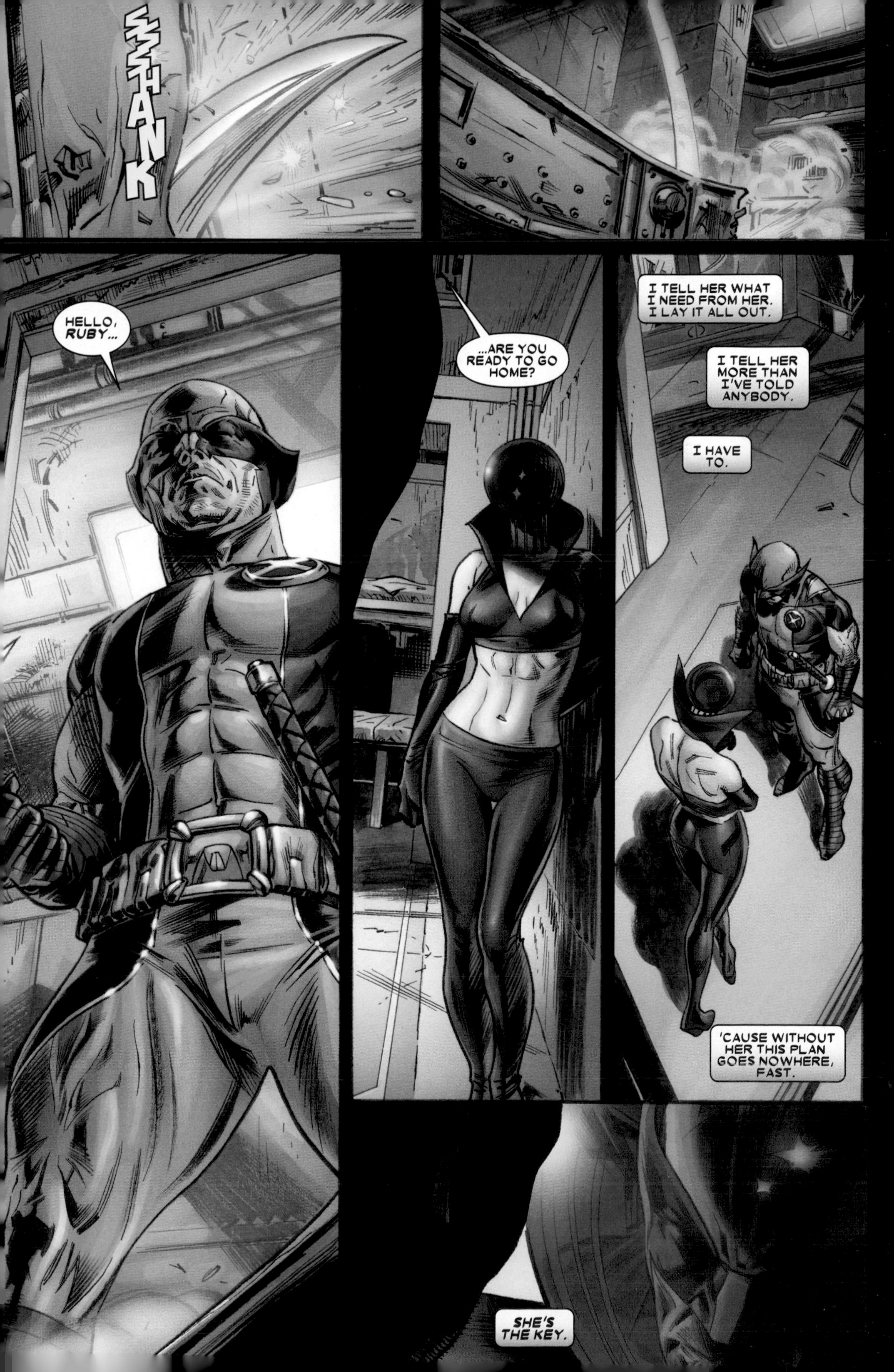
SSHANK
HELLO, RUBY...
...ARE YOU READY TO GO HOME?
I TELL HER WHAT I NEED FROM HER. I LAY IT ALL OUT.
I TELL HER MORE THAN I'VE TOLD ANYBODY.
I HAVE TO.
'CAUSE WITHOUT HER THIS PLAN GOES NOWHERE, FAST.
SHE'S THE KEY.

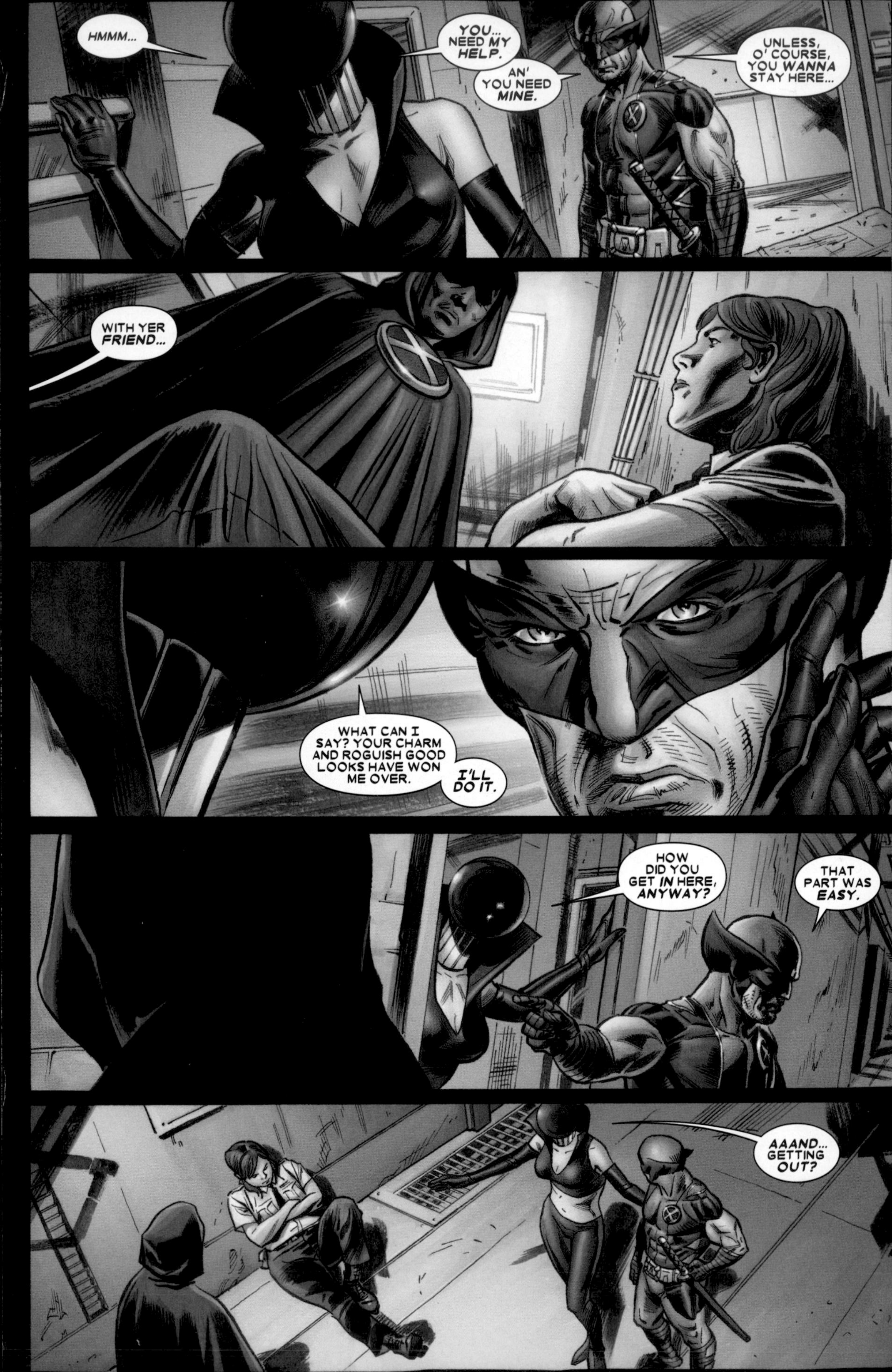
HMMM...
YOU... NEED MY HELP.
AN' YOU NEED MINE.
UNLESS, O' COURSE, YOU WANNA STAY HERE...
WITH YER FRIEND...
WHAT CAN I SAY? YOUR CHARM AND ROGUISH GOOD LOOKS HAVE WON ME OVER.
I'LL DO IT.
HOW DID YOU GET IN HERE, ANYWAY?
THAT PART WAS EASY.
AAAND... GETTING OUT?

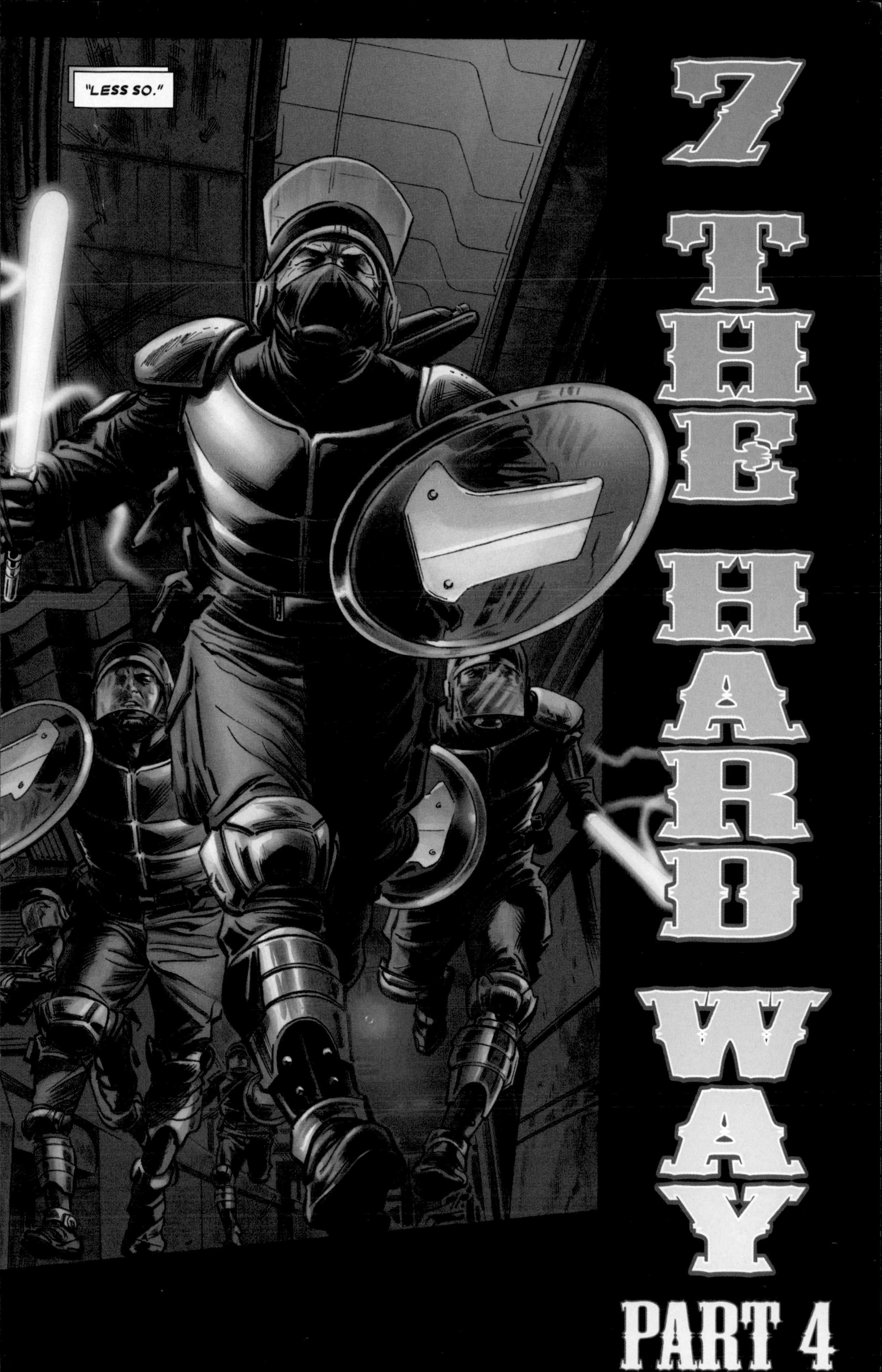
"LESS SO."
7 THE HARD WAY
PART 4

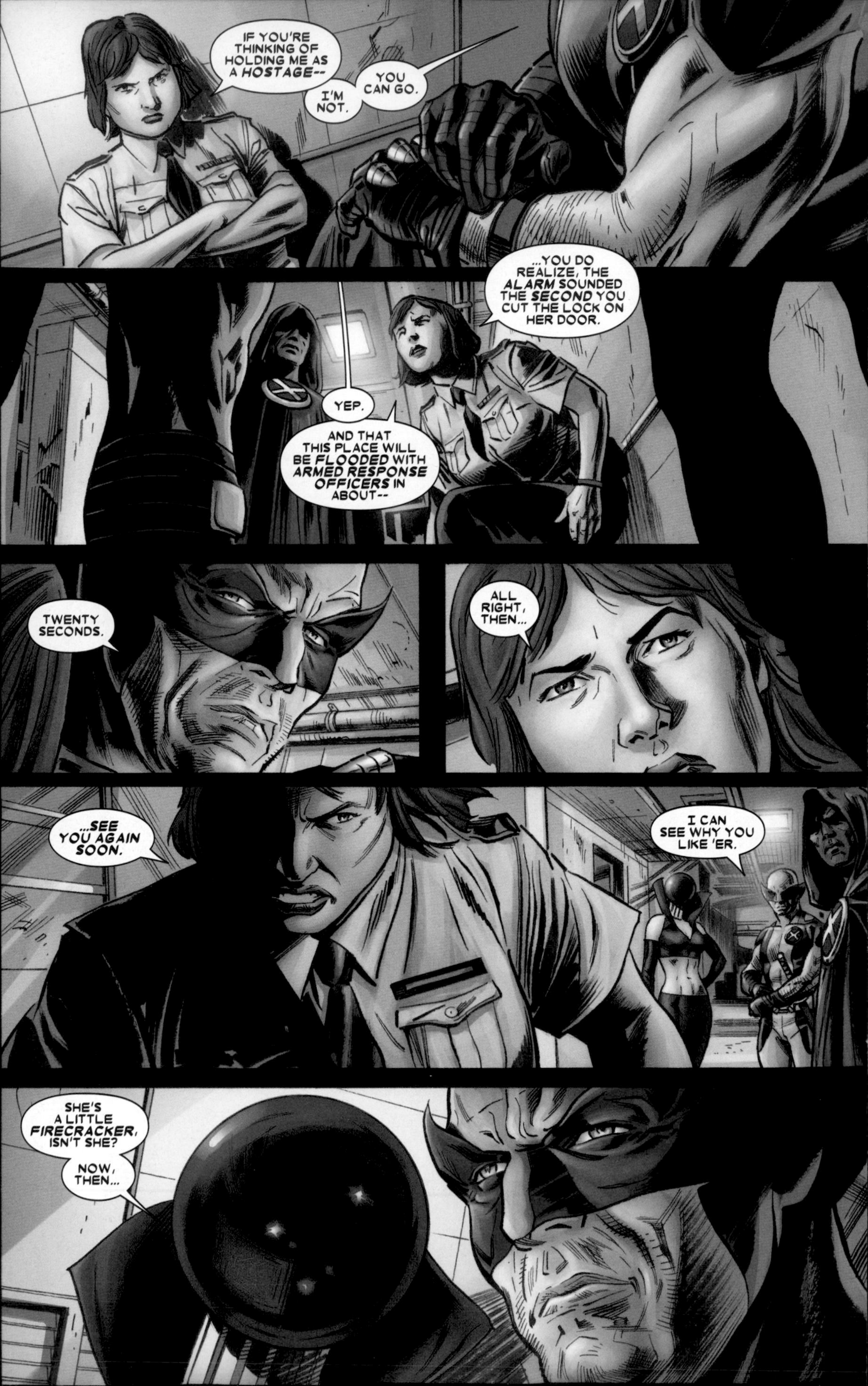

IF YOU'RE THINKING OF HOLDING ME AS A HOSTAGE--
I'M NOT.
YOU CAN GO.
...YOU DO REALIZE, THE ALARM SOUNDED THE SECOND YOU CUT THE LOCK ON HER DOOR.
YEP.
AND THAT THIS PLACE WILL BE FLOODED WITH ARMED RESPONSE OFFICERS IN ABOUT--
TWENTY SECONDS.
ALL RIGHT, THEN...
...SEE YOU AGAIN SOON.
I CAN SEE WHY YOU LIKE 'ER.
SHE'S A LITTLE FIRECRACKER, ISN'T SHE?
NOW, THEN...

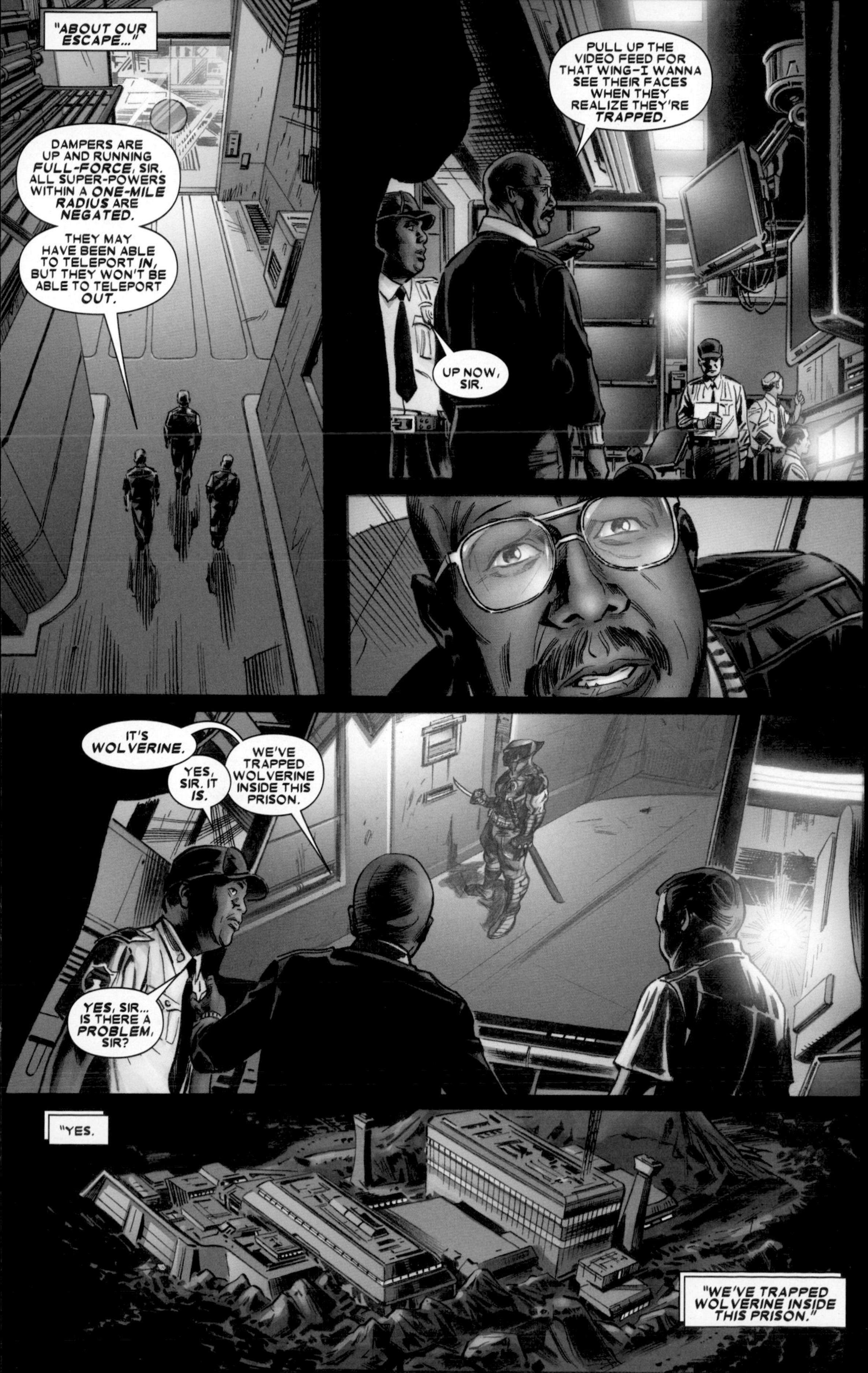
"ABOUT OUR ESCAPE..."
DAMPERS ARE UP AND RUNNING FULL-FORCE, SIR. ALL SUPER-POWERS WITHIN A ONE-MILE RADIUS ARE NEGATED.
THEY MAY HAVE BEEN ABLE TO TELEPORT IN, BUT THEY WON'T BE ABLE TO TELEPORT OUT.
PULL UP THE VIDEO FEED FOR THAT WING--I WANNA SEE THEIR FACES WHEN THEY REALIZE THEY'RE TRAPPED.
UP NOW, SIR.
IT'S WOLVERINE.
YES, SIR... IS THERE A PROBLEM, SIR?
YES, SIR. IT IS.
WE'VE TRAPPED WOLVERINE INSIDE THIS PRISON.
"YES.
"WE'VE TRAPPED WOLVERINE INSIDE THIS PRISON."

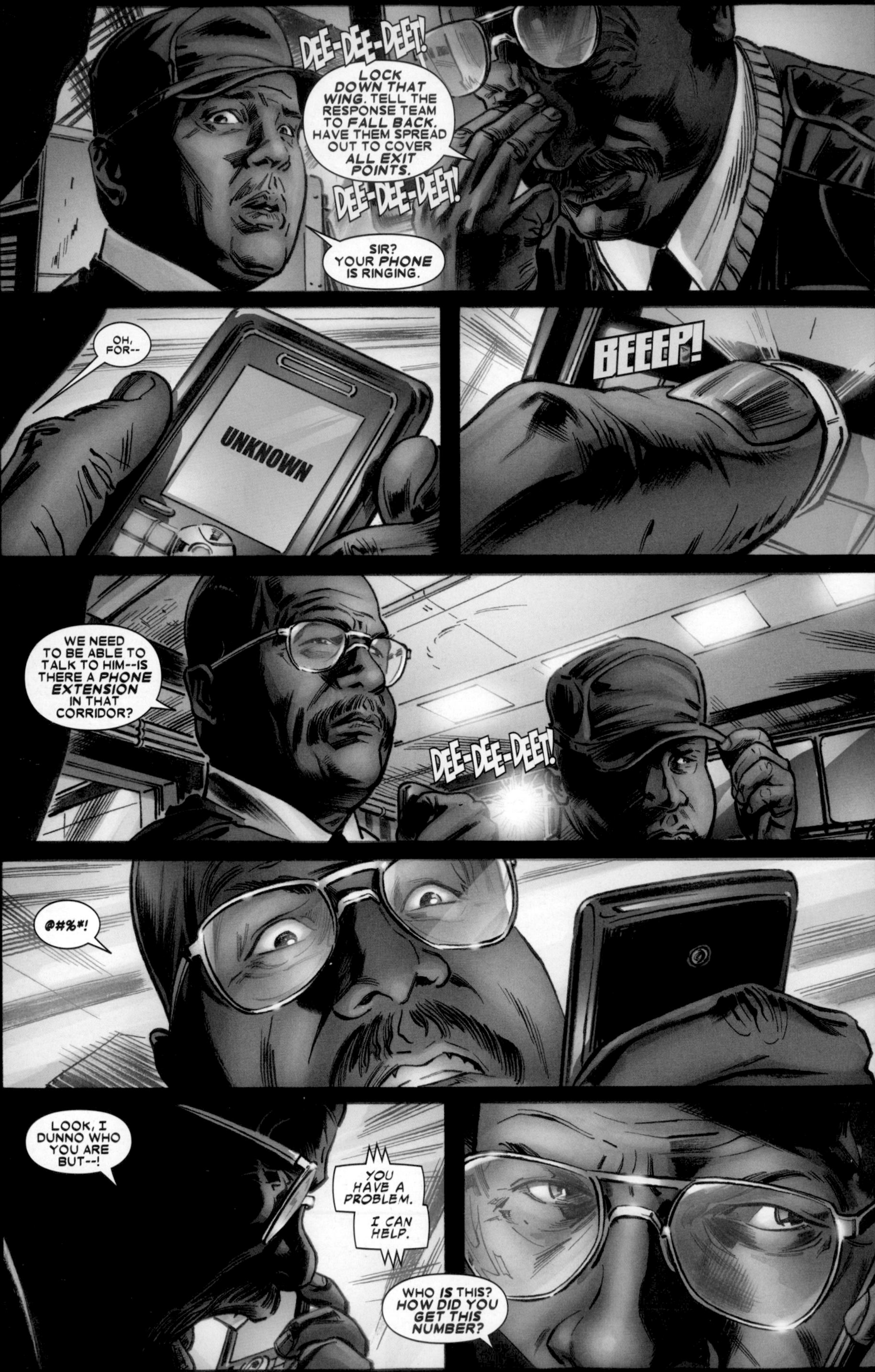
DEE-DEE-DEET!
LOCK DOWN THAT WING. TELL THE RESPONSE TEAM TO FALL BACK. HAVE THEM SPREAD OUT TO COVER ALL EXIT POINTS.
DEE-DEE-DEET!
SIR? YOUR PHONE IS RINGING.
OH, FOR--
UNKNOWN
BEEEP!
WE NEED TO BE ABLE TO TALK TO HIM--IS THERE A PHONE EXTENSION IN THAT CORRIDOR?
DEE-DEE-DEET!
@#%*!
LOOK, I DUNNO WHO YOU ARE BUT--!
YOU HAVE A PROBLEM.
I CAN HELP.
WHO IS THIS? HOW DID YOU GET THIS NUMBER?

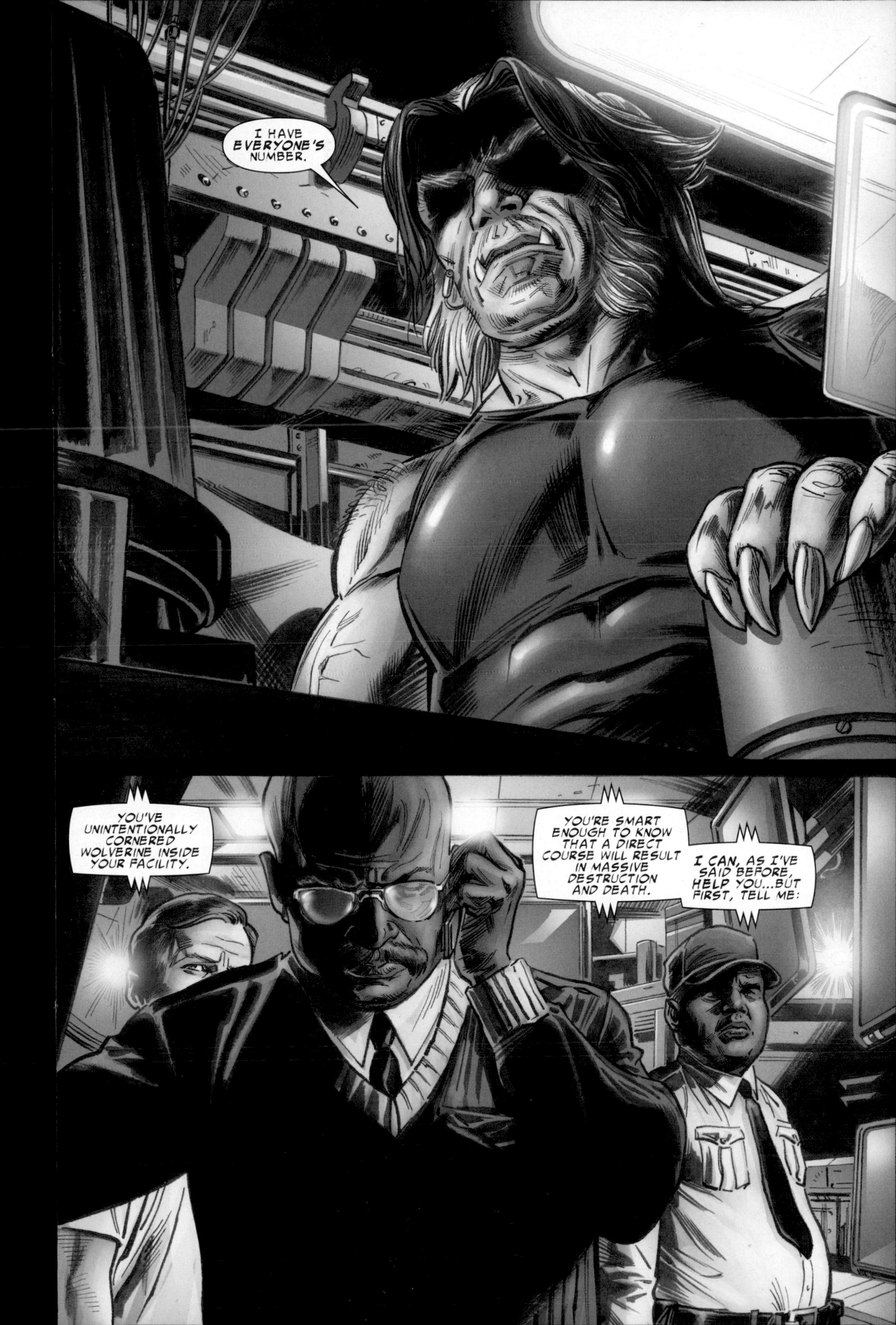
I HAVE **EVERYONE'S** NUMBER.
YOU'VE UNINTENTIONALLY CORNERED WOLVERINE INSIDE YOUR FACILITY.
YOU'RE SMART ENOUGH TO KNOW THAT A DIRECT COURSE WILL RESULT IN MASSIVE DESTRUCTION AND DEATH.
I CAN, AS I'VE SAID BEFORE, HELP YOU...BUT FIRST, TELL ME:

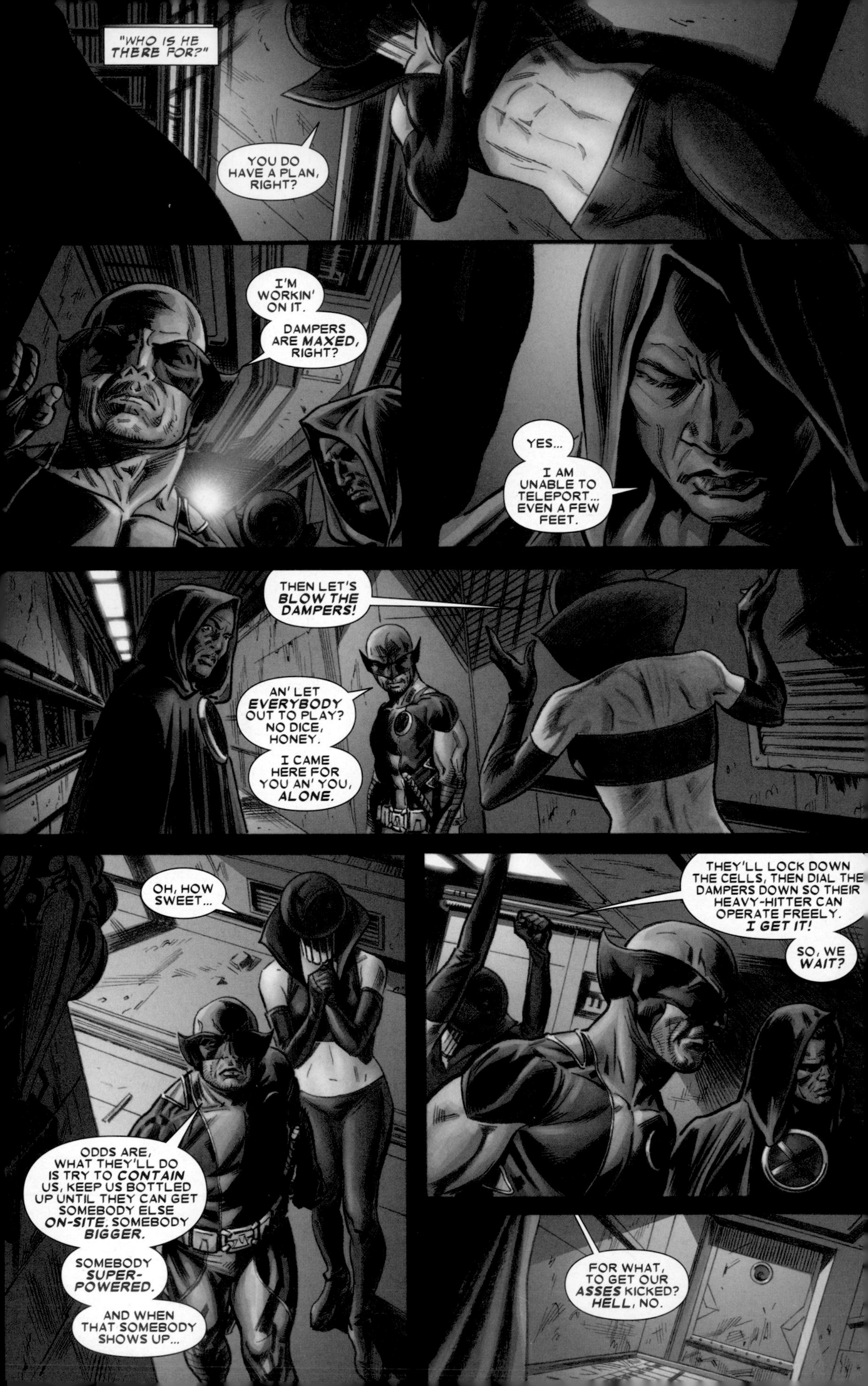
"WHO IS HE THERE FOR?"
YOU DO HAVE A PLAN, RIGHT?
I'M WORKIN' ON IT.
DAMPERS ARE MAXED, RIGHT?
YES...
I AM UNABLE TO TELEPORT... EVEN A FEW FEET.
THEN LET'S BLOW THE DAMPERS!
AN' LET EVERYBODY OUT TO PLAY? NO DICE, HONEY.
I CAME HERE FOR YOU AN' YOU, ALONE.
OH, HOW SWEET...
ODDS ARE, WHAT THEY'LL DO IS TRY TO CONTAIN US, KEEP US BOTTLED UP UNTIL THEY CAN GET SOMEBODY ELSE ON-SITE. SOMEBODY BIGGER.
SOMEBODY SUPER-POWERED.
AND WHEN THAT SOMEBODY SHOWS UP...
THEY'LL LOCK DOWN THE CELLS, THEN DIAL THE DAMPERS DOWN SO THEIR HEAVY-HITTER CAN OPERATE FREELY. I GET IT!
SO, WE WAIT?
FOR WHAT, TO GET OUR ASSES KICKED? HELL, NO.

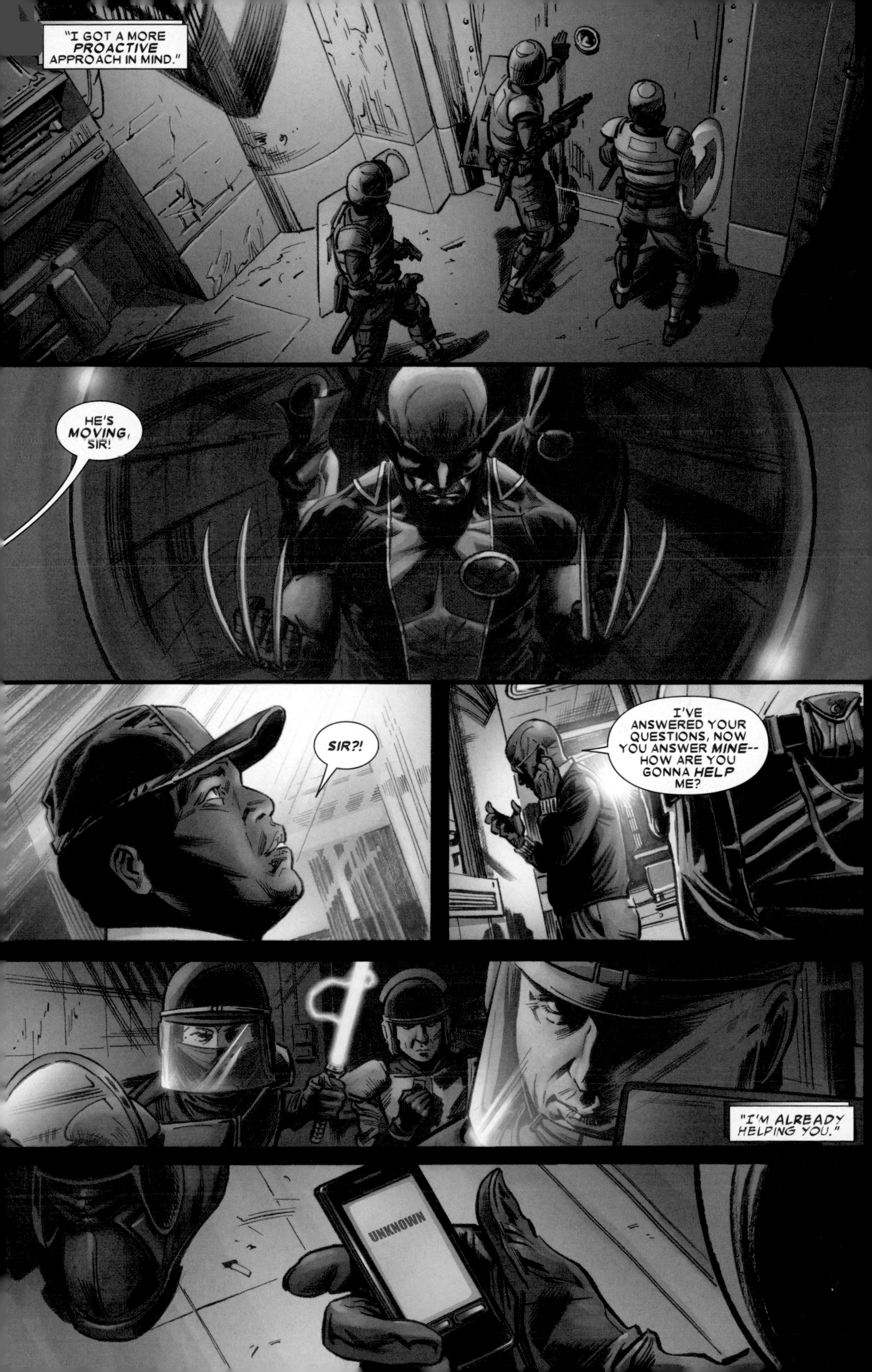
"I GOT A MORE PROACTIVE APPROACH IN MIND."
HE'S MOVING, SIR!
SIR?!
I'VE ANSWERED YOUR QUESTIONS, NOW YOU ANSWER MINE-- HOW ARE YOU GONNA HELP ME?
"I'M ALREADY HELPING YOU."
UNKNOWN

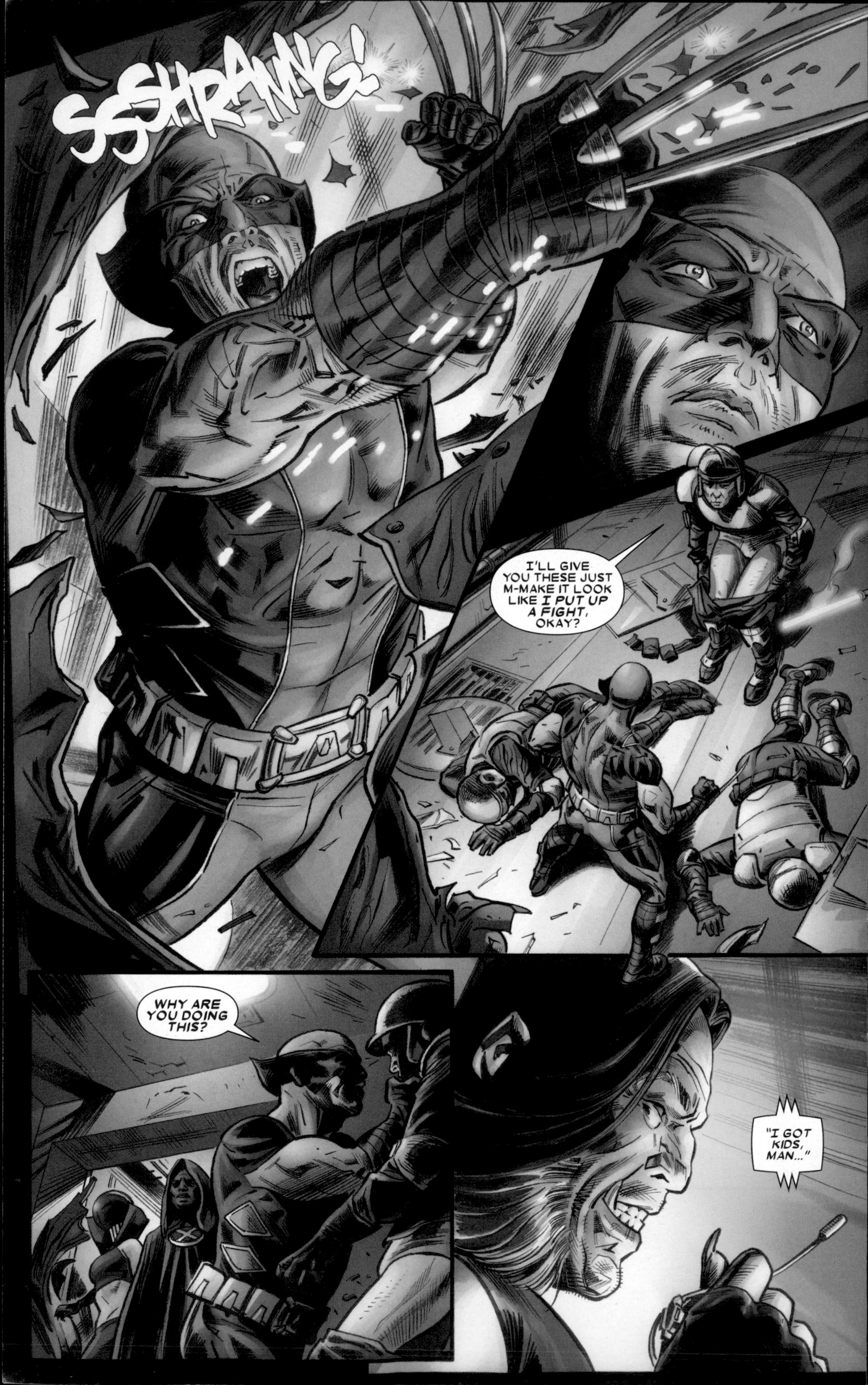
SSHRANNG!
I'LL GIVE YOU THESE JUST M-MAKE IT LOOK LIKE *I PUT UP A FIGHT,* OKAY?
WHY ARE YOU DOING THIS?
"I GOT KIDS, MAN..."

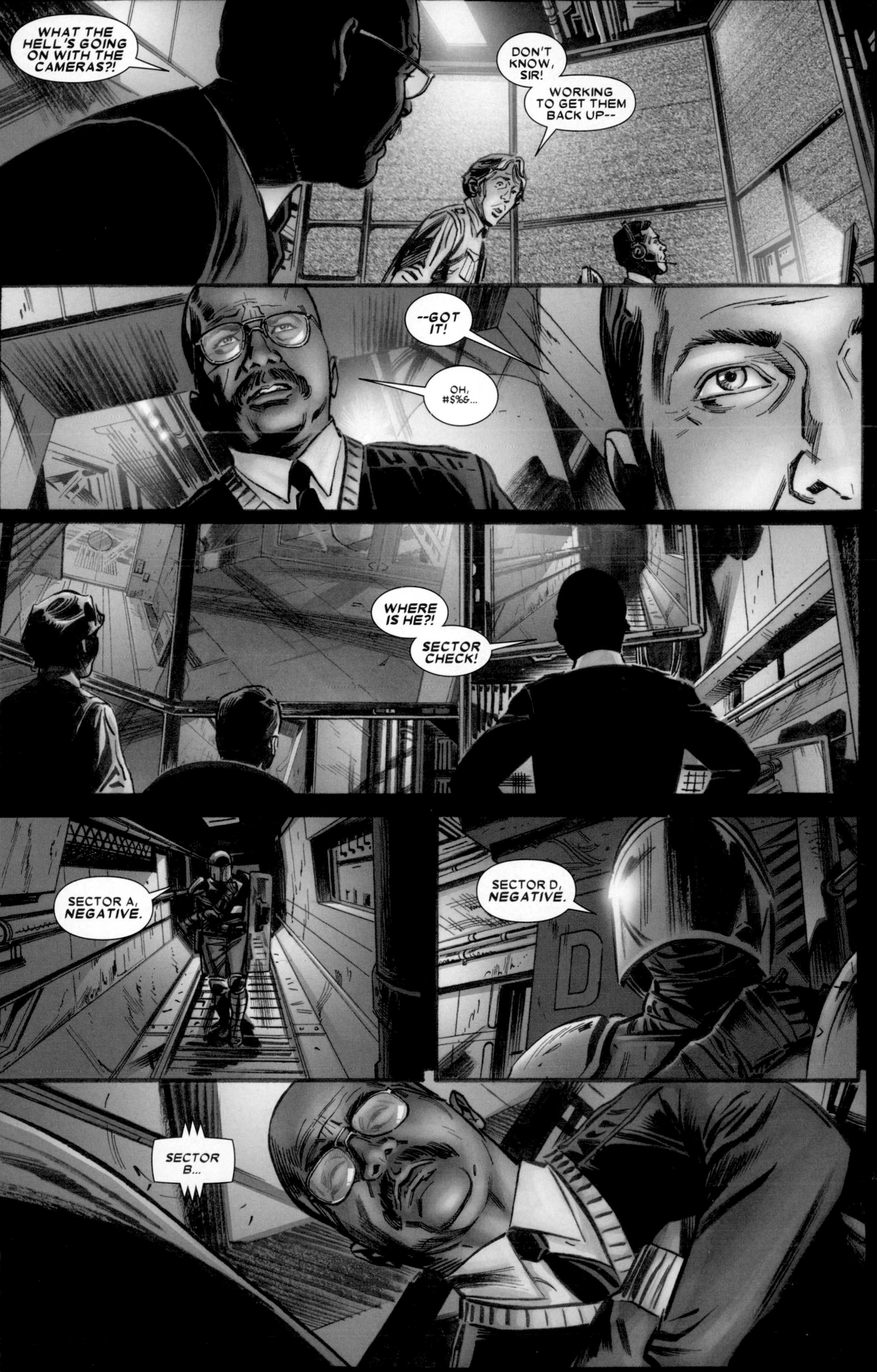
WHAT THE HELL'S GOING ON WITH THE CAMERAS?!
DON'T KNOW, SIR!
WORKING TO GET THEM BACK UP--
--GOT IT!
OH, #$%&...
WHERE IS HE?!
SECTOR CHECK!
SECTOR A, NEGATIVE.
SECTOR D, NEGATIVE.
D
SECTOR B...

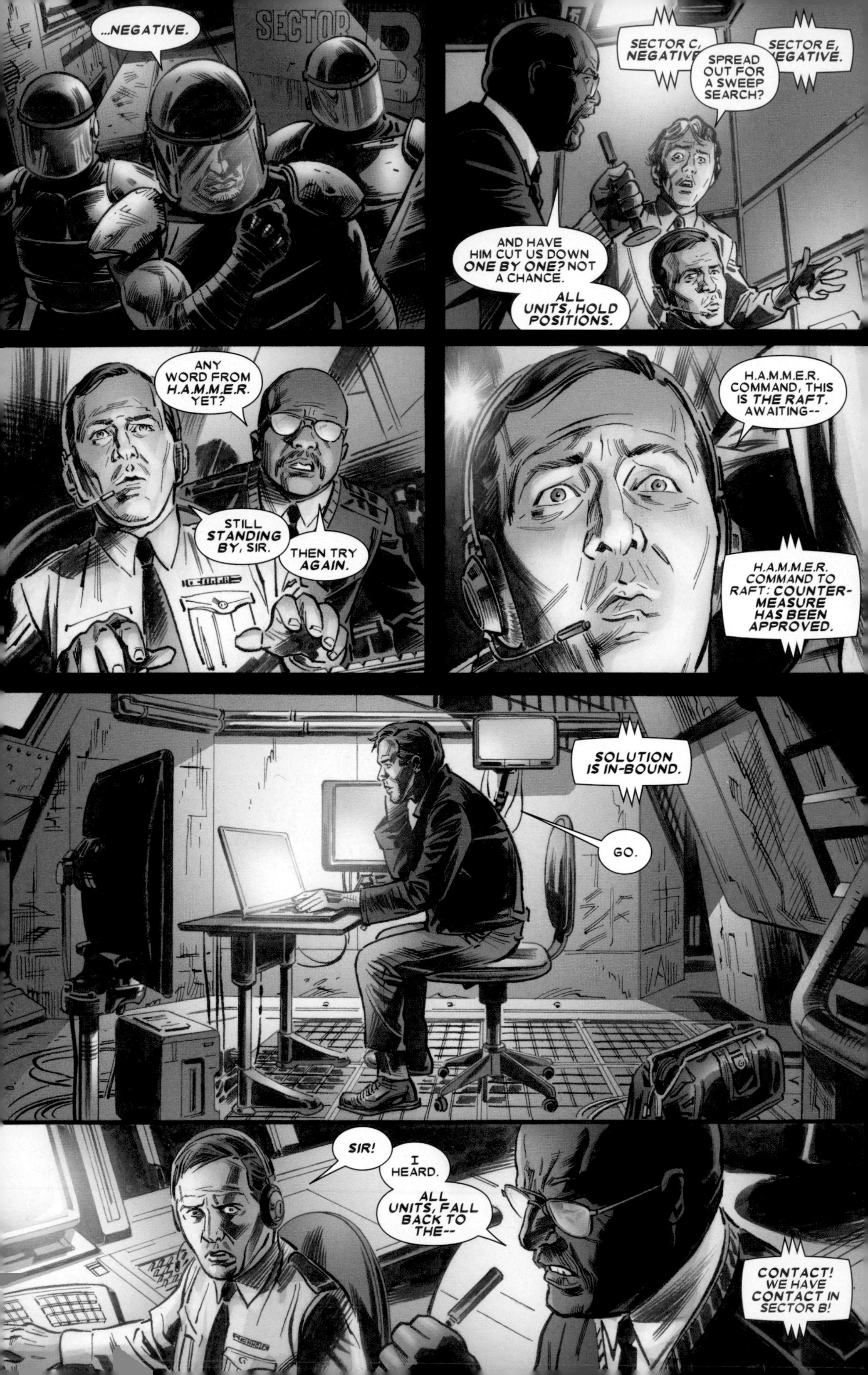
...NEGATIVE.
SECTOR B
SECTOR C, NEGATIVE.
SECTOR E, NEGATIVE.
SPREAD OUT FOR A SWEEP SEARCH?
AND HAVE HIM CUT US DOWN ONE BY ONE? NOT A CHANCE.
ALL UNITS, HOLD POSITIONS.
ANY WORD FROM H.A.M.M.E.R. YET?
STILL STANDING BY, SIR.
THEN TRY AGAIN.
H.A.M.M.E.R. COMMAND, THIS IS THE RAFT. AWAITING--
H.A.M.M.E.R. COMMAND TO RAFT: COUNTER-MEASURE HAS BEEN APPROVED.
SOLUTION IS IN-BOUND.
GO.
SIR!
I HEARD.
ALL UNITS, FALL BACK TO THE--
CONTACT! WE HAVE CONTACT IN SECTOR B!

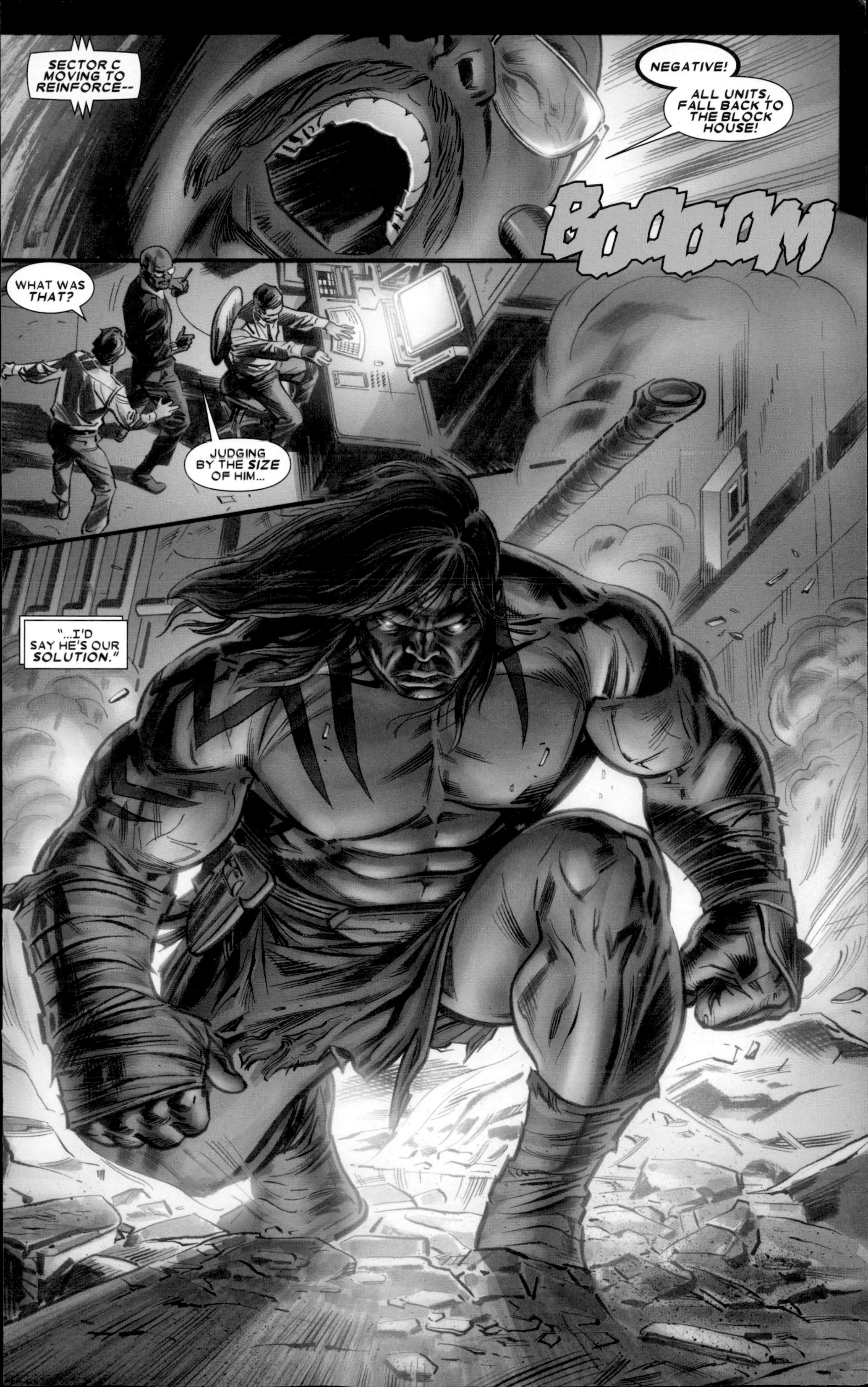
SECTOR C MOVING TO REINFORCE--
NEGATIVE!
ALL UNITS, FALL BACK TO THE BLOCK HOUSE!
BOOOOOM
WHAT WAS THAT?
JUDGING BY THE SIZE OF HIM...
"...I'D SAY HE'S OUR SOLUTION."

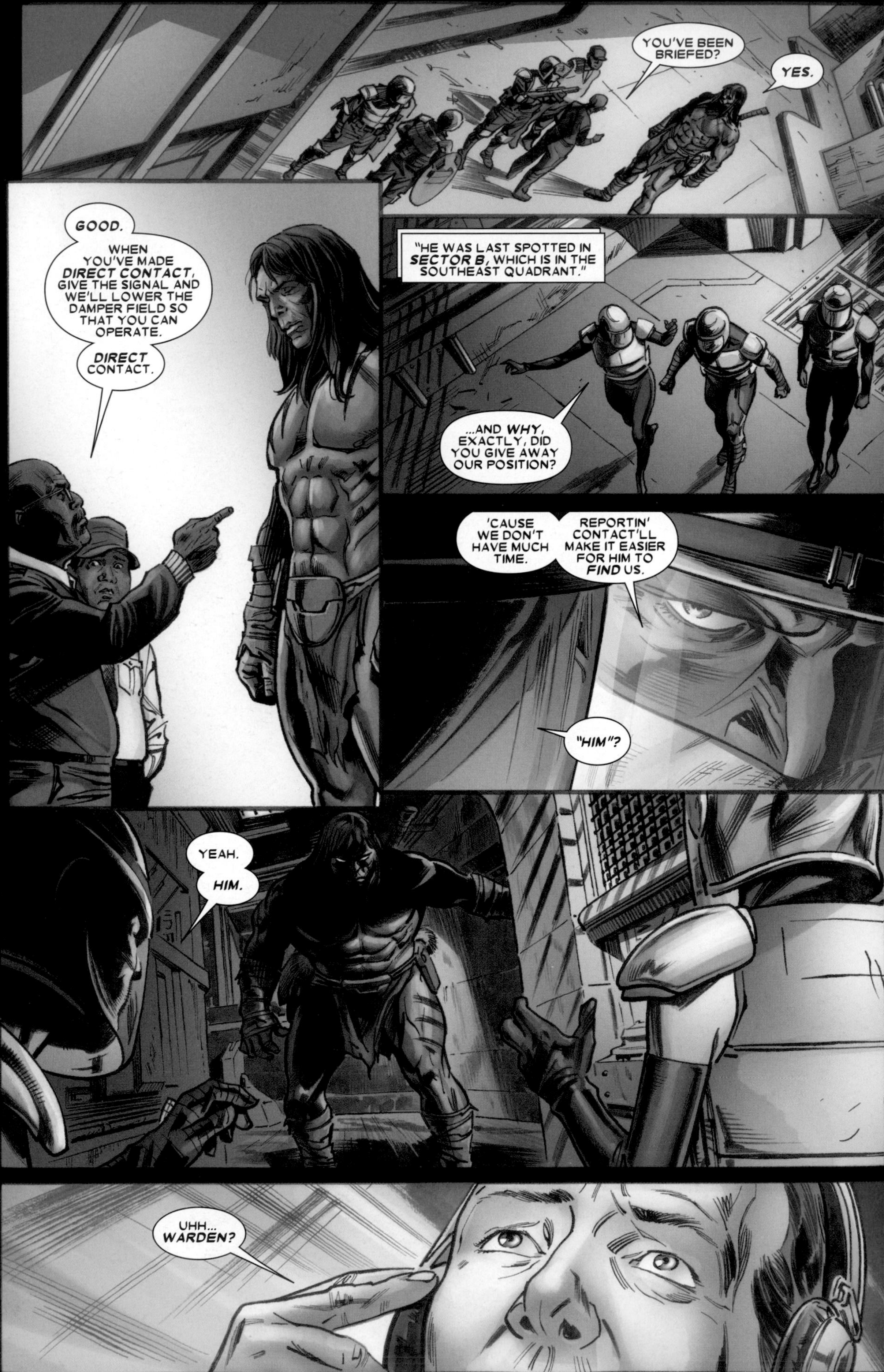
YOU'VE BEEN BRIEFED?
YES.
GOOD.
WHEN YOU'VE MADE DIRECT CONTACT, GIVE THE SIGNAL AND WE'LL LOWER THE DAMPER FIELD SO THAT YOU CAN OPERATE.
DIRECT CONTACT.
"HE WAS LAST SPOTTED IN SECTOR B, WHICH IS IN THE SOUTHEAST QUADRANT."
...AND WHY, EXACTLY, DID YOU GIVE AWAY OUR POSITION?
'CAUSE WE DON'T HAVE MUCH TIME.
REPORTIN' CONTACT'LL MAKE IT EASIER FOR HIM TO FIND US.
"HIM"?
YEAH.
HIM.
UHH... WARDEN?

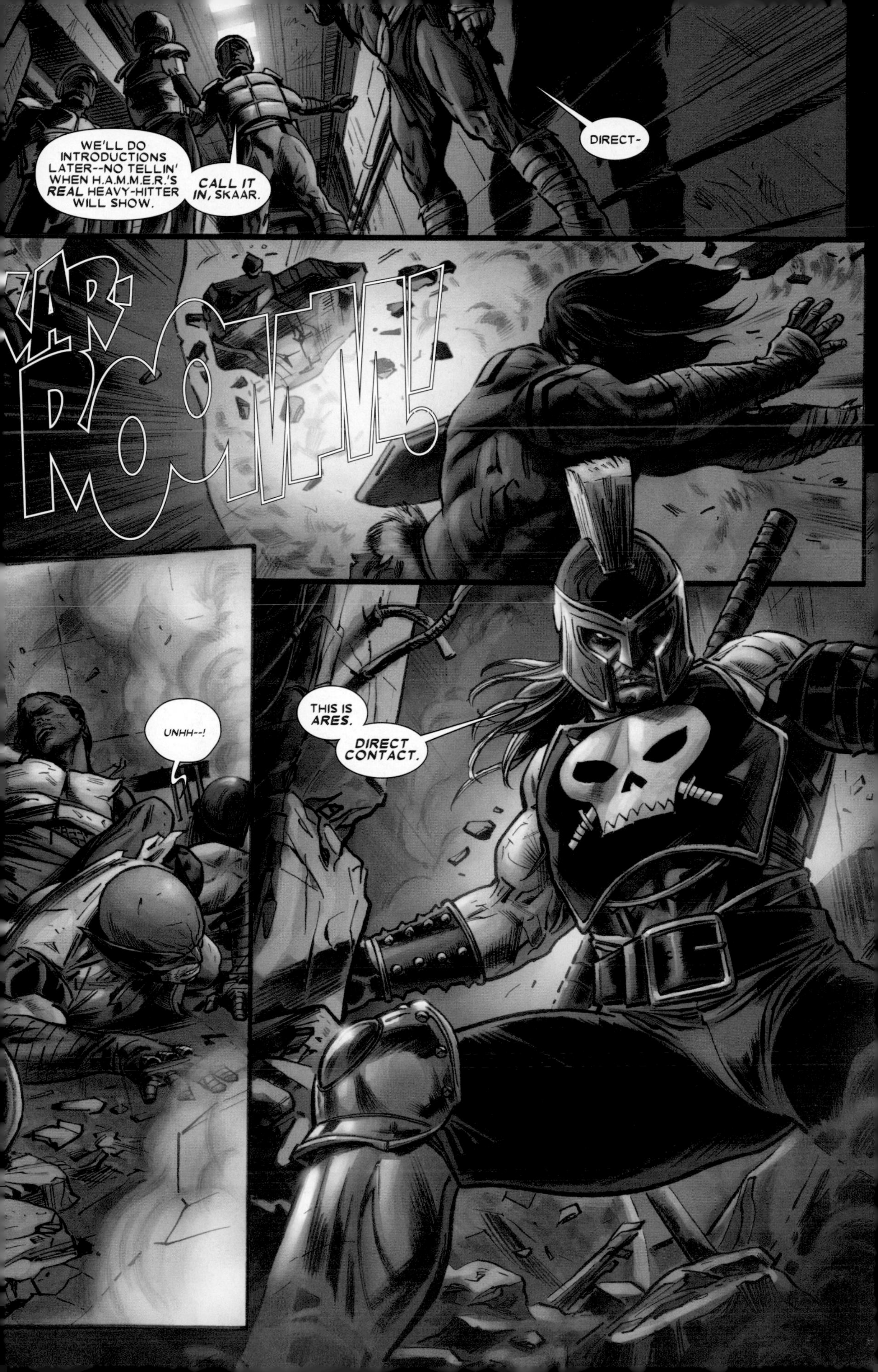
WE'LL DO INTRODUCTIONS LATER--NO TELLIN' WHEN H.A.M.M.E.R.'S *REAL* HEAVY-HITTER WILL SHOW.
CALL IT IN, SKAAR.
DIRECT-
KAR-ROOOM!
UNHH--!
THIS IS *ARES*.
DIRECT CONTACT.

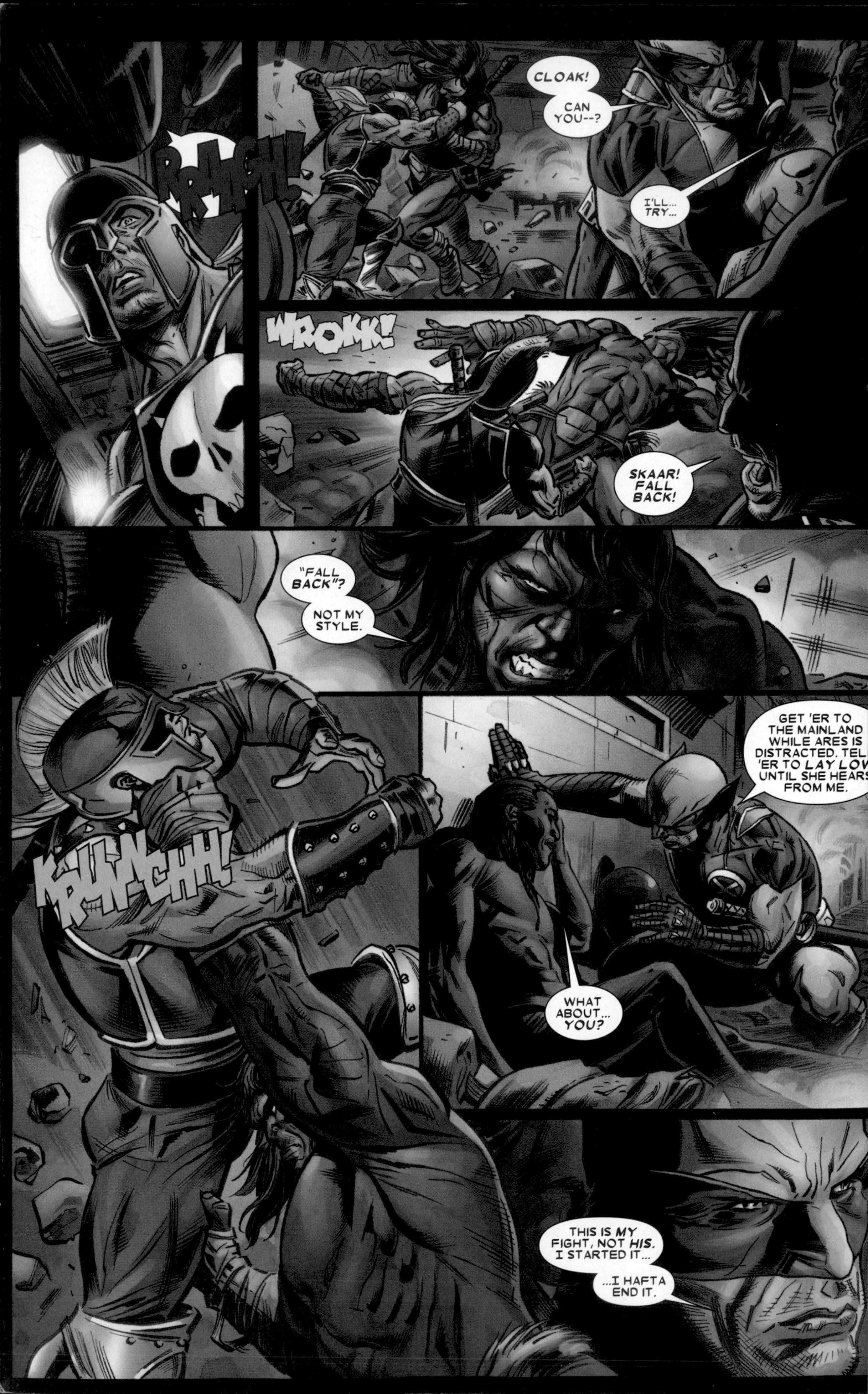

RRAAGH!
CLOAK!
CAN YOU--?
I'LL... TRY...
WROKK!
SKAAR! FALL BACK!
"FALL BACK"?
NOT MY STYLE.
KRUNCHH!
GET 'ER TO THE MAINLAND WHILE ARES IS DISTRACTED. TELL 'ER TO LAY LOW UNTIL SHE HEARS FROM ME.
WHAT ABOUT... YOU?
THIS IS MY FIGHT, NOT HIS. I STARTED IT...
...I HAFTA END IT.

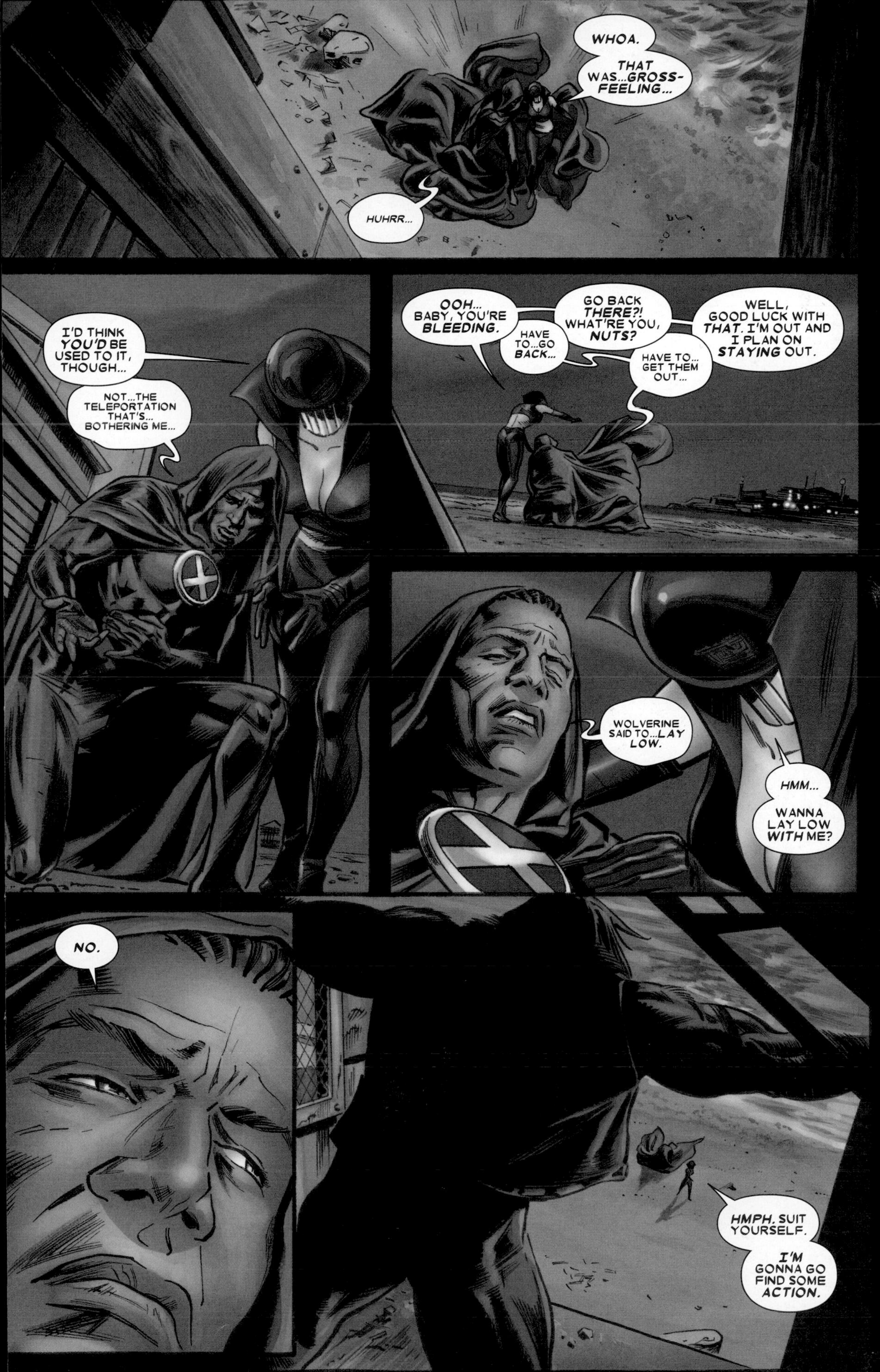
WHOA.
THAT WAS...GROSS-FEELING...
HUHRR...
I'D THINK YOU'D BE USED TO IT, THOUGH...
NOT...THE TELEPORTATION THAT'S... BOTHERING ME...
OOH... BABY, YOU'RE BLEEDING.
HAVE TO...GO BACK...
GO BACK THERE?! WHAT'RE YOU, NUTS?
HAVE TO... GET THEM OUT...
WELL, GOOD LUCK WITH THAT. I'M OUT AND I PLAN ON STAYING OUT.
WOLVERINE SAID TO...LAY LOW.
HMM...
WANNA LAY LOW WITH ME?
NO.
HMPH. SUIT YOURSELF.
I'M GONNA GO FIND SOME ACTION.

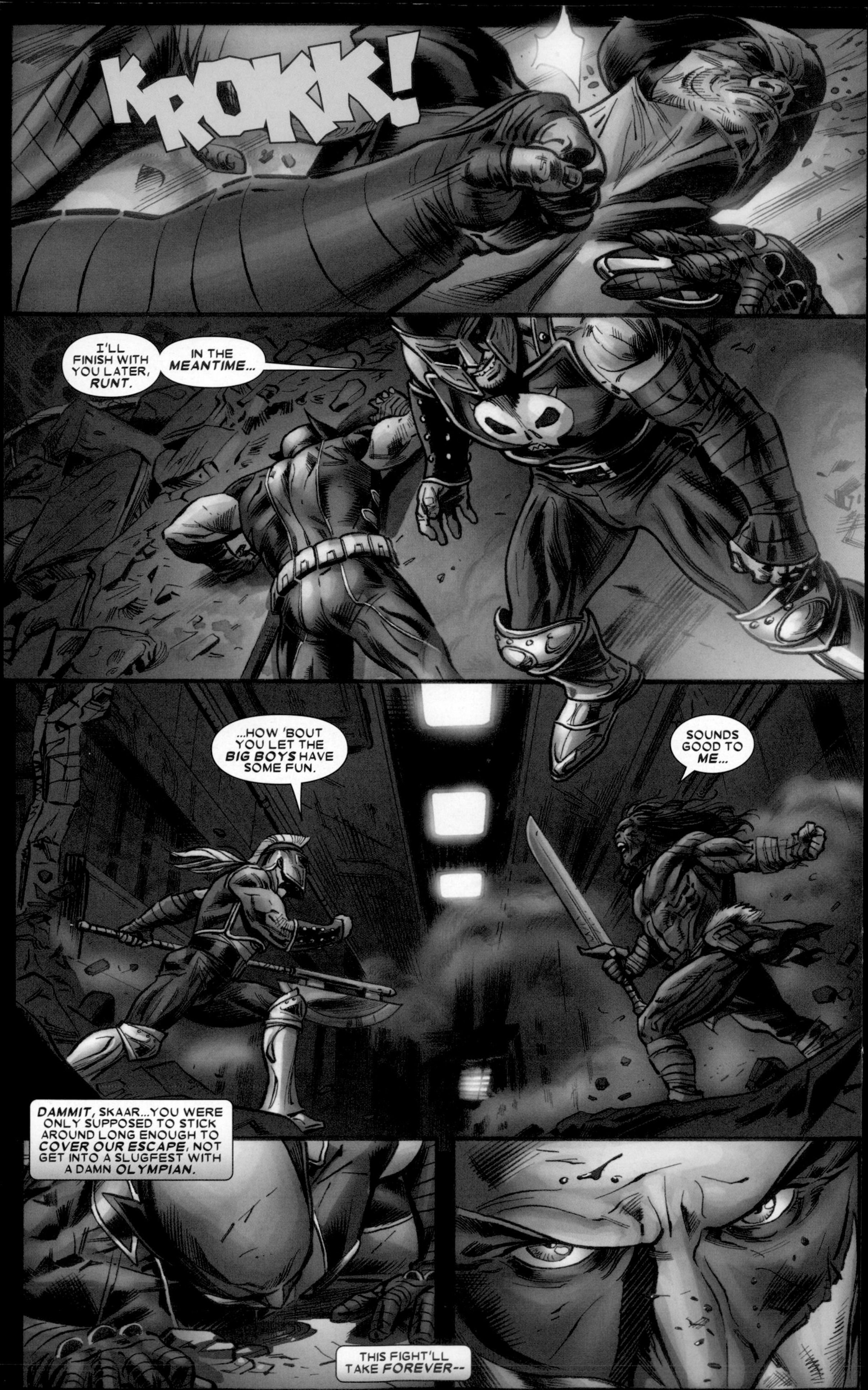
KROKK!
I'LL FINISH WITH YOU LATER, RUNT.
IN THE MEANTIME...
...HOW 'BOUT YOU LET THE BIG BOYS HAVE SOME FUN.
SOUNDS GOOD TO ME...
DAMMIT, SKAAR...YOU WERE ONLY SUPPOSED TO STICK AROUND LONG ENOUGH TO COVER OUR ESCAPE, NOT GET INTO A SLUGFEST WITH A DAMN OLYMPIAN.
THIS FIGHT'LL TAKE FOREVER--

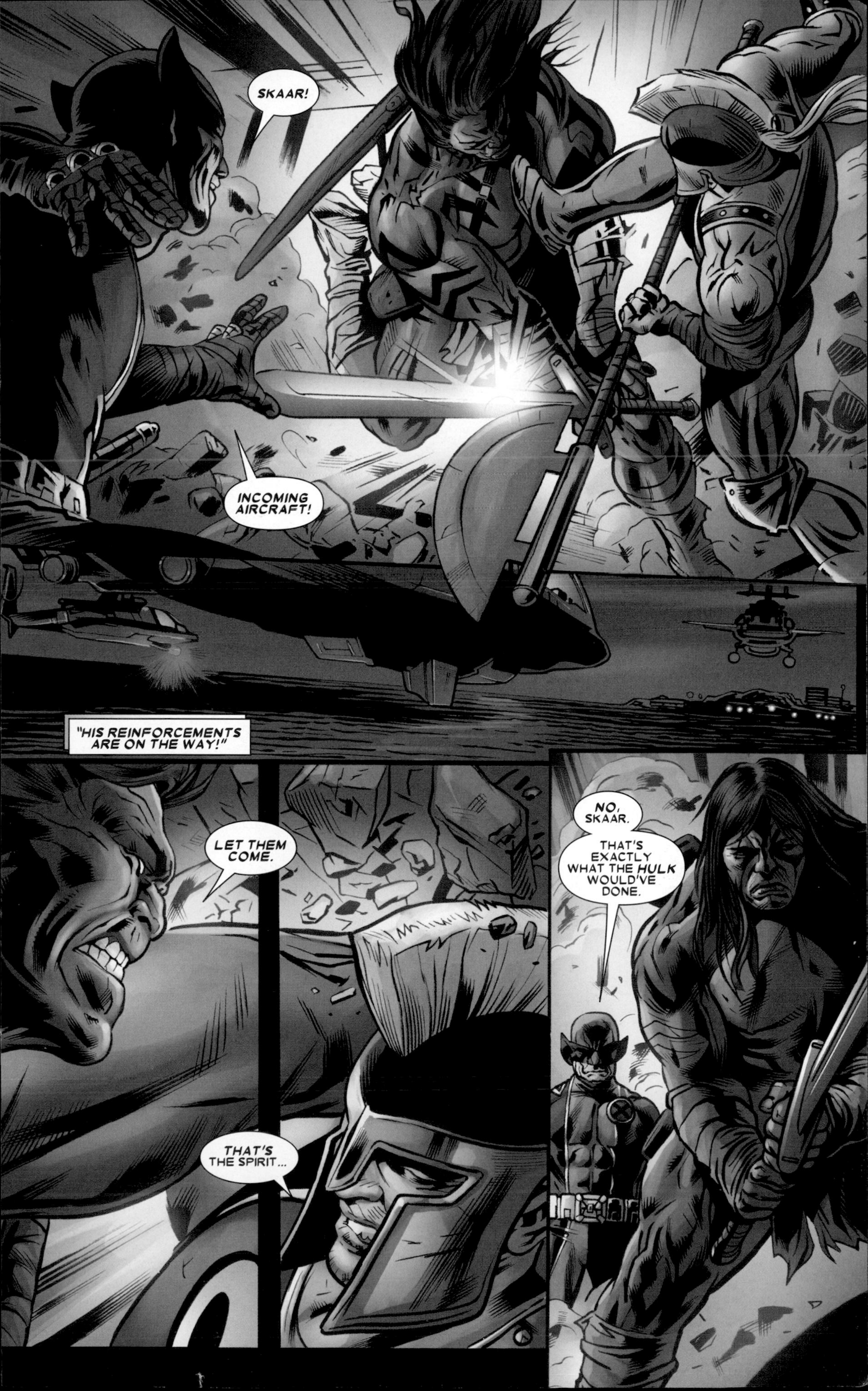
SKAAR!
INCOMING AIRCRAFT!
"HIS REINFORCEMENTS ARE ON THE WAY!"
LET THEM COME.
THAT'S THE SPIRIT...
NO, SKAAR.
THAT'S EXACTLY WHAT THE HULK WOULD'VE DONE.

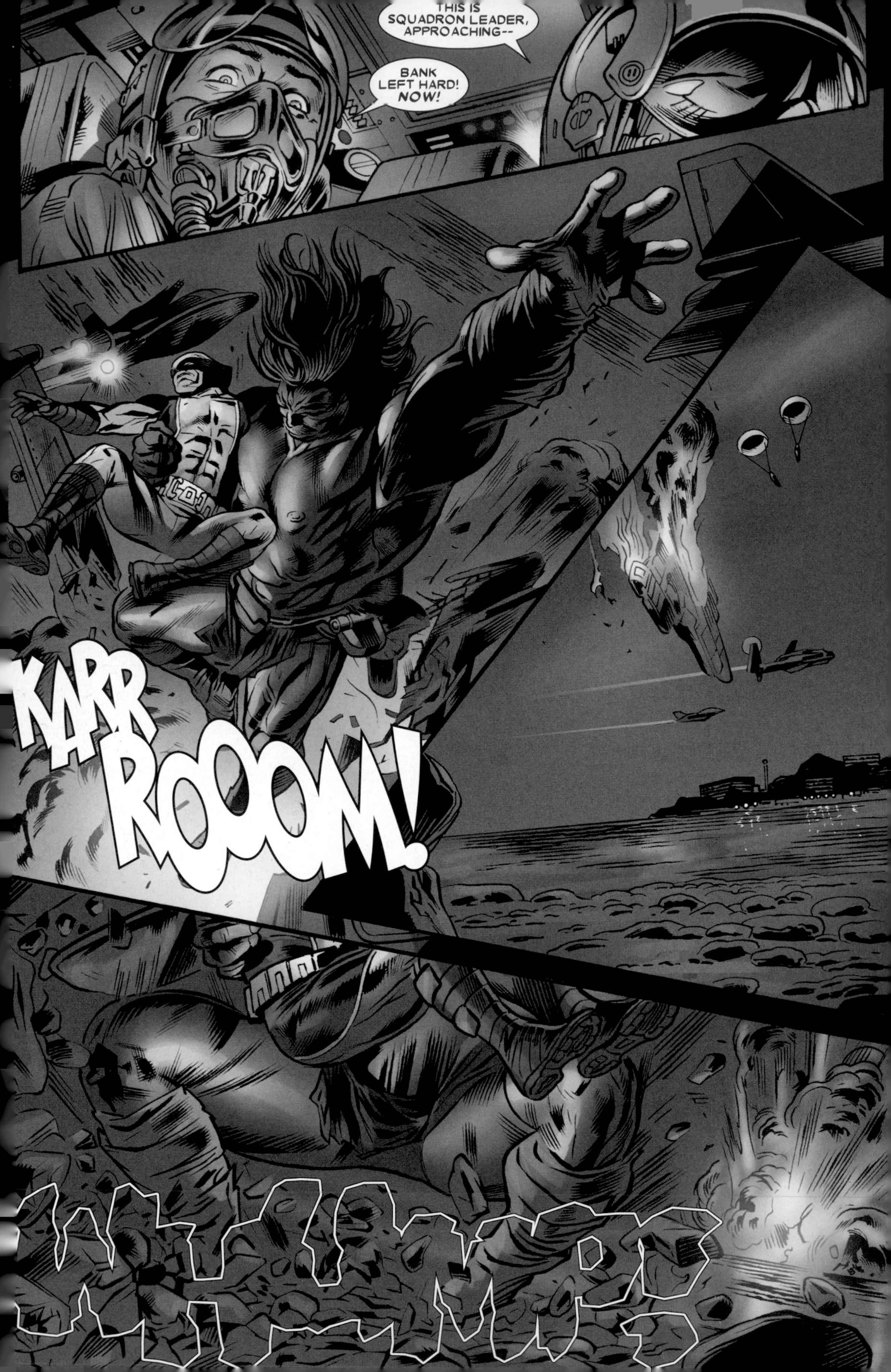
THIS IS SQUADRON LEADER, APPROACHING--
BANK LEFT HARD! NOW!
KARR ROOOM!

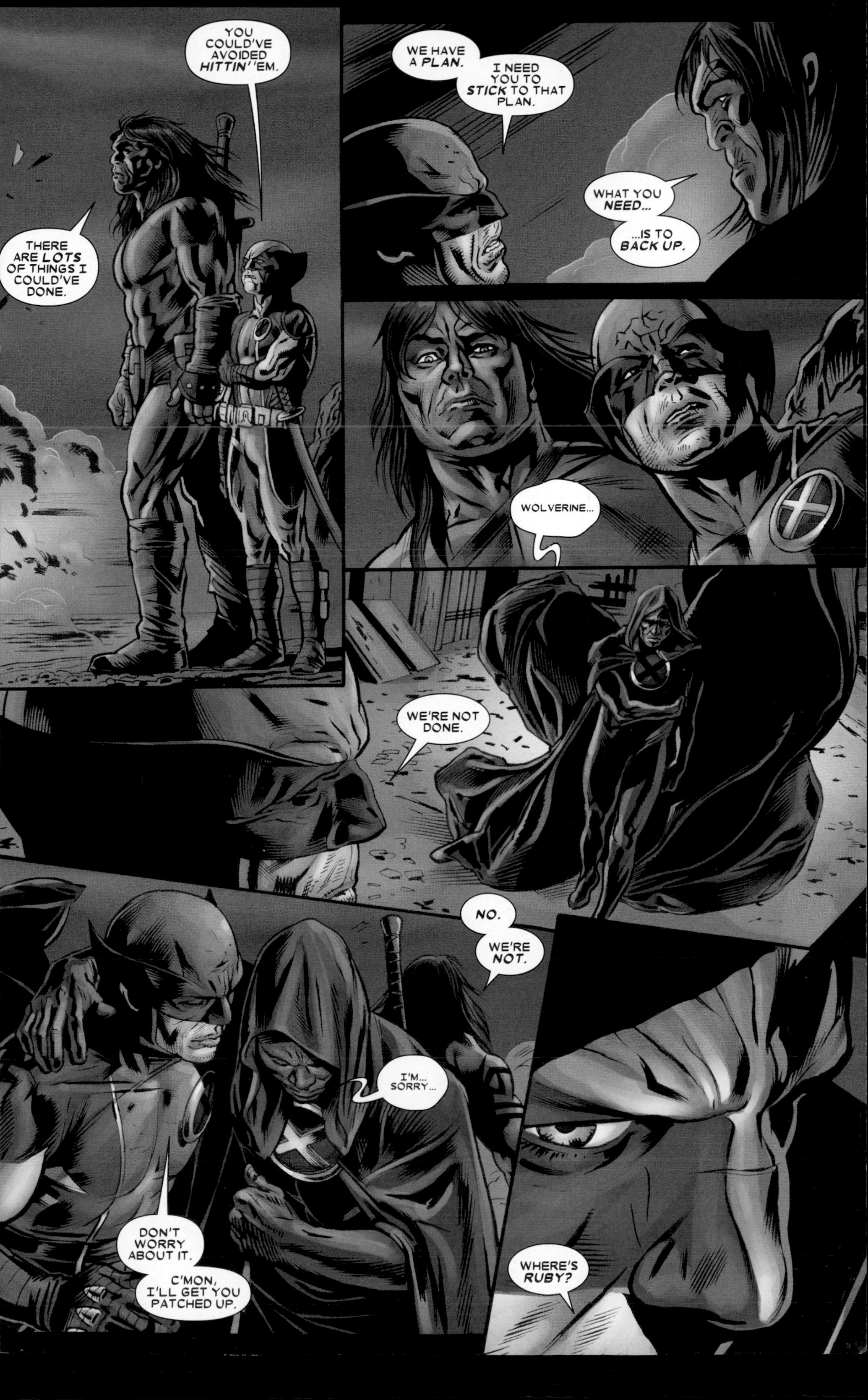
YOU COULD'VE AVOIDED HITTIN' 'EM.
THERE ARE LOTS OF THINGS I COULD'VE DONE.
WE HAVE A PLAN.
I NEED YOU TO STICK TO THAT PLAN.
WHAT YOU NEED...
...IS TO BACK UP.
WOLVERINE...
WE'RE NOT DONE.
NO.
WE'RE NOT.
I'M... SORRY...
DON'T WORRY ABOUT IT.
C'MON, I'LL GET YOU PATCHED UP.
WHERE'S RUBY?

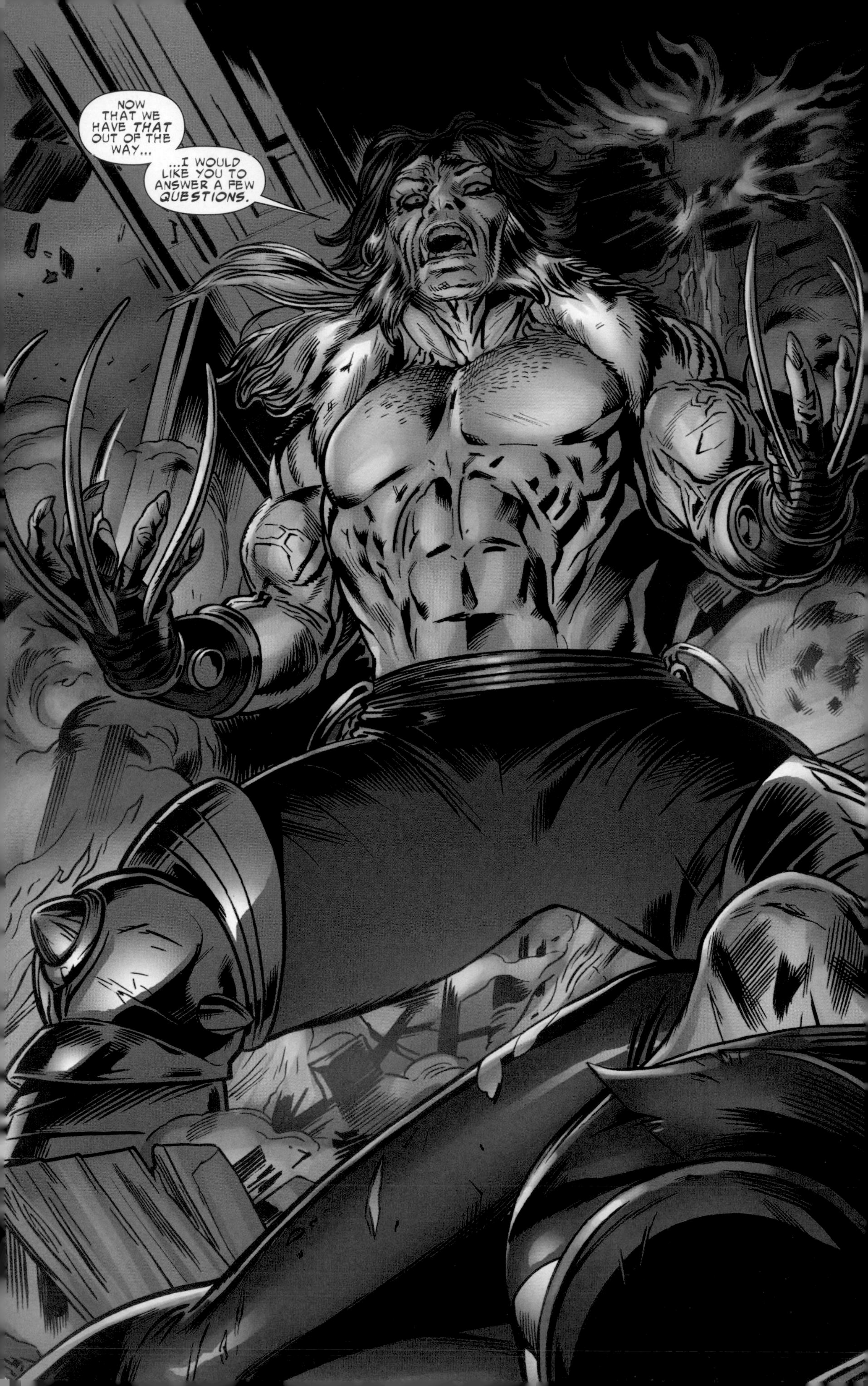
NOW THAT WE HAVE THAT OUT OF THE WAY...
...I WOULD LIKE YOU TO ANSWER A FEW QUESTIONS.

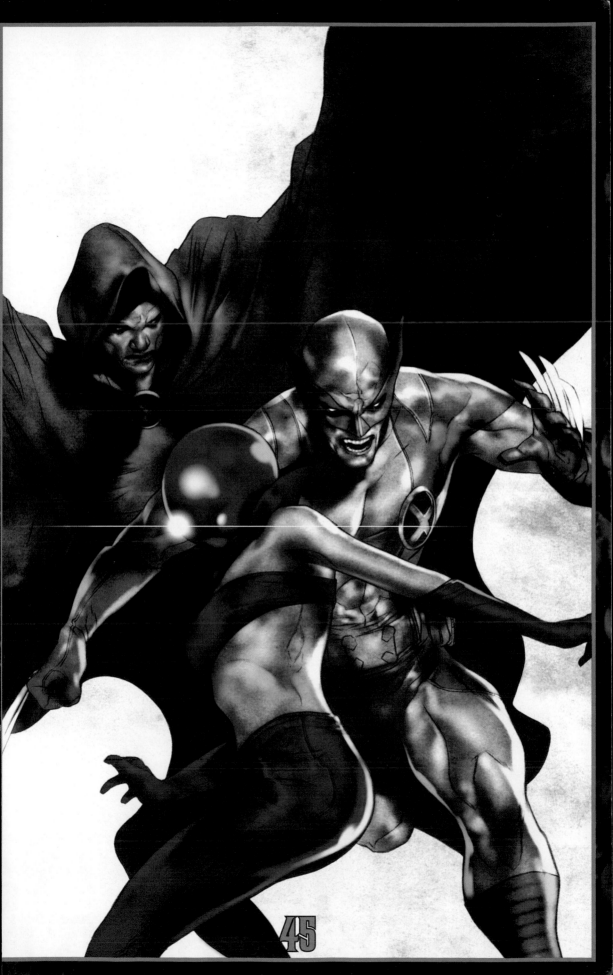

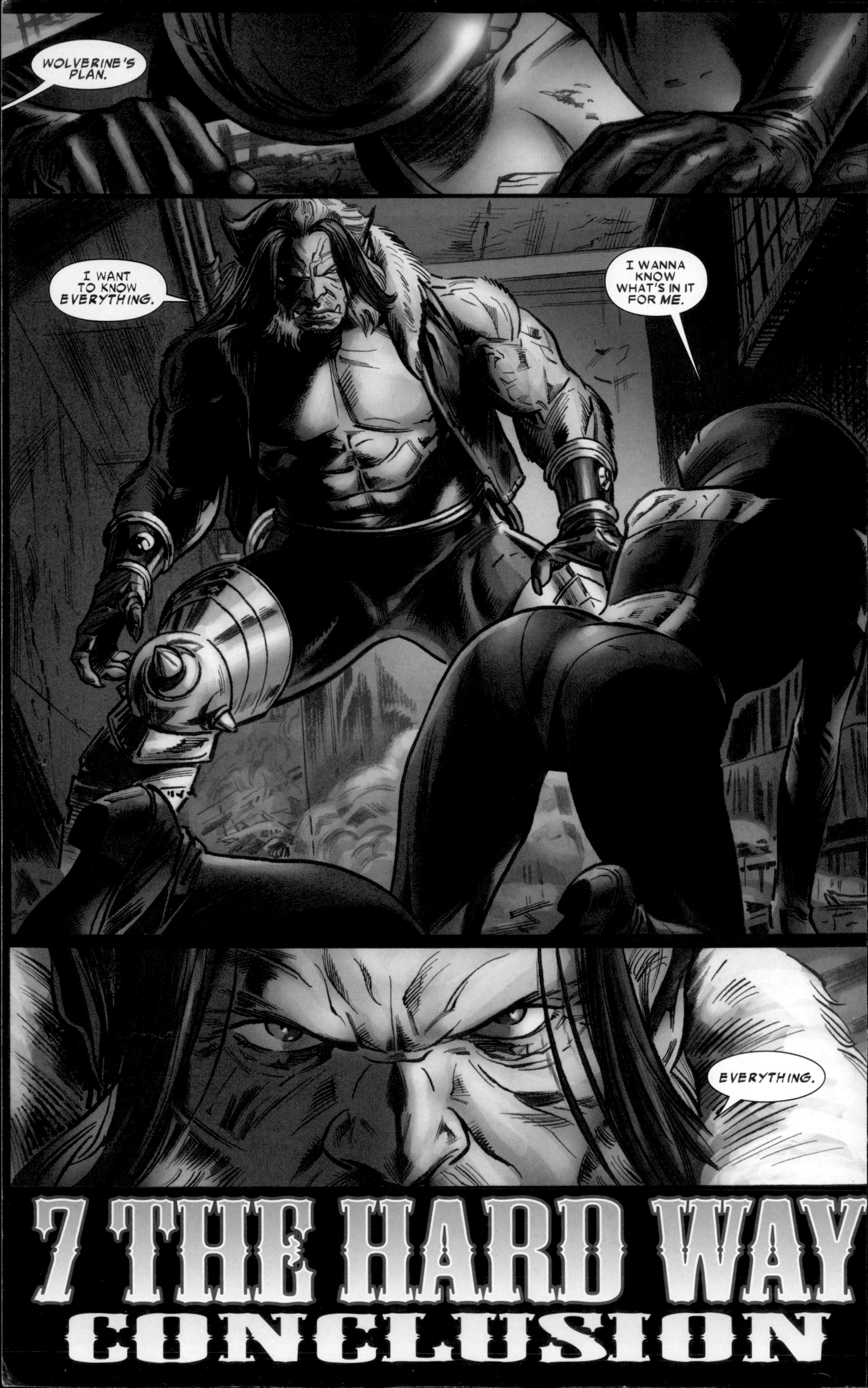
WOLVERINE'S PLAN.
I WANT TO KNOW EVERYTHING.
I WANNA KNOW WHAT'S IN IT FOR ME.
EVERYTHING.
7 THE HARD WAY
CONCLUSION

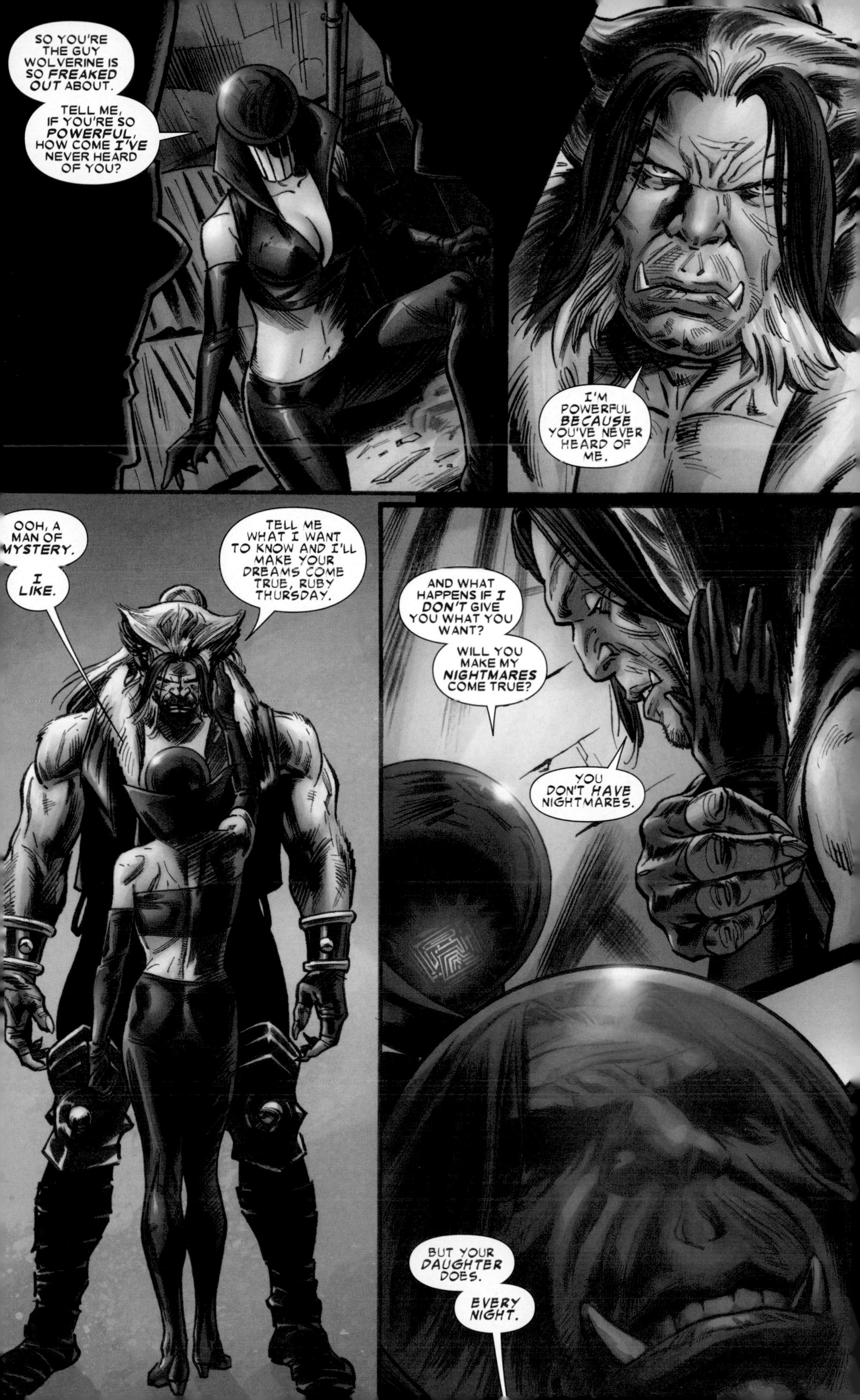
SO YOU'RE THE GUY WOLVERINE IS SO FREAKED OUT ABOUT.
TELL ME, IF YOU'RE SO POWERFUL, HOW COME I'VE NEVER HEARD OF YOU?
I'M POWERFUL BECAUSE YOU'VE NEVER HEARD OF ME.
OOH, A MAN OF MYSTERY.
I LIKE.
TELL ME WHAT I WANT TO KNOW AND I'LL MAKE YOUR DREAMS COME TRUE, RUBY THURSDAY.
AND WHAT HAPPENS IF I DON'T GIVE YOU WHAT YOU WANT?
WILL YOU MAKE MY NIGHTMARES COME TRUE?
YOU DON'T HAVE NIGHTMARES.
BUT YOUR DAUGHTER DOES.
EVERY NIGHT.

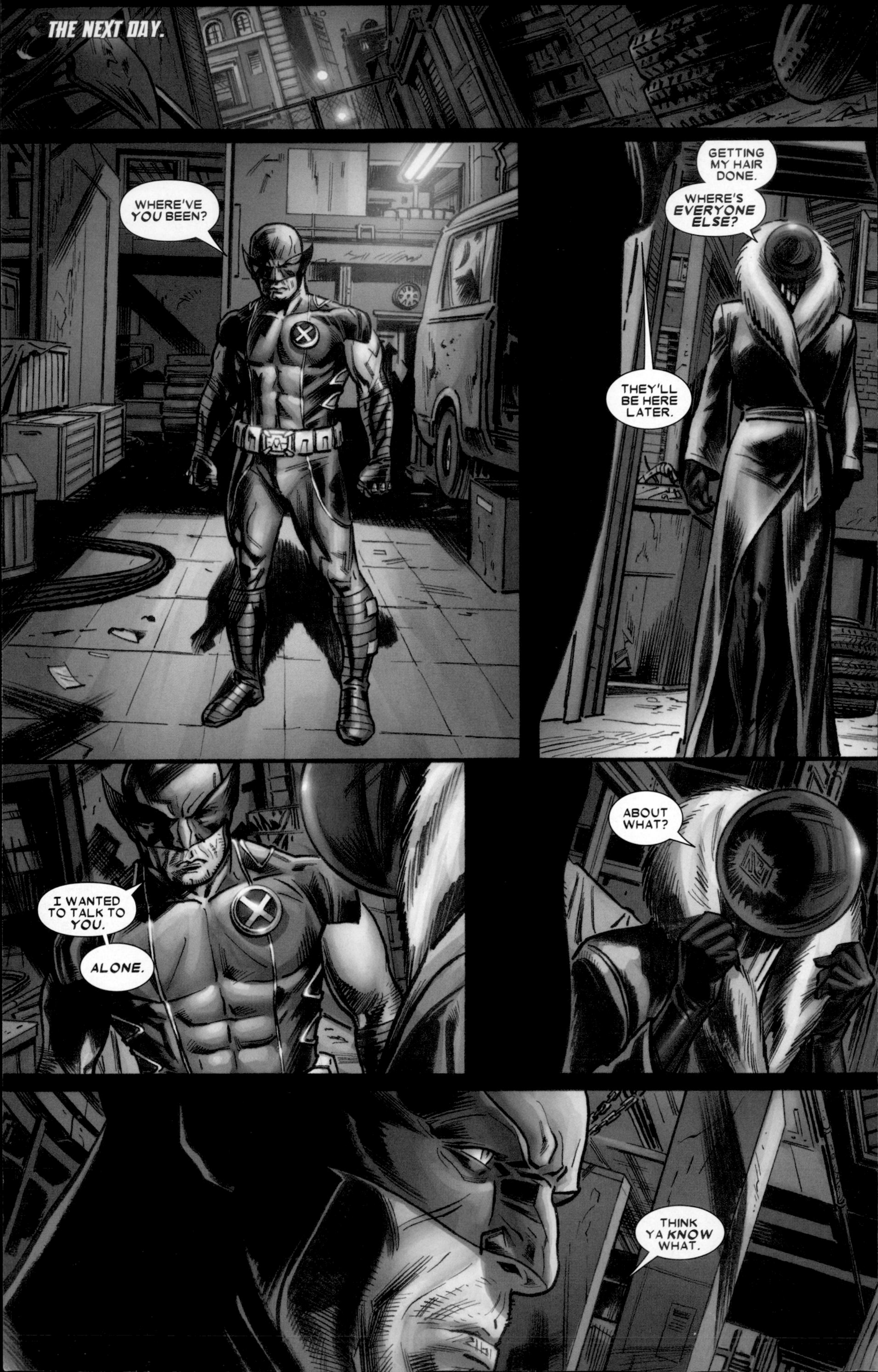
THE NEXT DAY.
WHERE'VE YOU BEEN?
GETTING MY HAIR DONE.
WHERE'S EVERYONE ELSE?
THEY'LL BE HERE LATER.
I WANTED TO TALK TO YOU.
ALONE.
ABOUT WHAT?
THINK YA KNOW WHAT.

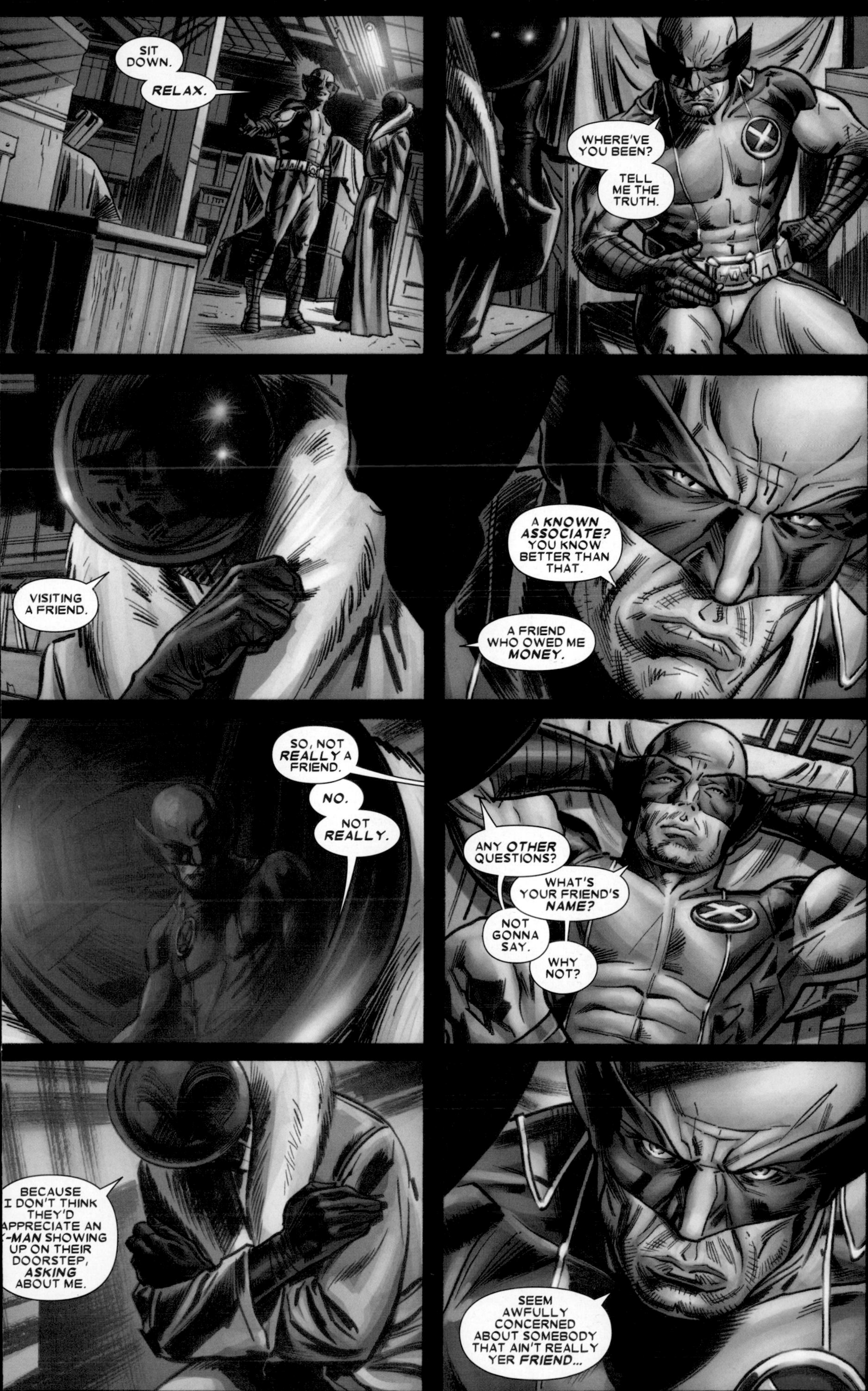
SIT DOWN.
RELAX.
WHERE'VE YOU BEEN?
TELL ME THE TRUTH.
VISITING A FRIEND.
A KNOWN ASSOCIATE? YOU KNOW BETTER THAN THAT.
A FRIEND WHO OWED ME MONEY.
SO, NOT REALLY A FRIEND.
NO.
NOT REALLY.
ANY OTHER QUESTIONS?
WHAT'S YOUR FRIEND'S NAME?
NOT GONNA SAY.
WHY NOT?
BECAUSE I DON'T THINK THEY'D APPRECIATE AN X-MAN SHOWING UP ON THEIR DOORSTEP, ASKING ABOUT ME.
SEEM AWFULLY CONCERNED ABOUT SOMEBODY THAT AIN'T REALLY YER FRIEND...

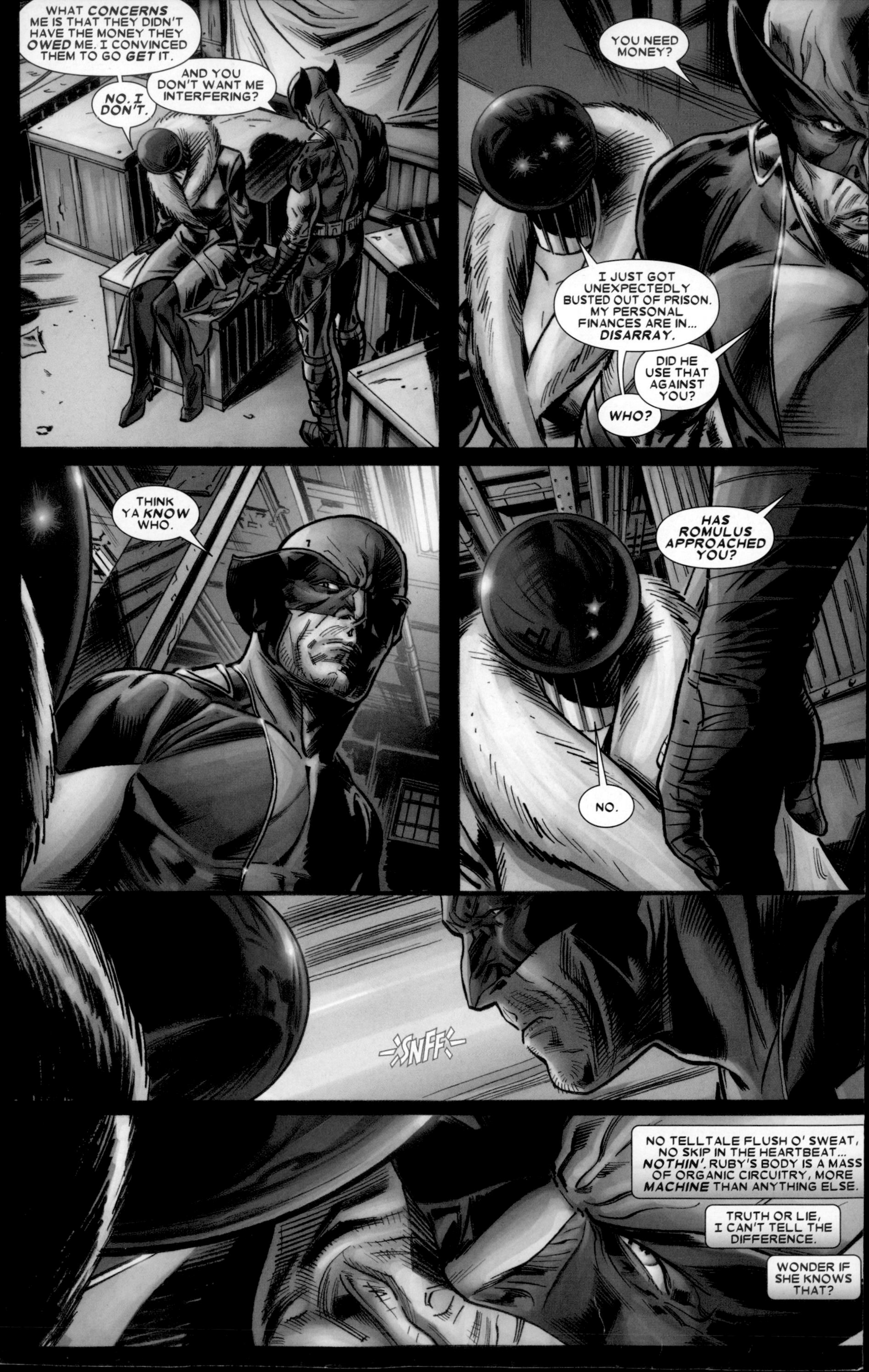

WHAT CONCERNS ME IS THAT THEY DIDN'T HAVE THE MONEY THEY OWED ME. I CONVINCED THEM TO GO GET IT.
AND YOU DON'T WANT ME INTERFERING?
NO. I DON'T.
YOU NEED MONEY?
I JUST GOT UNEXPECTEDLY BUSTED OUT OF PRISON. MY PERSONAL FINANCES ARE IN... DISARRAY.
DID HE USE THAT AGAINST YOU?
WHO?
THINK YA KNOW WHO.
HAS ROMULUS APPROACHED YOU?
NO.
SNFF
NO TELLTALE FLUSH O' SWEAT, NO SKIP IN THE HEARTBEAT... NOTHIN'. RUBY'S BODY IS A MASS OF ORGANIC CIRCUITRY, MORE MACHINE THAN ANYTHING ELSE.
TRUTH OR LIE, I CAN'T TELL THE DIFFERENCE.
WONDER IF SHE KNOWS THAT?

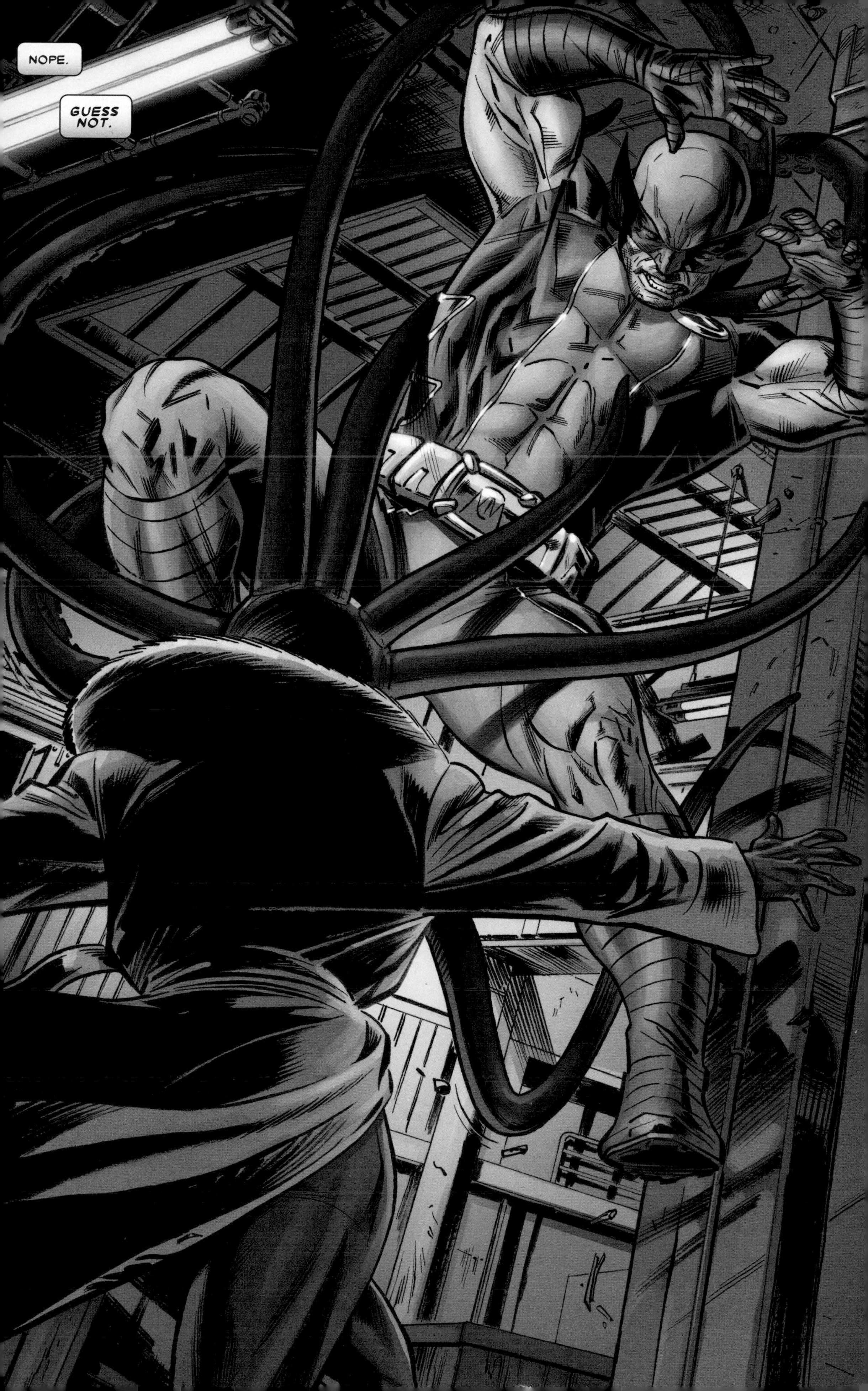
NOPE.
GUESS NOT.

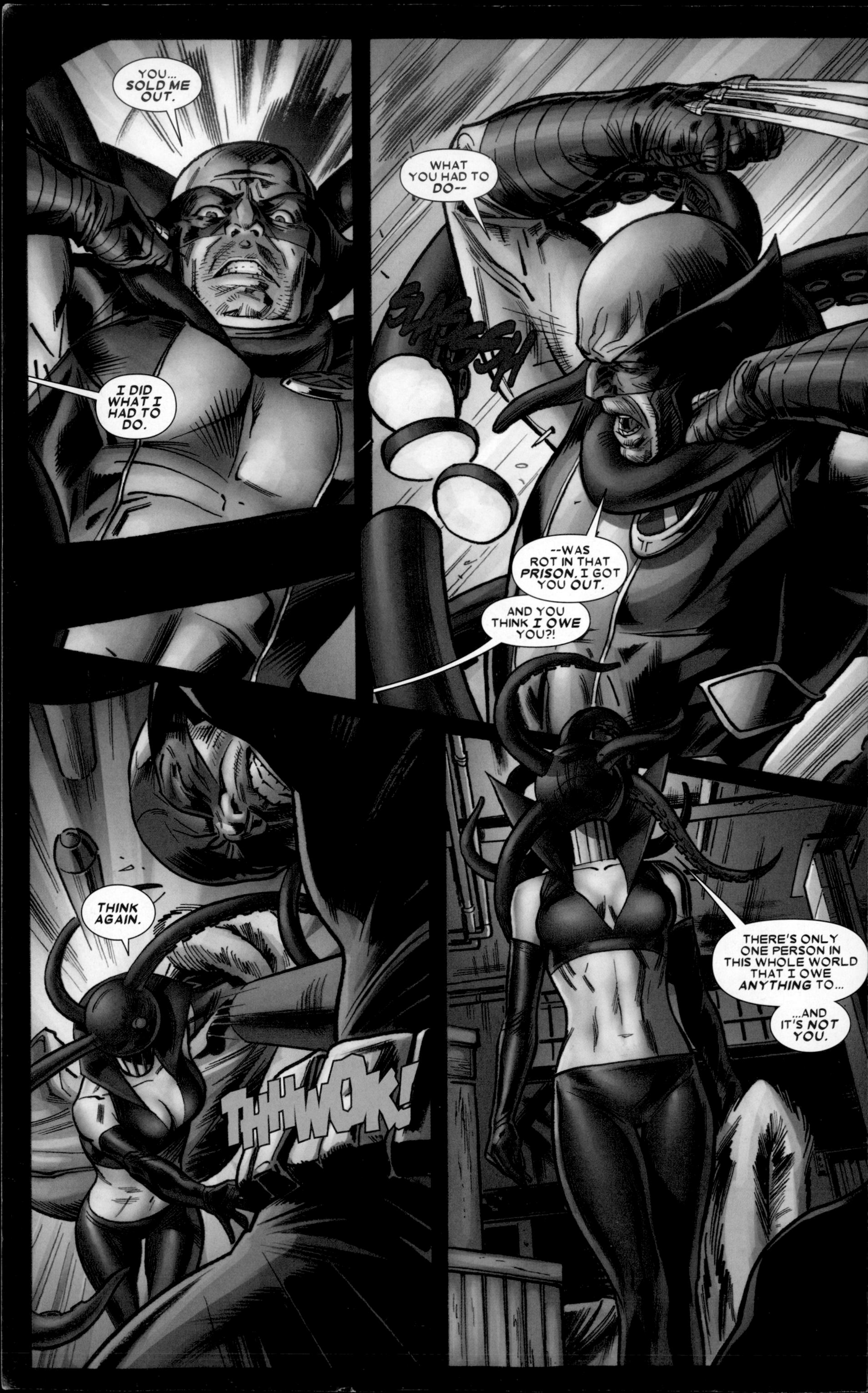
YOU... SOLD ME OUT.
I DID WHAT I HAD TO DO.
WHAT YOU HAD TO DO--
--WAS ROT IN THAT PRISON. I GOT YOU OUT.
AND YOU THINK I OWE YOU?!
THINK AGAIN.
THHWOK!
THERE'S ONLY ONE PERSON IN THIS WHOLE WORLD THAT I OWE ANYTHING TO...
...AND IT'S NOT YOU.

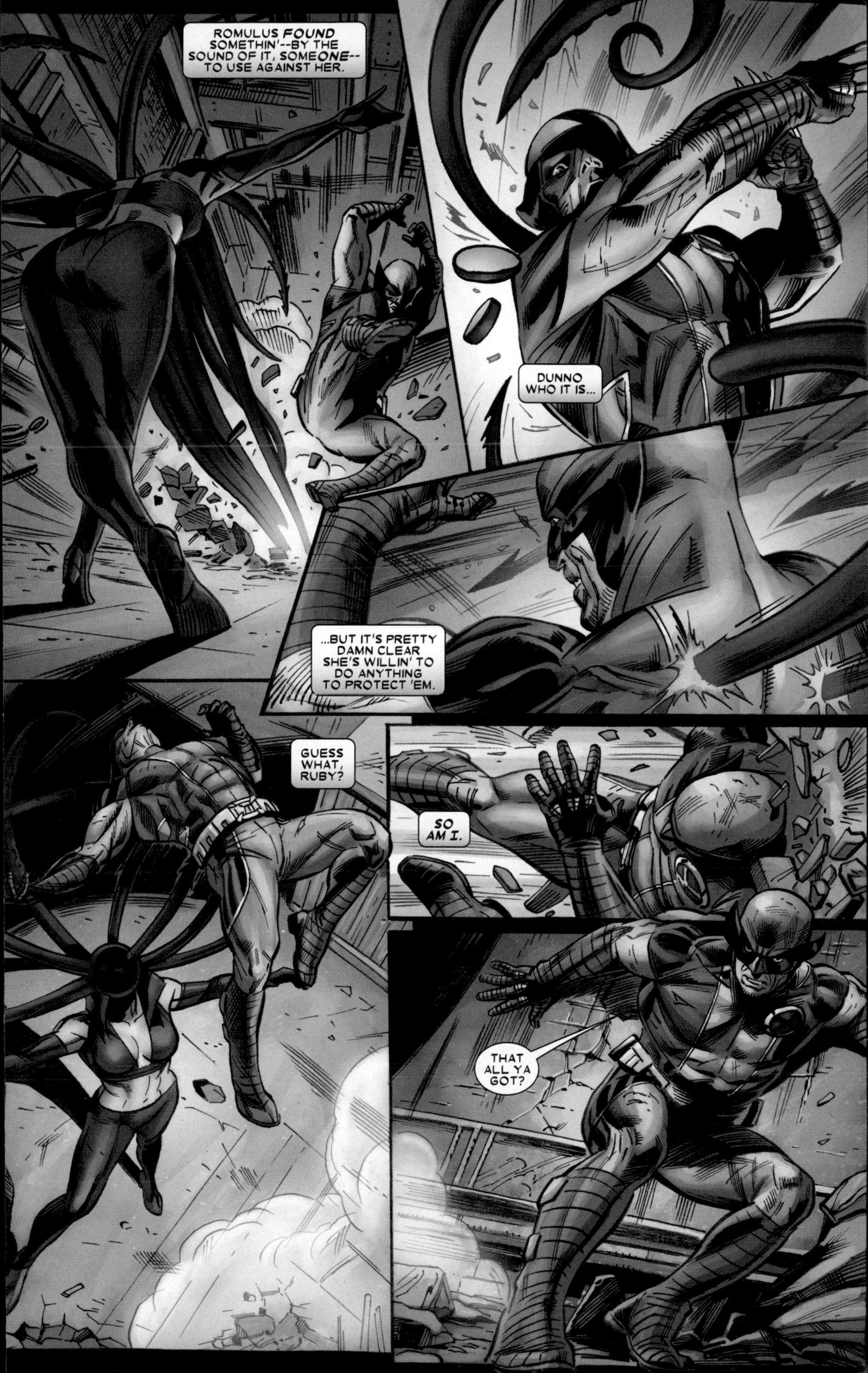
ROMULUS *FOUND* SOMETHIN'--BY THE SOUND OF IT, SOME*ONE*--TO USE AGAINST HER.
DUNNO WHO IT IS...
...BUT IT'S PRETTY DAMN CLEAR SHE'S WILLIN' TO DO ANYTHING TO PROTECT 'EM.
GUESS WHAT, RUBY?
SO AM I.
THAT ALL YA GOT?

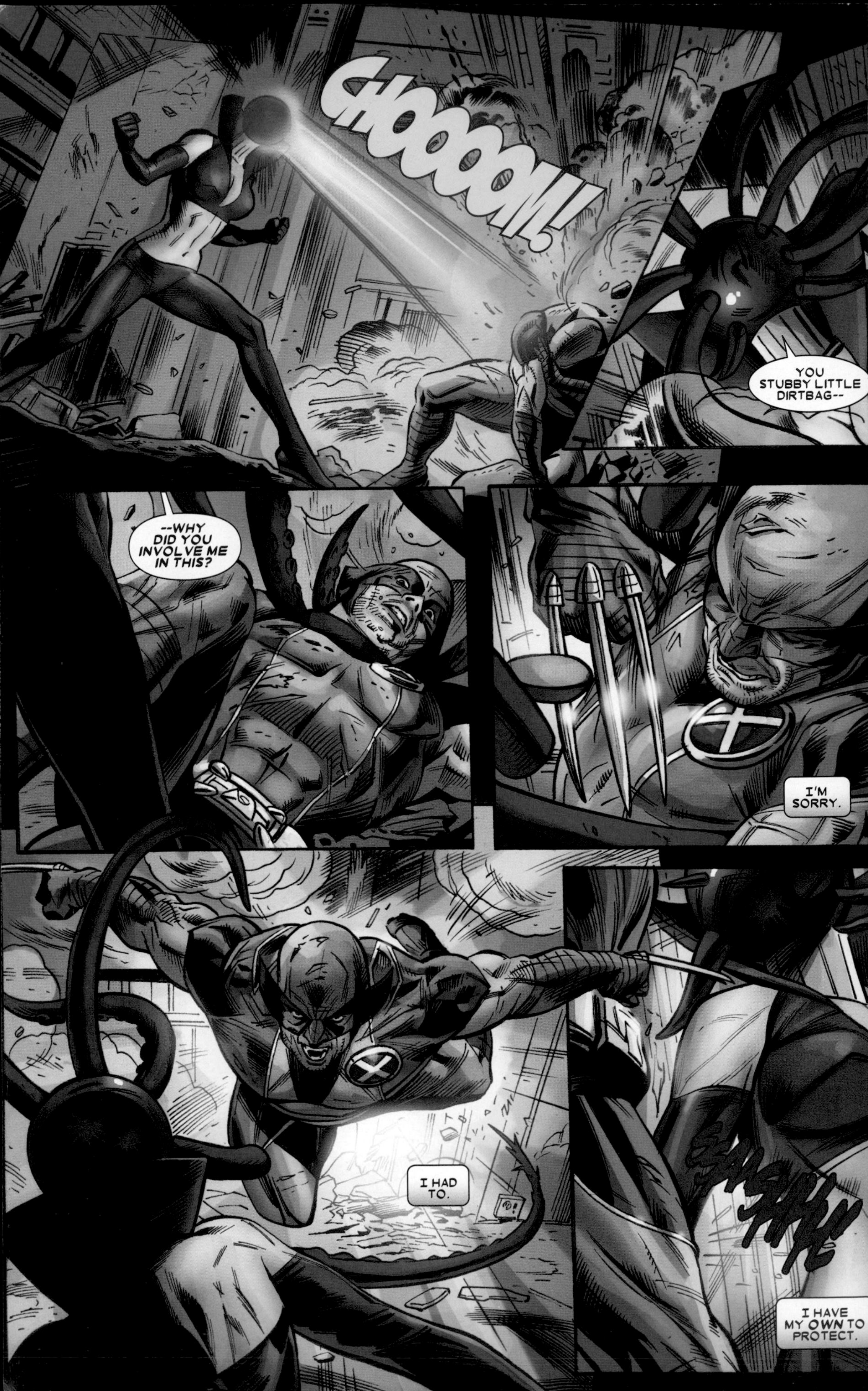
CHOOOOM!!
YOU STUBBY LITTLE DIRTBAG--
--WHY DID YOU INVOLVE ME IN THIS?
I'M SORRY.
I HAD TO.
I HAVE MY OWN TO PROTECT.

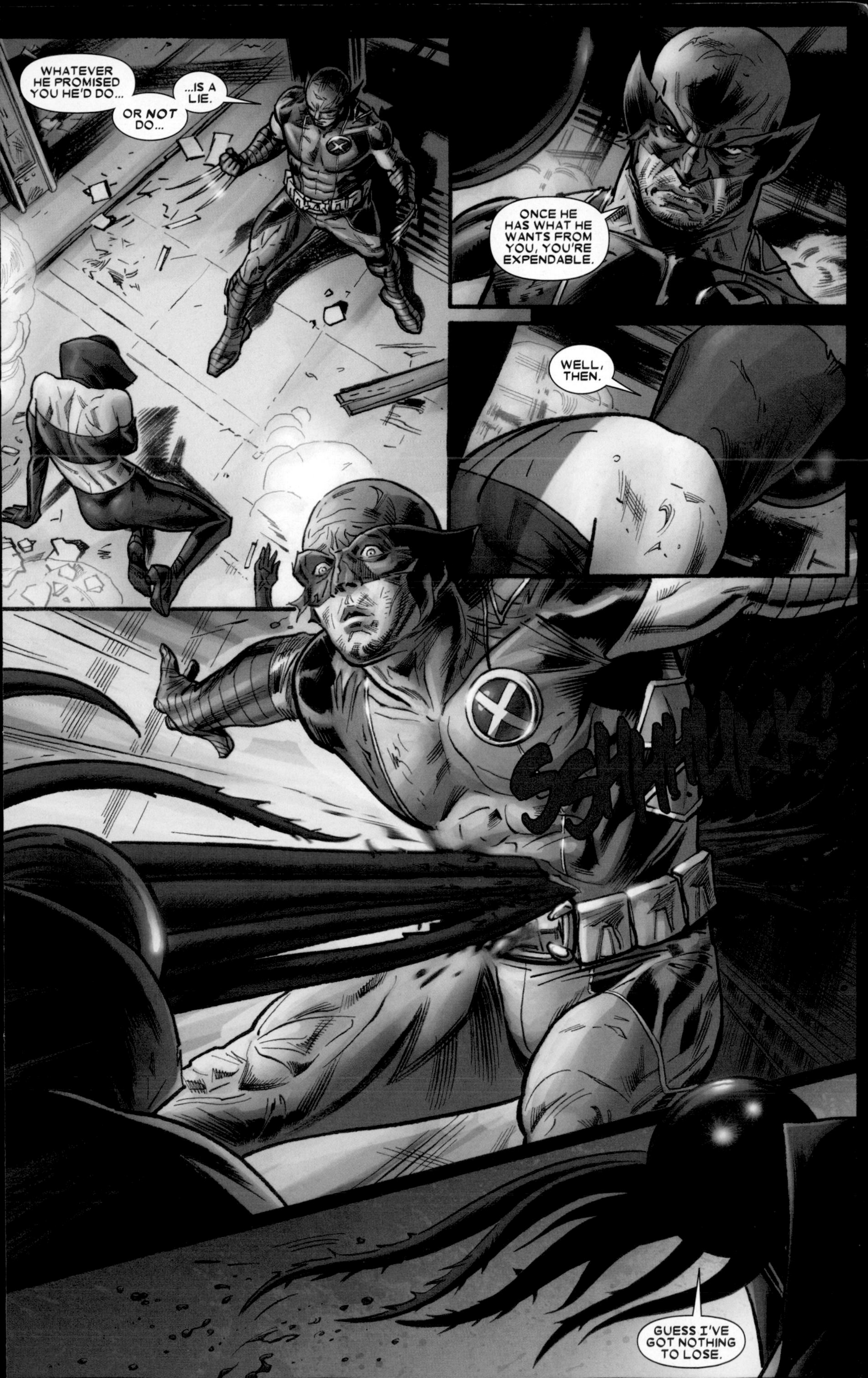
WHATEVER HE PROMISED YOU HE'D DO...
OR NOT DO...
...IS A LIE.
ONCE HE HAS WHAT HE WANTS FROM YOU, YOU'RE EXPENDABLE.
WELL, THEN.
GUESS I'VE GOT NOTHING TO LOSE.

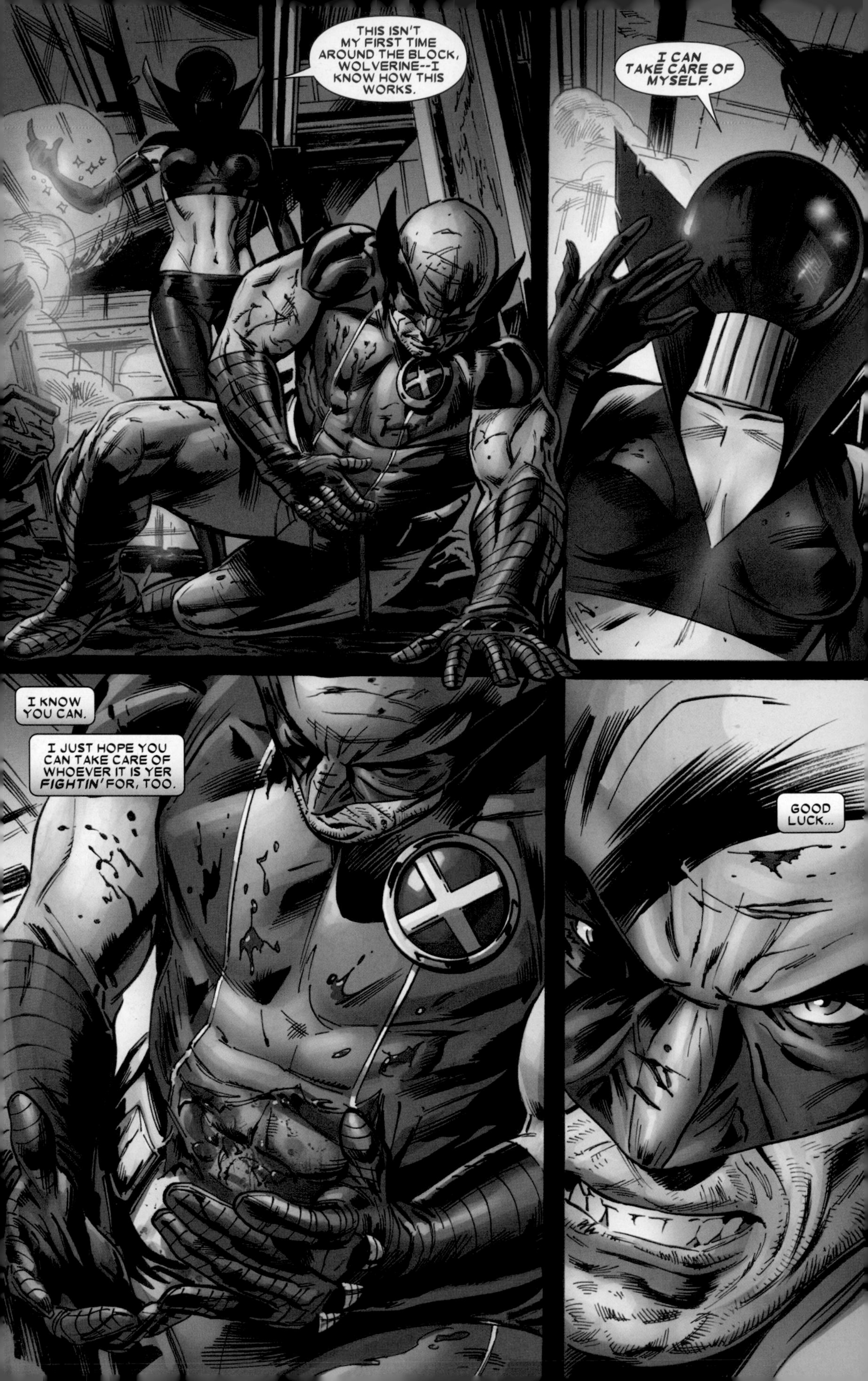
THIS ISN'T MY FIRST TIME AROUND THE BLOCK, WOLVERINE--I KNOW HOW THIS WORKS.
I CAN TAKE CARE OF MYSELF.
I KNOW YOU CAN.
I JUST HOPE YOU CAN TAKE CARE OF WHOEVER IT IS YER FIGHTIN' FOR, TOO.
GOOD LUCK...

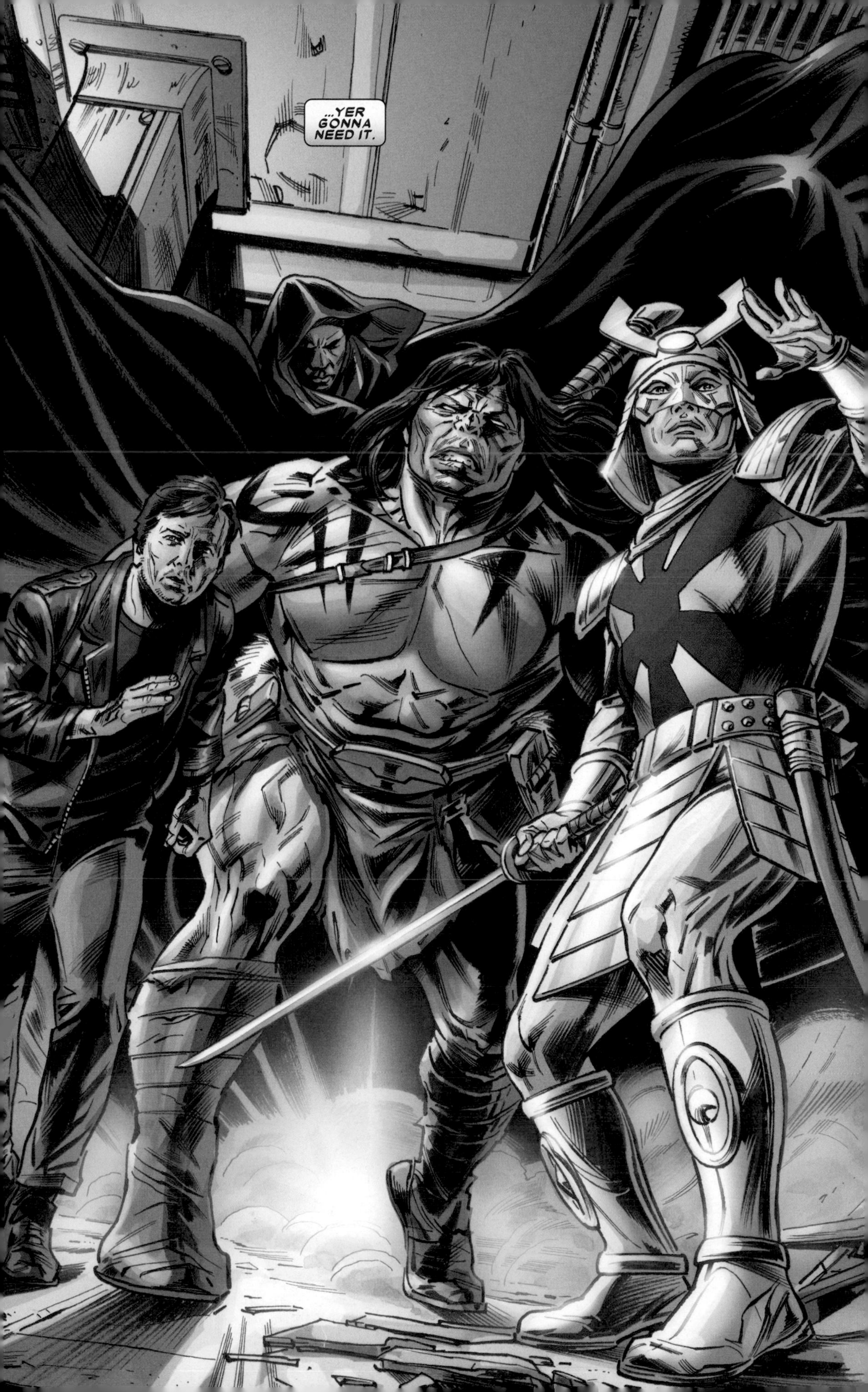
...YER GONNA NEED IT.

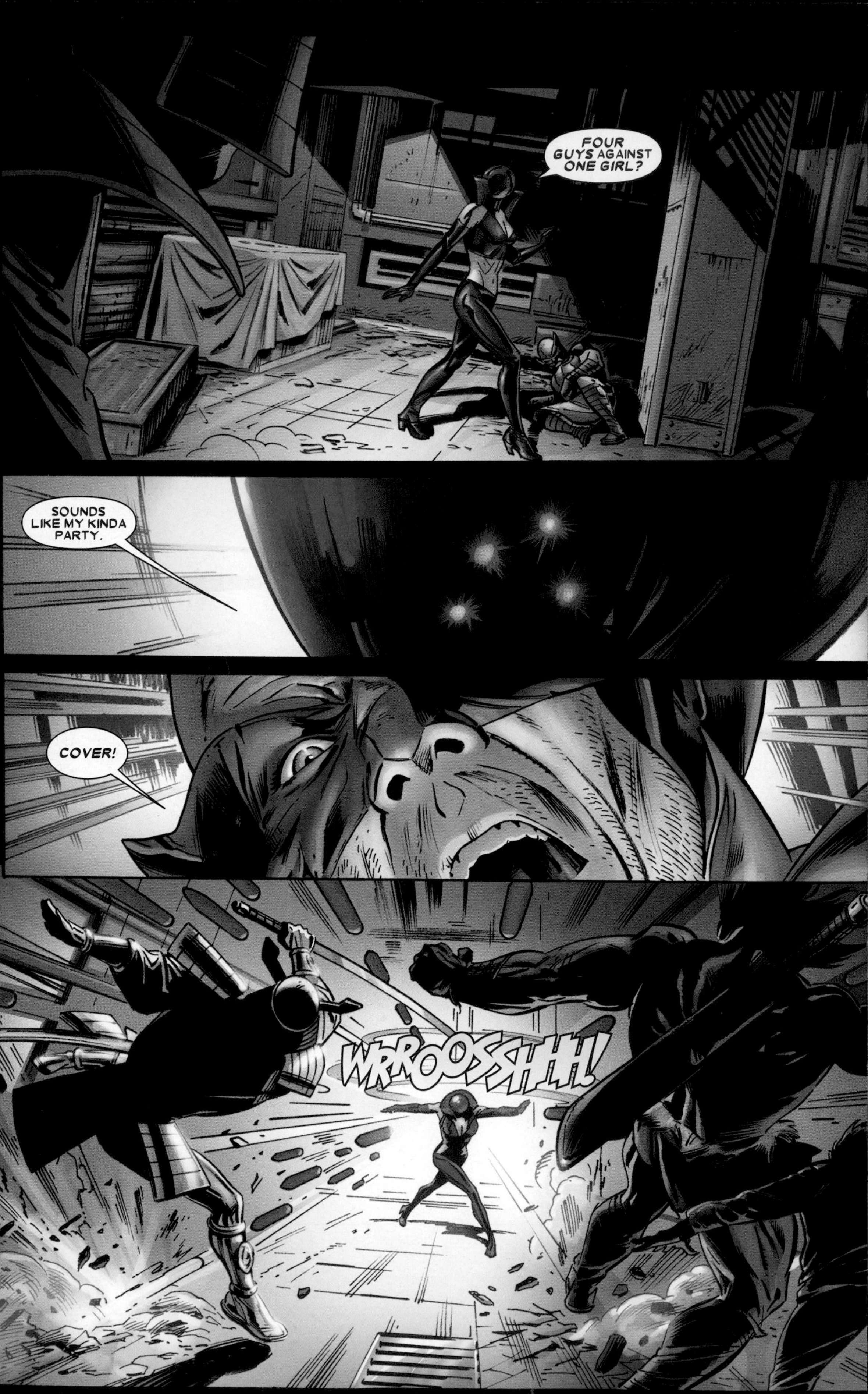
FOUR GUYS AGAINST ONE GIRL?
SOUNDS LIKE MY KINDA PARTY.
COVER!
WRROOSSHHH!

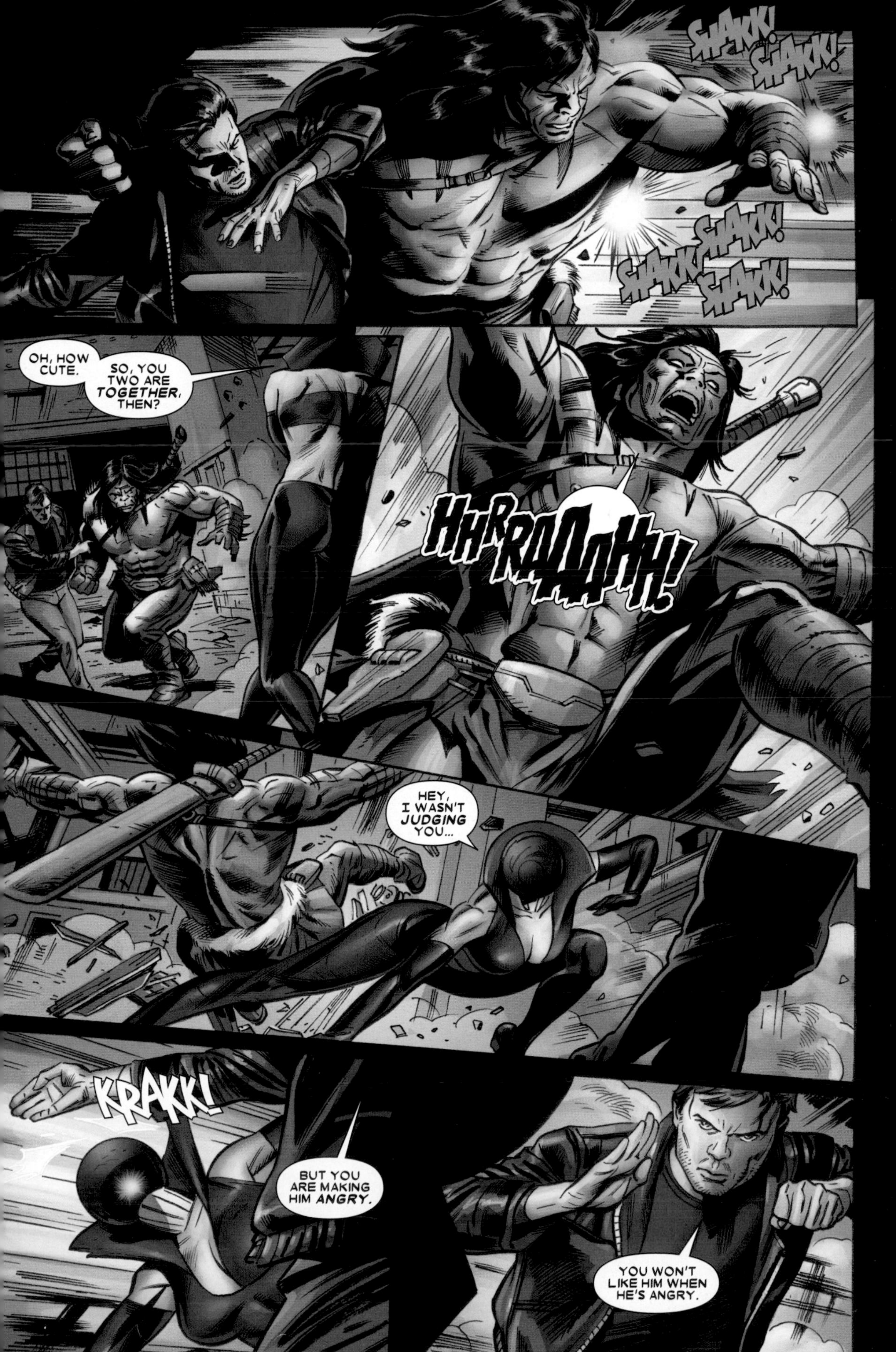
SHAKK! SHAKK!
SHAKK! SHAKK!
SHAKK! SHAKK!
OH, HOW CUTE.
SO, YOU TWO ARE TOGETHER, THEN?
HHRRAAAHH!
HEY, I WASN'T JUDGING YOU...
KRAKK!
BUT YOU ARE MAKING HIM ANGRY.
YOU WON'T LIKE HIM WHEN HE'S ANGRY.

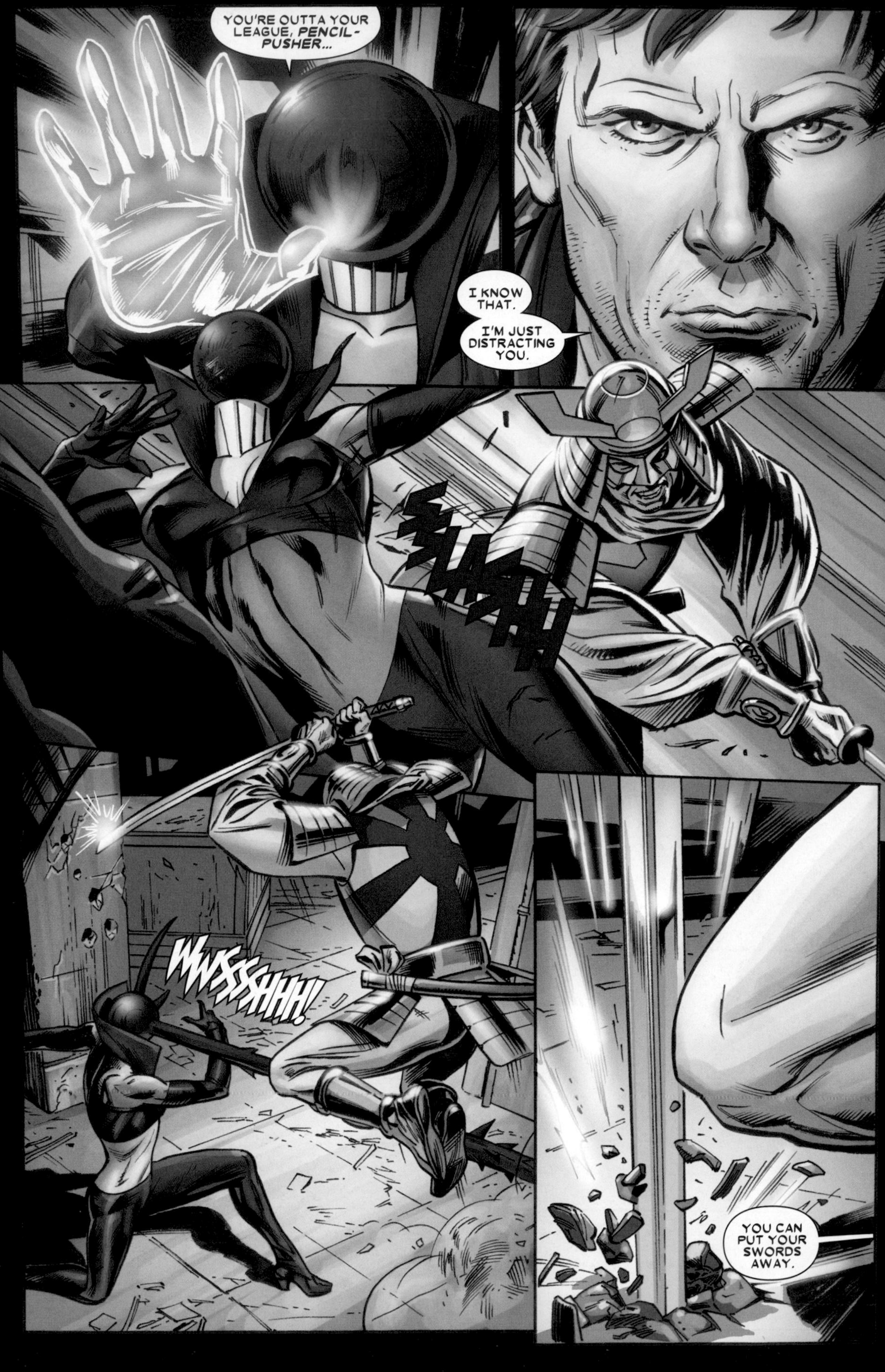
YOU'RE OUTTA YOUR LEAGUE, PENCIL-PUSHER...
I KNOW THAT.
I'M JUST DISTRACTING YOU.
SHASHH
WHSSSHHH!
YOU CAN PUT YOUR SWORDS AWAY.

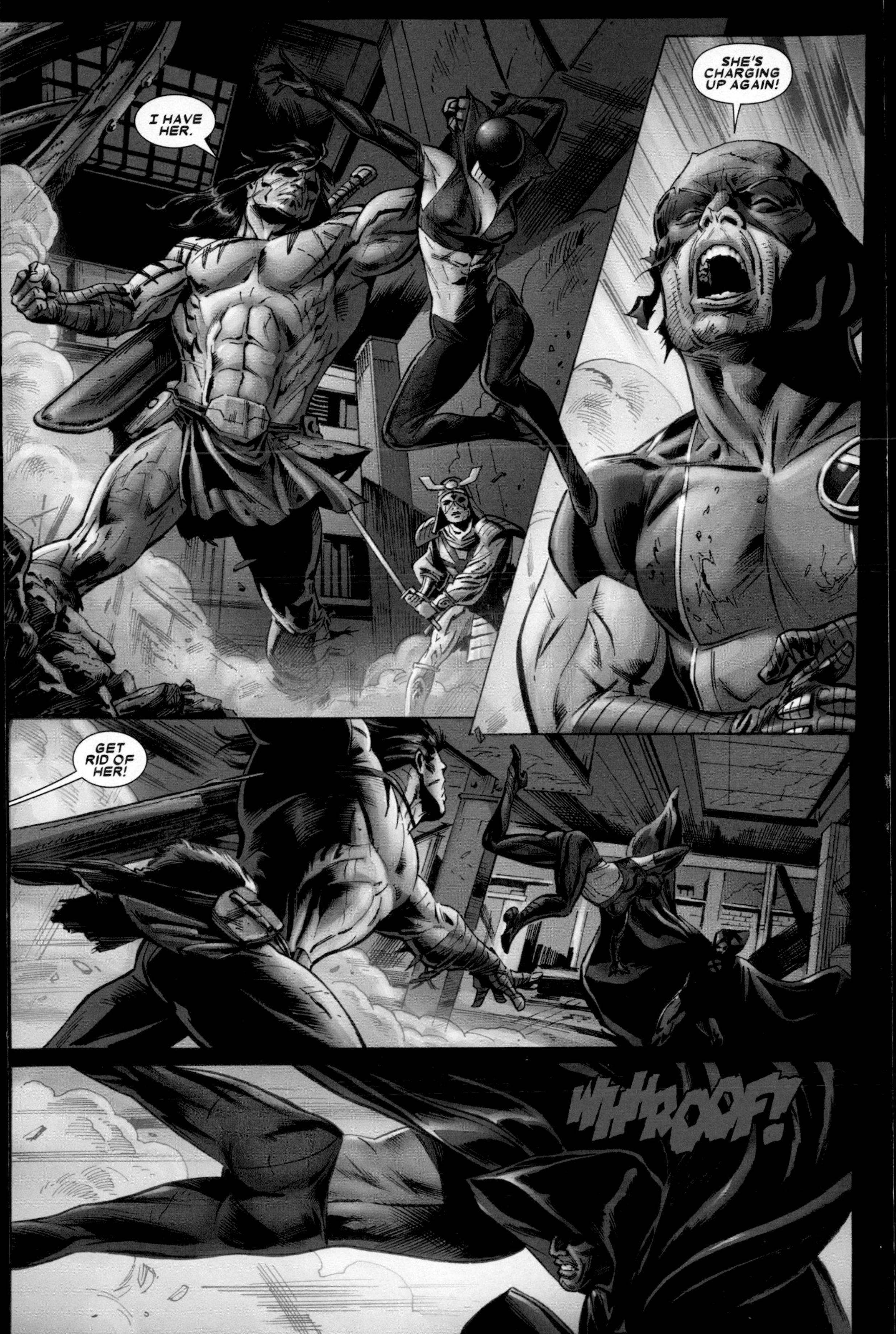
I HAVE HER.
SHE'S CHARGING UP AGAIN!
GET RID OF HER!
WHROOF!

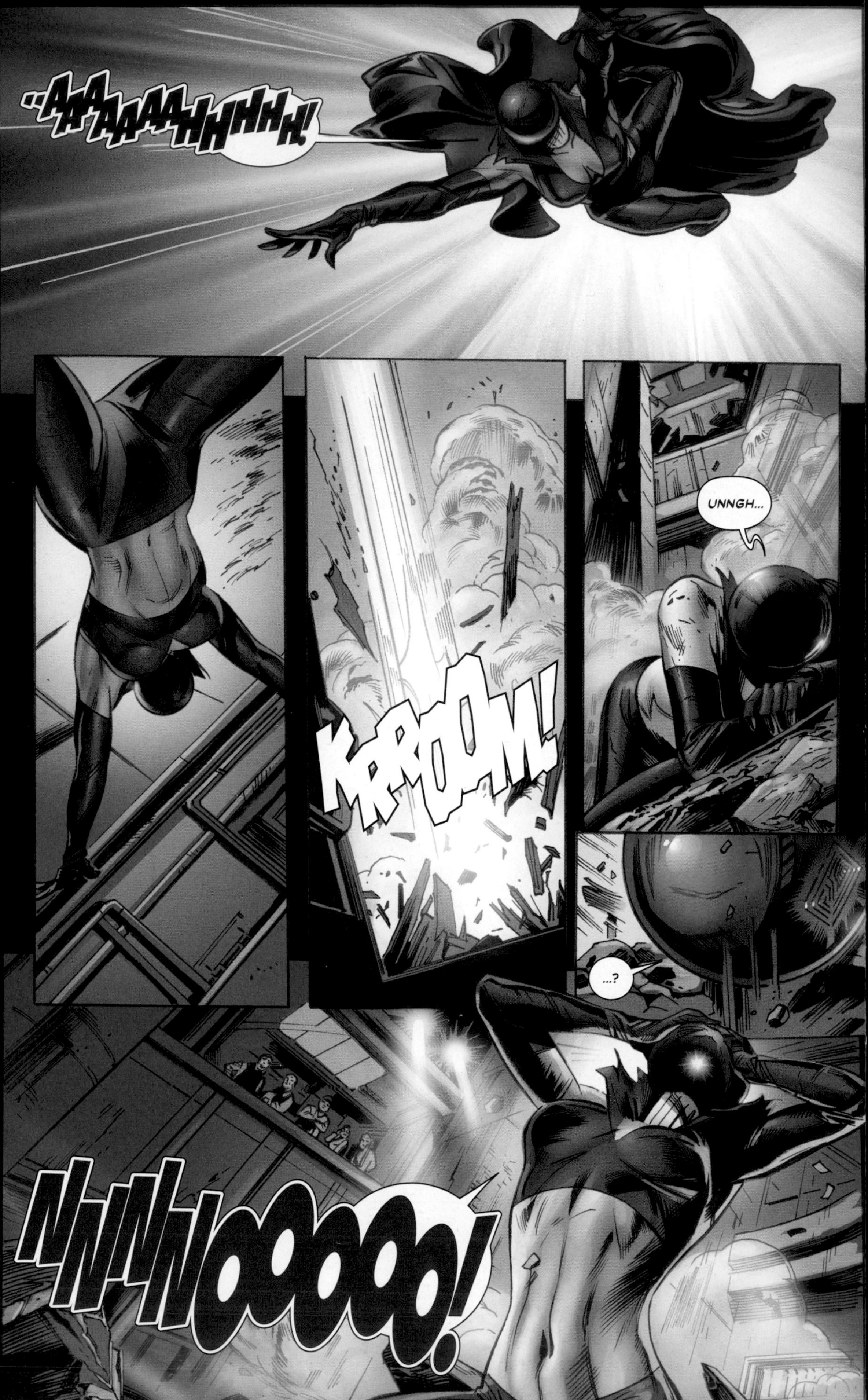

..AAAAAAAAHHHHH!
KRROOM!
UNNGH...
...?
NNNNOOOOO!

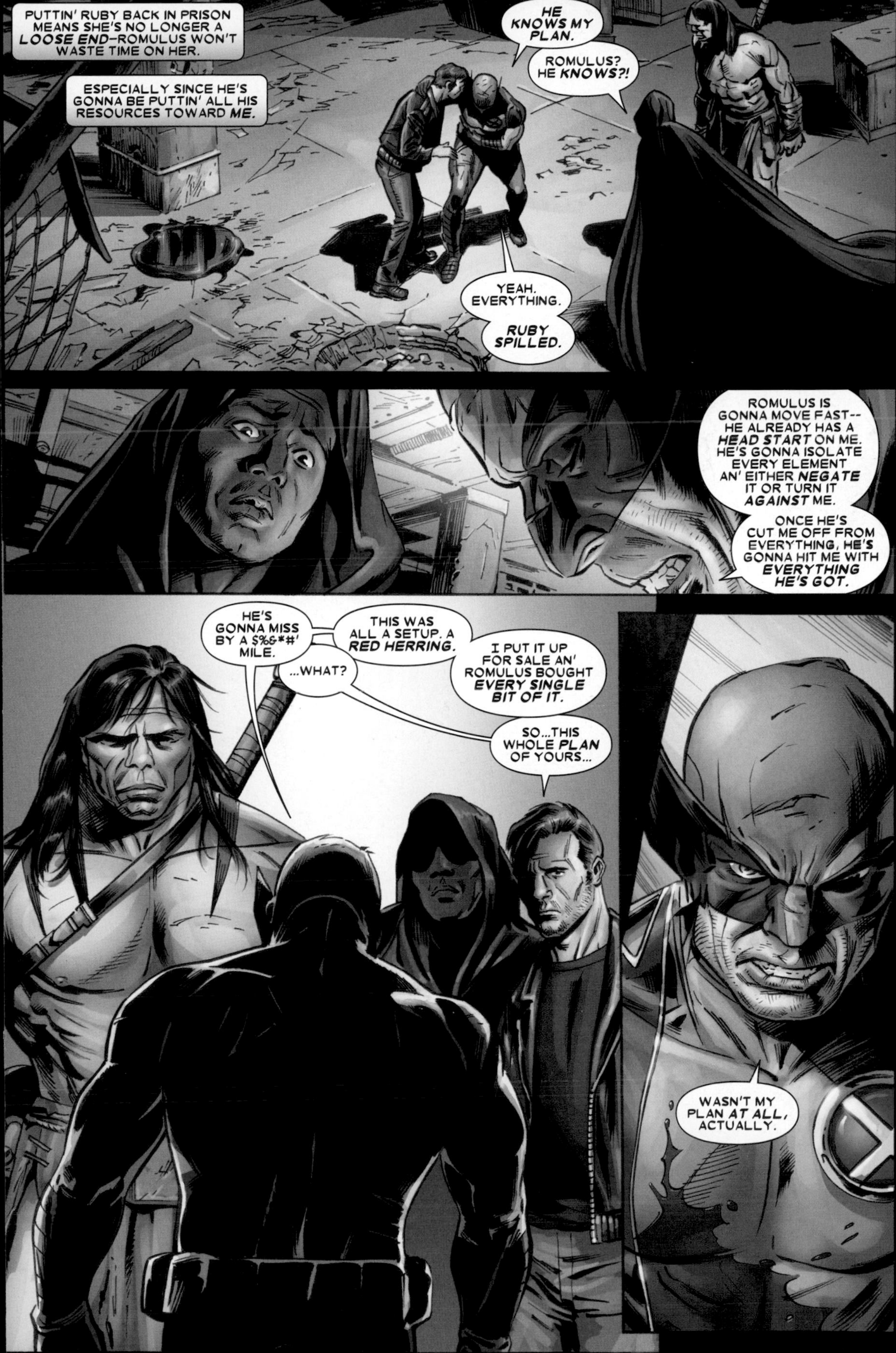
PUTTIN' RUBY BACK IN PRISON MEANS SHE'S NO LONGER A LOOSE END--ROMULUS WON'T WASTE TIME ON HER.
ESPECIALLY SINCE HE'S GONNA BE PUTTIN' ALL HIS RESOURCES TOWARD ME.
HE KNOWS MY PLAN.
ROMULUS? HE KNOWS?!
YEAH. EVERYTHING.
RUBY SPILLED.
ROMULUS IS GONNA MOVE FAST-- HE ALREADY HAS A HEAD START ON ME. HE'S GONNA ISOLATE EVERY ELEMENT AN' EITHER NEGATE IT OR TURN IT AGAINST ME.
ONCE HE'S CUT ME OFF FROM EVERYTHING, HE'S GONNA HIT ME WITH EVERYTHING HE'S GOT.
HE'S GONNA MISS BY A $%&*#' MILE.
THIS WAS ALL A SETUP. A RED HERRING.
...WHAT?
I PUT IT UP FOR SALE AN' ROMULUS BOUGHT EVERY SINGLE BIT OF IT.
SO...THIS WHOLE PLAN OF YOURS...
WASN'T MY PLAN AT ALL, ACTUALLY.

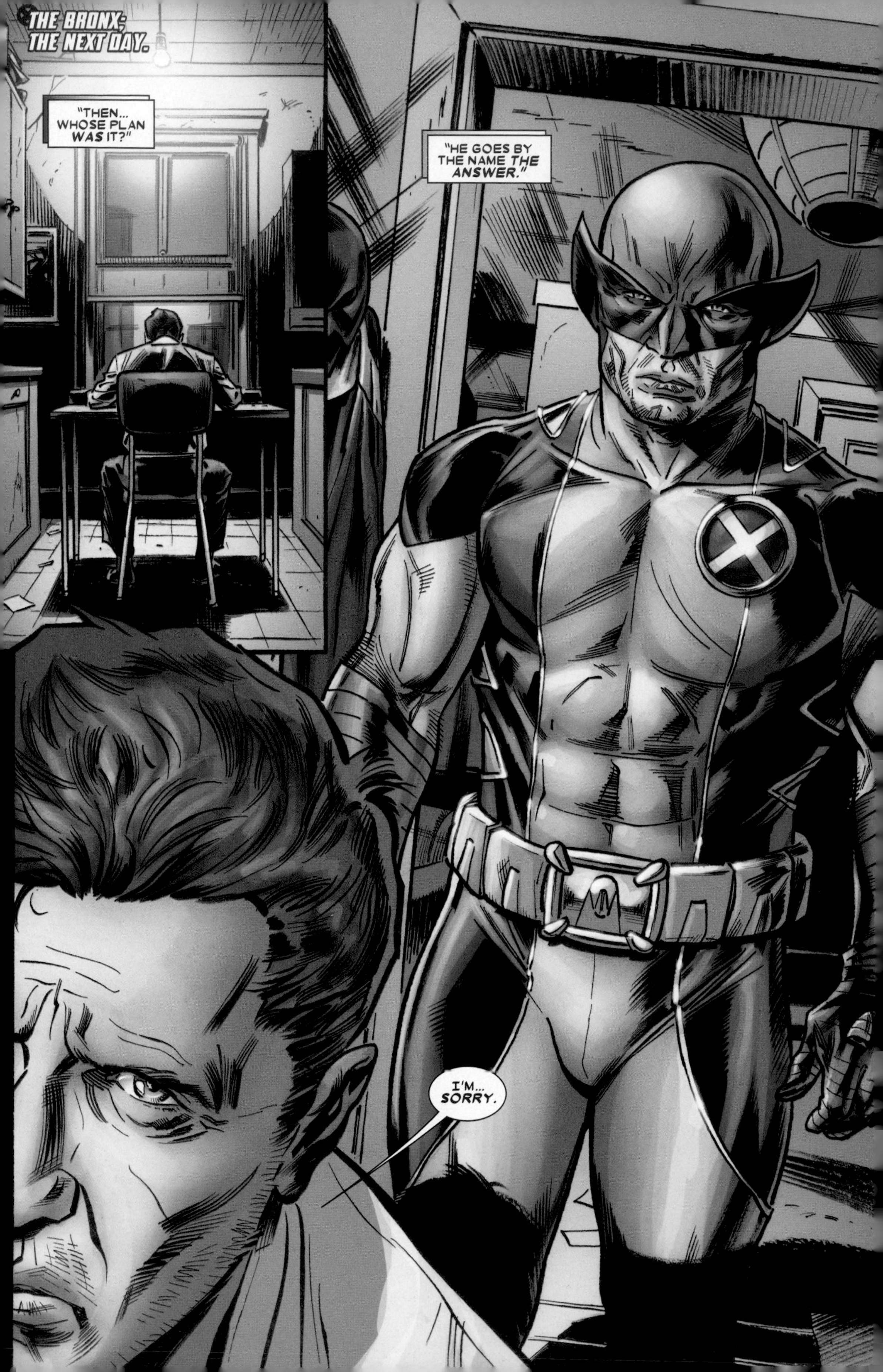
THE BRONX, THE NEXT DAY.
"THEN... WHOSE PLAN WAS IT?"
"HE GOES BY THE NAME THE ANSWER."
I'M... SORRY.

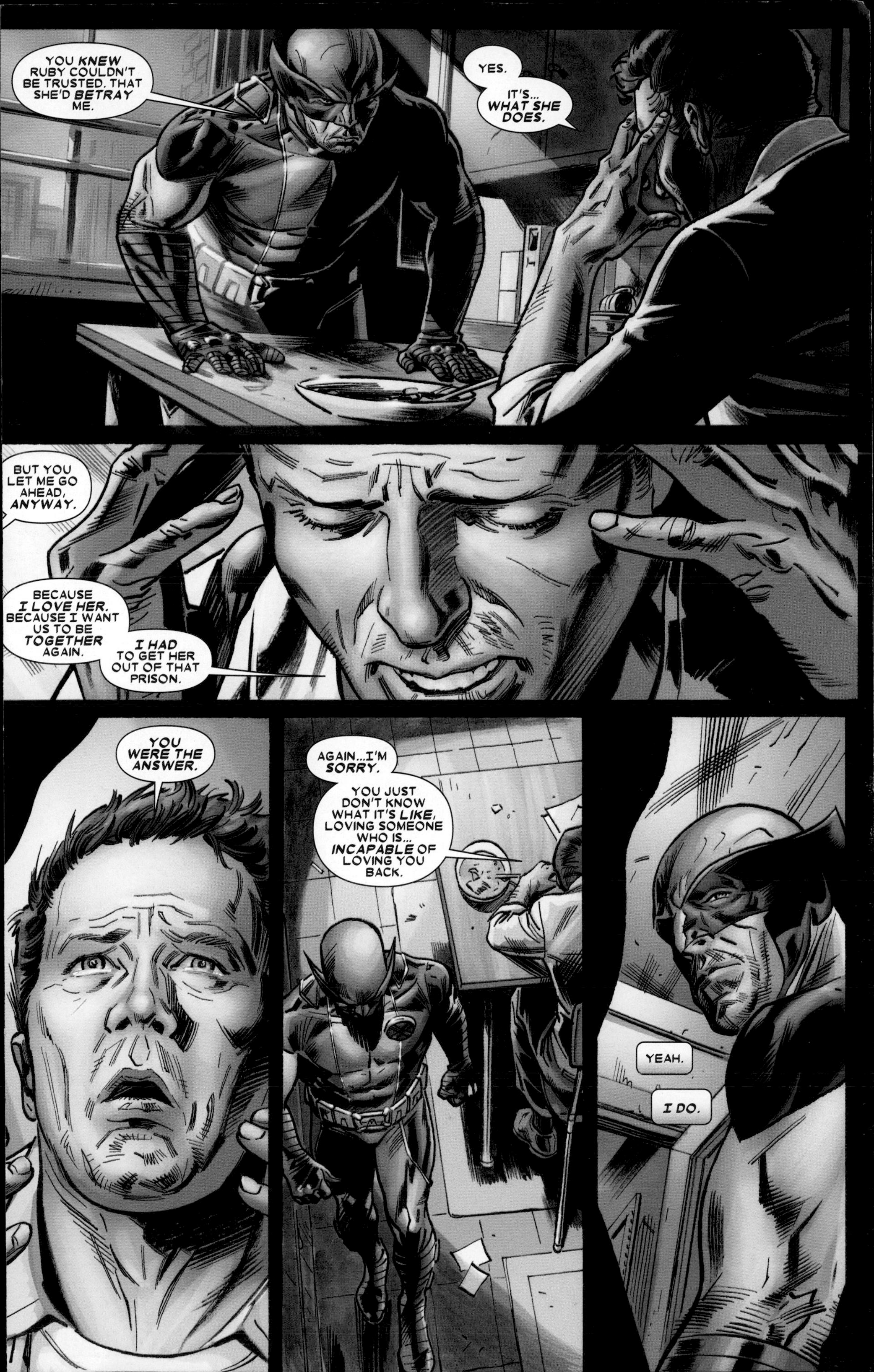

YOU KNEW RUBY COULDN'T BE TRUSTED. THAT SHE'D BETRAY ME.
YES.
IT'S... WHAT SHE DOES.
BUT YOU LET ME GO AHEAD, ANYWAY.
BECAUSE I LOVE HER. BECAUSE I WANT US TO BE TOGETHER AGAIN.
I HAD TO GET HER OUT OF THAT PRISON.
YOU WERE THE ANSWER.
AGAIN...I'M SORRY.
YOU JUST DON'T KNOW WHAT IT'S LIKE, LOVING SOMEONE WHO IS... INCAPABLE OF LOVING YOU BACK.
YEAH.
I DO.

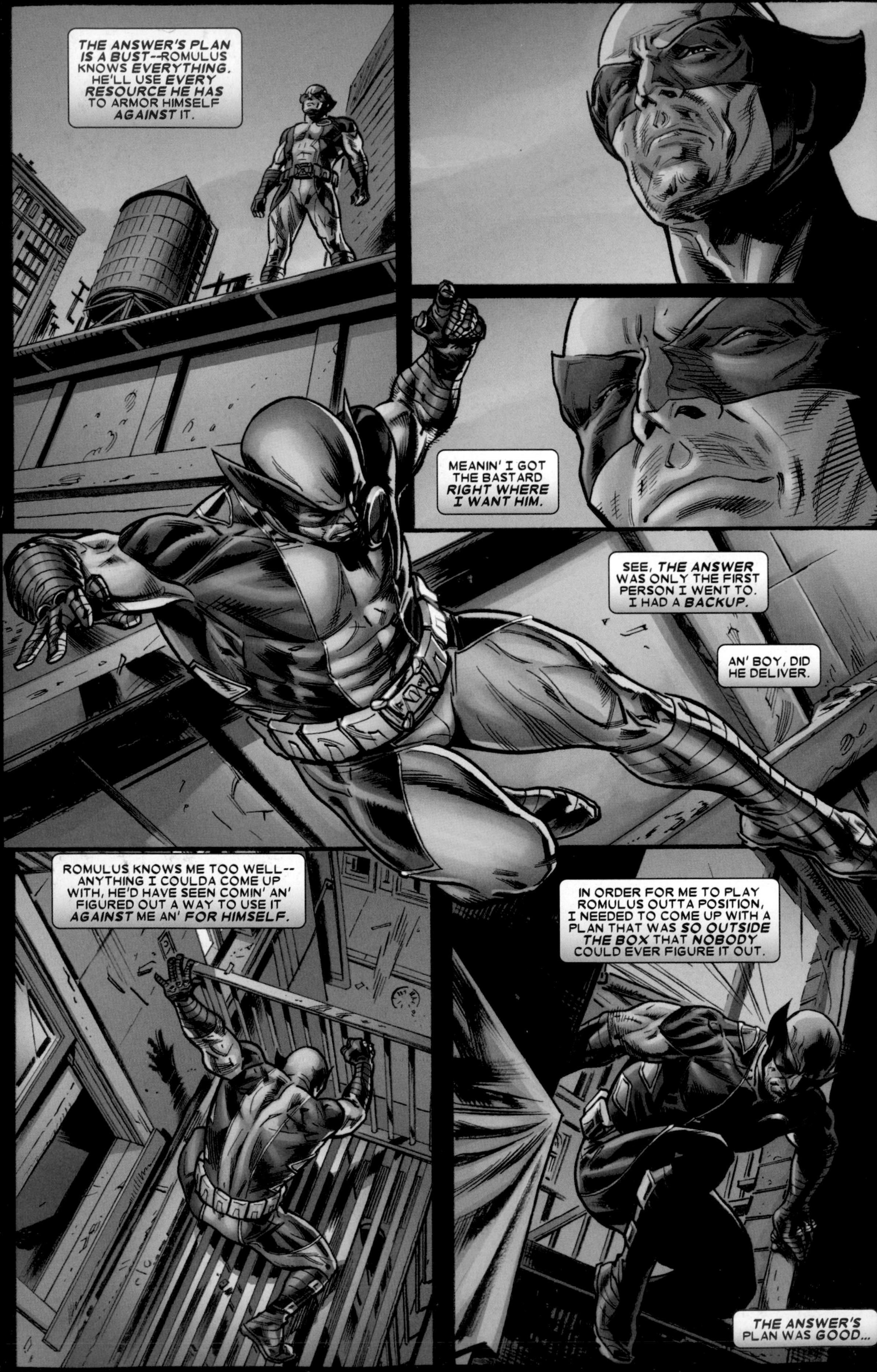
THE ANSWER'S PLAN IS A BUST--ROMULUS KNOWS EVERYTHING. HE'LL USE EVERY RESOURCE HE HAS TO ARMOR HIMSELF AGAINST IT.
MEANIN' I GOT THE BASTARD RIGHT WHERE I WANT HIM.
SEE, THE ANSWER WAS ONLY THE FIRST PERSON I WENT TO. I HAD A BACKUP.
AN' BOY, DID HE DELIVER.
ROMULUS KNOWS ME TOO WELL-- ANYTHING I COULDA COME UP WITH, HE'D HAVE SEEN COMIN' AN' FIGURED OUT A WAY TO USE IT AGAINST ME AN' FOR HIMSELF.
IN ORDER FOR ME TO PLAY ROMULUS OUTTA POSITION, I NEEDED TO COME UP WITH A PLAN THAT WAS SO OUTSIDE THE BOX THAT NOBODY COULD EVER FIGURE IT OUT.
THE ANSWER'S PLAN WAS GOOD...

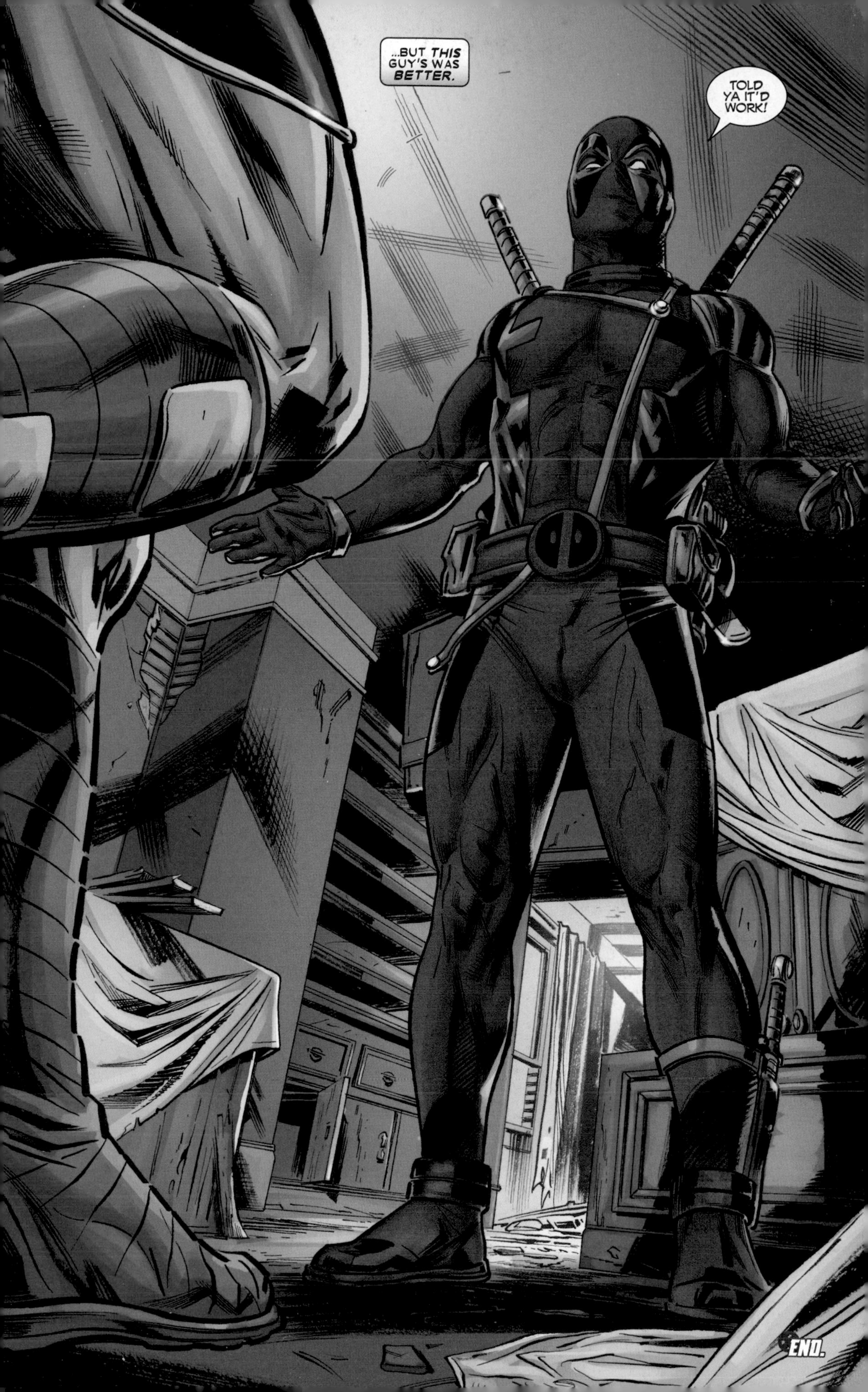

...BUT THIS GUY'S WAS BETTER.
TOLD YA IT'D WORK!
END.

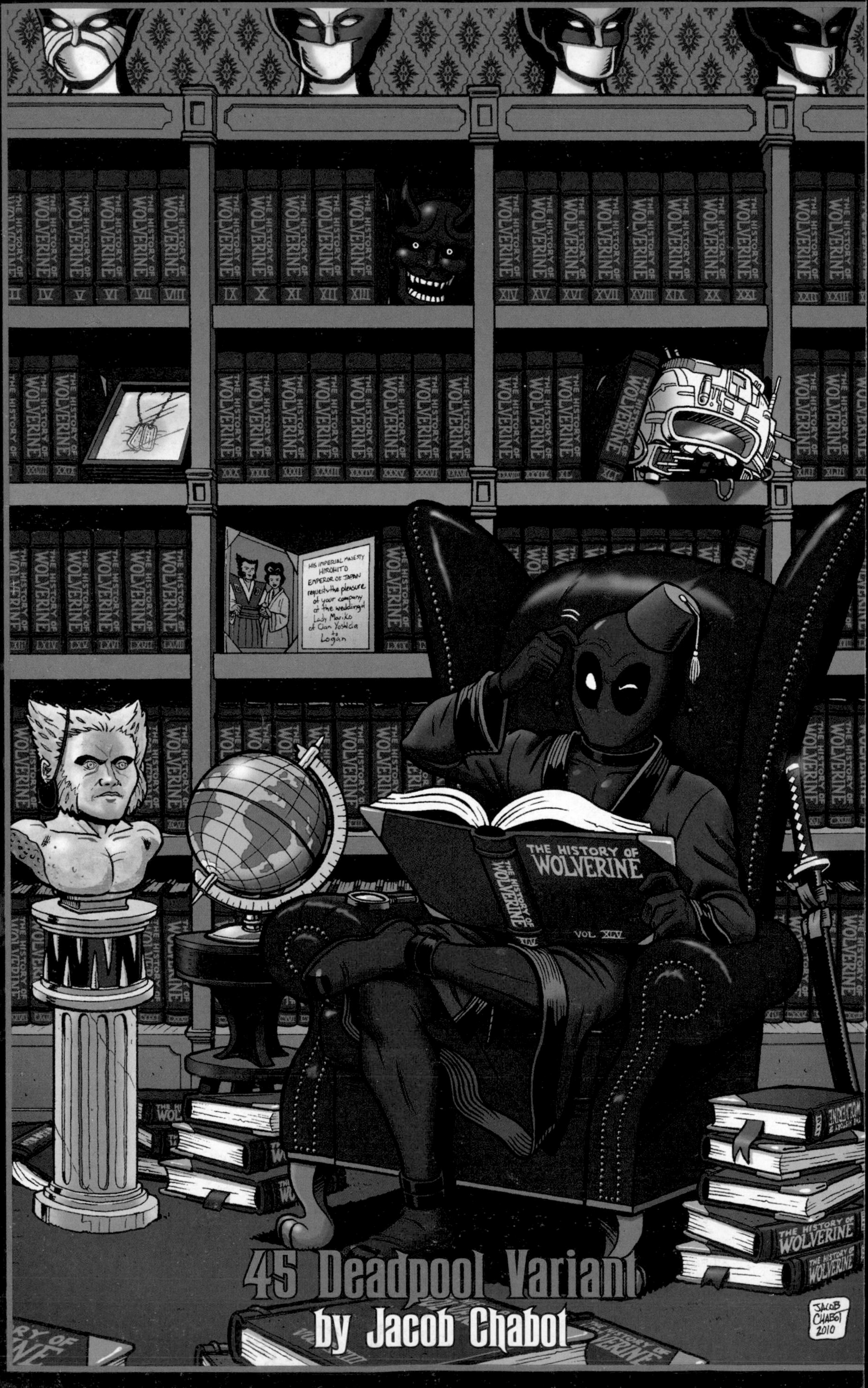
HIS IMPERIAL MAJESTY HIROHITO EMPEROR OF JAPAN requests the pleasure of your company at the wedding of Lady Mariko of Clan Yoshida to Logan
THE HISTORY OF WOLVERINE
VOL. XLV
JACOB CHABOT 2010

45 Deadpool Variant
by Jacob Chabot